*Revitalizing
American Governance*

Revitalizing American Governance

REQUIRED: MODERATION, COMMON SENSE, AND COURAGE

CHARLES BINGMAN

REVITALIZING AMERICAN GOVERNANCE
REQUIRED: MODERATION, COMMON SENSE, AND COURAGE

iUniverse books may be ordered through booksellers or by contacting:

iUniverse
1663 Liberty Drive
Bloomington, IN 47403
www.iuniverse.com
1-800-Authors (1-800-288-4677)

Because of the dynamic nature of the Internet, any web addresses or links contained in this book may have changed since publication and may no longer be valid. The views expressed in this work are solely those of the author and do not necessarily reflect the views of the publisher, and the publisher hereby disclaims any responsibility for them.

Any people depicted in stock imagery provided by Getty Images are models, and such images are being used for illustrative purposes only. Certain stock imagery © Getty Images.

ISBN: 978-1-5320-4193-8 (sc)
ISBN: 978-1-5320-4194-5 (e)

Library of Congress Control Number: 2018901950

Print information available on the last page.

iUniverse rev. date: 02/20/2018

CONTENTS

PART TWO

PART ONE

═══════════ ★ ═ ★ ═ ★ ═══════════

* "Just powers devived from the consent of the governed"

Thomas Jefferson

    * "The great difficulty is this: you must first enable
the government to control the governed; and in
the next place oblige it to control itself."

James Madison

    * "If anything can go wrong, it will go wrong"

Murphy

THE WORLD IS CHANGING

=★=★=★=

THE AMERICAN ECONOMY AND society are experiencing a rapid period of change – but of course, they has always been changing. Gone are the horse and carriage, and in have come the horseless carriages by the millions. Gone are the canals, and in are super highways. Education no longer peaks at the 6th grade or the 12th grade but at the post-doctoral level. The wood stove has become the home heating/cooling system. The ice box is out, and the refrigerator is in, and full up.

"Governance" is far broader than just the governments themselves since it encompasses the involvement of individuals in some form of involvement with the affairs of governments. Governance also includes the roles of corporations, interest groups and non-government institutions as well. The whole thing starts with a great debate: what is it the government is really supposed to do?

In the past, the answer has ranged from "nothing" to "everything"; from letting the peasants starve, to government "from the cradle to the grave". By UN definition, there are 196 countries in the world. Perhaps 40-50 of them are very small, or remote islands, important for those living there, but not weighty in world affairs. There are thus about 150 substantial governments, and all of them are run from the top down by centrist elites, and about 105 of them are in deep trouble. "Deep trouble" is defined as involving wars, insurrections, seriou internal conflict, deliberate skewing of wealth, lack of social justice, and lack of social services and public infrastructure. Most of these governments suffer from poor management, bumbling incompetence and rampant corruption. Most of them suffer from problems created and extended by the governments themselves out of motives of greed, viciousness and an insatiable lust for power.

In its totality, the American national government system is unbelievably huge and complex, sophisticated, complicated, muddled and notoriously fragmented and yet interrelated. It is probably unwise to think of it as "the government" since it is literally hundreds of governments, program by program and place by place. In short it has never been a coherent entity designed to be "managed" as that term is understood in other contexts. The best way to evaluate government is first from the top down, and second from the middle down. From the top down, governments are created and designed not for management effectiveness but for political interpretations, and as discussed earlier, the political view of the world is often markedly different from the professional management view. Thus, public managers are faced with conditions far different than those face by the executives and managers in the private sector, and they are usually far more complicated.

The President is, by order of the Constitution, the Chief Executive of the government, and yet not even the President can really manage the totality the way a chief executive of corporations can manage. Much of the operational power and authority for specific government programs is vested by law not in the President but in the head of the government agency that delivers the program. Cabinet secretaries and agency heads may "work for" the President and be appointed by him, but each also "works for" the Congress which defines his or her programs, dictates agency structure, defines many of its processes, and ultimately controls its finances. The President cannot order his leaders to violate the law, and should be careful not to try.

The U. S. became an economic powerhouse through the world's finest manufacturing capacity. But manufacturiing has gradually been overtaken by its own success because it financed the surge of the consumer economy that dominates the economic horizon today. More and more of the total economy is commercial, including banking and insurance, higher education, government, and millions of jobs in offices, retail establishments and "brain" occupations. The picks and shovels have largely been replaced by the telephone and the computer.

More and more, the future has become the cities. In 1930, XX% of the U. S. population lived on farms and in rural communities and small towns. Today, that number is down to about XX%.

The world is awakening to the fact that the future will be increasingly urban, and neither central governments nor cities themselves seem fully ready to cope. Many of the world's largest cities are already overwhelmed. All over the world, massive shifts of population are occurring from rural and village life to urban life. This movement has been largely stabilized in the most developed countries, but in the less developed countries, a serious decline of primary level jobs (i.e. agriculture, mining, forestry, and fishing) is taking place because of the low economic value derived from these occupations, and this decline is forcing millions to move to cities in the hope of finding a better livelihood. This movement is spontaneous and irreversible. This creates two kinds of problems: first, the overburden and potential collapse of urban economies and infrastructure; and second, the collapse of rural society, despite efforts of many countries to subsidize and prop up rural economies and enhance rural development.

The huge surge of people to cities has meant that especially the largest and most densely populated cities has dramatically increased the need for high quality public infrastructure has risen in importance, and as cities fall behind the power curve, it has become harder and harder to catch up again. When states fail and collapse, the process of disintegration mutilates institutions and destroys the underlying understandings between the government and the governed. This is precisely why state rebuilding must be sustained, and requires time, massive capacity building, large sums from the outside, debt relief, and appropriate forms of tutoring. But note: not even the U. N. or the U. S. can be held responsible for rebuilding other governments around the world. Many humanitarian voices advocate exactly that, but the only way to resurrect more than a hundred failed of floundering states is for each to remain responsible for their own fate.

The whole world including the United States is experiencing a huge surge in population. Almost every sector of economy is becoming more sophisticated and more productive, and despite the most ominous of predictions, the world has almost never run out of critical resources. There have been major improvements, worldwide, in technology, education, the body of usable knowledge, in managerial skills, and in the value added nature of economic sectors. There is less reliance on primary economic sectors (farming, fishing, mining, forestry) and a movement upscale to more value added secondary and tertiary levels of economic activity. Here are some of the most important ways in which the world has become better:

1. Transportation: air travel has grown beyond belief; hundreds of millions of people now have their own automobiles; thousands of miles of highways and urban streets have been provided; the number of air line passengers is simply staggering; and in all modes, the cost per unit mile of travel is, remarkably, down.

2. Despite repeated ominous predictions of world wide starvation, food is far more widely available. New techniques, better farming equipment, new fertilizers and insecticides have allowed far greater productionon far frewer acres under cultivation. Food is available in remarkable variation at far more affordable cost.

3. The expected life span of humans in 1900 was 41. In 2000, it was 77, and it is close to 80 now.

4. Millions of women have entered the workforce. In 2015, 74% of working age women were in the labor force, compared to about 35% in 1946.

5. Almost all forms of medicine are unbelievably advanced. Most of the horrible diseases of the past – plagues, small pox, measles, polio, influenza have largely been eliminated. New problems such as obesity, drug addition and AIDS are being dealt with as individual problems.

6. Humans are more willing and able to move to improve their lives. Immigration and emmigration, while difficult in the short run, prove to be invaluable in the longer term. The tragedy is the fact that "mobiliity" is now so often the fate of refugees and displaced persons, but there is a substantial record of humane efforts to deal with these problems.

7. Machines that replace human labor have multiplied, and greatly reduced the cost of producing most "things". Machines have enabled the greater expansion of economies, creating more wealth and new forms of work.

8. Communications have experienced a remarkable revolution, especially in the form of computers and cell phones, and the world of the average person will never be the same.

9. Home ownership is much more likely, and homes are totally better and more convenient: heating and air conditioning, sanitation, labor saving appliances, furniture, clothing – at greatly reduced costs.

10. The base of formal education and further access to knowledge has been greatly expanded. An exceptional number of young people are now able to go to college.

11. The openness of society has been increasing. The roles of women and minorities have become more equal, more permissive and more relaxed.

12. As a result of these changes, real incomes have doubled between 1900 andtoday. In 1900, the "middle class" was just about 1% of the population. Now it is over 23%.

13. There is a very special reality that, through the 1980s and '90s, the U. S. accepted more than a million legal immigrants per year – more legal immigrants than all other nations of the world combined. In addition, there has been a huge flow of illegal immigrants. 11% of the U. S. population is foreign born – about 40 million people.

14. Factoring out immigration, the rise of American inequality disappears; for 89% of the American population, that is, native born, income inequality is declining since the 1960's. For African-Americans, family median incomes are finally currently rising twice as fast as the population as a whole.

15. 80% of the U. S. population has graduated from high school, and 25% have a college degree. The U. S. averages 12.3 years of education – the highest in the world. The current drop out rate is about 10%; but prior to 1940, most children dropped out – in order to work.

16. Health insurance did not exist until after WW I. In 1900, 42% of workers were in primary sectors of the economy; 38% were in industry; and 20 % were in "white collar" occupations. 47% of women's employment was as domestics. 58% of men and 52% of women are now in service sector. In 1850, the average work week was 66 hours; in 1900, it was 53 hours; in 2000, it was 42 hours. House keeping chores took 4 hours a day for 90% of housholds in 1900; in 2000, it is about 14%.

THE WORLD IS FULL OF HORROR

━━━━━━━━━━━━━━━ ★ ═ ★ ═ ★ ━━━━━━━━━━━━━━━

Yes, THE WORLD IS changing, sometimes for the better, but still it is a world full of the incomprehensible conflicts of wars, rebellions, insurrections, tribal conflict, and vicious terrorist cruelty. During the lifetime of our people, consider the horrible list of serious conflicts around the world, in no particular order:

1. WW II and the subsequent Cold War
2. The Iran-Iraq war
3. The internal wars of Rwanda, Burundi, the Democratic Republic of Congo
4. The Korean War
5. The Vietnam War
6. The Syrian civil war
7. India vs. Pakistan – forever
8. Thousands of conflicts between Sunni and Shia Muslims
9. The Lebanese civil war
10. The Sudanese civil war
11. Three Arab-Israeli wars
12. Liberia vs. Sierra Leone
13. The Algerian civil war
14. The U. S. – Iraq war
15. The Tunesian rebellion
16. Revolts in Central African Republic
17. Soviet invasion of Afghanistan
18. Iraqi invasion of Kuwait
19. Mali Muslim insurrections

20. Wars in Laos
21. Revolution in Cambodia
22. Civil war in Chad
23. Indonesian invasion of E. Timor
24. Russia vs. Chechnya
25. Ethiopia vs. Eritrea
26. Ethiopia vs. Somalia
27. Israel vs. the regime in Gaza
28. Russia vs. Kosovo
29. Civil war in Nepal
30. Nigeria vs. Boko Haram
31. Internal war in Peru
32. Philippine revolt of Maoist rebels
33. Civil war in Yemen
34. Civil war in Sri Lanka
35. War and rebellion in Tajikistan
36. War and civil conflict in Thailand

In addition to this seemingly endless list of major armed conflicts, there is a second also endless list of hundreds of thousands of minor conflicts and oppressions by and against almost every government in the world.

A VITAL LESSON IN GOVERNANCE:
THE DECLINE OF STATE SOCIALISM

=★=★=★=

AFTER WWII, MANY OF the governments of the world adopted some form or level of state socialist government, promising care of all people "from the cradle to the grave". But then, this tide of state socialism faded and declined, and left much of the world wondering what was next. In the end, State Owned Enterprises (SOE) as the chosen form of economic organizations deployed by Socialist governments proved not to be so much the efficient instruments of economic performance as the ineffective political entities for mounting public programs. In country after country, the success of the state socialist economic policies proved limited, and a discouraging number of SOEs proved to be failed instruments. But the political leadership that created them felt that it was politically vital to defend and protect them and they could not admit their failures. So governments went to extraordinary lengths to prop them up, subsidize them and conceal their difficulties. In China, at times, more than 50% of their 400,000 SOES were operating at a deficit and had to be subsidized with government funds that were desperately needed for other national priorities. In India, a similar pattern of SOE deficits burdens the government, and in fact the problems of SOEs plague most of the governments around the world that relied most heavily on their use.

Defining which states were in fact Socialist is both difficult and probematic. Many governments defined themselves as representative democracies and not socialist states, but yet they employed many of the most defining Socialist policies and philosophies. These governments here are defined as "semi-socialist" states, especially where they have made extensive use of that most serious economic tool of socialist regimes, the

State Owned Enterprise (SOE). The following list is offered as a reasonable identification:

Albania
Angola
Argentina
Azergaijan
Belize
Bolivia
Bulgaria
Cambodia
Chile
China
Croatia
Cuba
Czech
Denmark
Dominian
Egypt
El Salvador
Eritria
Estonia
Ethiopia
France
Greenland
Guyana
Hungary
India
Indonesia
Iraq
Iran
Italy
Jordan
Kazakhstan
Laos
Latvia

Russia
Serbia
Slovakia
Slovenia
South Africa
Republic Spain
Sudan
Republic Sweden
Syria
Tajikistan
Tanzania
Turkmenistan
United Kingdom
Uzbekistan
Venezuela
Vietnam
Yemen
Zambia
Zimbabwe

Lithuania
Macedonia
Moldava
Maliwi
Mexico
Montegregro
Mozambique
Myanmar
Nicaragua
Norway
Oman
Papua New Guinea
Peru
Poland
Portugal
Romania

This is 78 countries. Obviously, it is difficult to decide which countries should be on this list and really had Socialist or Semi-Socialist governments. Many of their governments consistently maintain that they have an open economically competitive economy, and most of the systemic elements of democratic and representative governments. But all of the 78 countries listed here have been heavily committed to substantial elements of State Socialist philosophy and policy, especially in the widespread use of State Owned Enterprises to run critical elements of the economy. These countries have also maintained the top down "cradle to grave" socialist policies in the deliverance of social services. These "maybe" states are therefore designated here as "semi-Socialist States".

It is equally complicated and difficult to evaluate the success of these 78 countries over a broad range of their politics, economies, and social services provision. Some countries have been, and continue to be obviously unredeemably horrible. Some remain very bad in many ways, but have made some badly needed improvements. If the question is asked "have any of these Socialist states significantly improved themselves under State Socialist governance, the answer is "perhaps 12-15." In answer to the question "how many are very substantially worse", a tolerable assessment would be probably 30. Of the remaining 36, few are real successes. Most of those which have showed measurable improvement, almost all of them improved only after they were forced to retreat from stringent state domination of the economy toward a more open and competitive economy. In some cases, the nature of the Socialist leadership also changed toward more top down freedom, driven by the shift of economic elements into private hands, and the liberation of the workforce.

There is a lot of disagreement over what constitutes "failure", but a reasonably usable list of failed Socialist regimes would include the following:

Albania	Macedonia
Azerbajian	Moldava
Belarus	Mongolia
Bosnia	N. Korea
Bulgaria	Poland
Chechnya	Romania
China	Russia
Croatia	Slovakia
Czechoslavakia	Slovenia
Czech Republic	Tajikistan
Estonia	Ukraine
Georgia	Uzbekistan
Hungary	Vietnam
Kazakhstan	Yugoslavia
Krgyakhstan	Serbia
Lituuania	

In theory, SOEs were expected to capture the income value of the economy and make it available to the government for the public good. In fact, governments have been forced to subsidize most of their SOEs is a whole series of ways: guaranteed loans, subsidized loans, loan forgiveness, special government lending institutions, subsidized resources (i.e. power, fuel, transport, raw materials, etc.), cross subsidization between SOEs, import protection, controlled access to markets, export subsidy, waived profits, monopoly advantage, controlled marketing advantages, preferences for supplies and materials, an overvalued exchange rate, artificially low prices for supplies and artificially high prices for outputs.

In order to protect their status, SOEs have been made virtually risk free. Their deficits are covered by the government; their borrowing is virtually guaranteed; SOEs cannot "fail" in the private sector sense, and the government usually takes all of the heat for failure or incompetence. On the other hand, the government also forced many dysfunctions: unmanageable debt-equity ratios, sales forced at subsidized prices, labor redundancy, forced location of production, SOEs required to provide social services, regulated pricing, excessive wage levels, mandated raw materials prices – in other words, a pattern of political interference in what were supposed to be business-like enterprises. According to Robert Rothberg in his book When States Fail", "The empirical record seems to show that managers of public assets doctor their books, hoard goods, evade taxes, hide profits, and collude with other enterprises to delude or defraud the government. "They are poorly monitored, notoriously overstaffed, riddled with corruption, a big part of the patronage machine, chronic loss-makers, and financially sick in that their debt are often in excess of their real net worth."

In China and elsewhere around the world, SOEs relying on heavy duty political protection have turned arrogant and established an extraordinarily bad management reputation.

The lesson to be learned out of all of this in the U. S. is that state enterprises are dangerous,and it is fortunate that, for us, it was a road not taken. But more importantly, it has taught us that it is at the very great advantage of our government to become active stimulators of private enterprise – as opposed to a government of negativism and control. As argued earlier, government regulations that constrain, or taxes that confiscate are the worst possible public policies. Taxation, yes, but not "too much". Regulation, yes, but not beyond reason. Encouragement yes, but not subsidization.

THE AMERICAN ALTERNATIVE

================ ★ = ★ = ★ ================

W HAT IS THE ALTERNATIVE to the Socialist cradle-to-grave government? It is what Americans have really always wanted it to be—for people to learn to take care of themselves, with the government in a supportive or "safety net" role of smoothing the way, and taking care of the those not able to care for themselves. Much of what is happening in America today centers on the struggle to redefine the relationships between governments and citizens along this watershed. Governments are being forced to choose what they can and cannot do, and this is politically tough and distasteful. What is the "objective" of this struggle? It is not really for governments to eliminate poverty. It is for societies to become middle class—to which the poor aspire, and from which the rich emerge. The middle class is that class that, over a long span of history since the Industrial Revolution has been willing and capable of self reliance. The middle class is essentially what powers the developed countries, and it is beginning to serve the same role in many of the less developed countries. But there are ominous trends. A study by the congressional Joint Economic Committee (JEC) reports tha marriages are down, and births to single mothers by 2015 to 40%; fewer Americans are members of a church or religious organization, and fewer people volunteer for service. The economy is increasingly difficult for people who lack more advanced education or work skills designed to serve the new commercial/consumer economy that now dominates the American scene.

The same motivations exist, but under their own imperatives, within the African American community. As stated by U. of Washington professor, Nikhil Pal Singh, "Black is a Country", shaping its own mores, desires, motivations, beliefs and cultural elements. Blacks don't want to be whites;

they want to be better and more successful blacks. What they see as white prejudice may also be a clash between what each wants out of society, often separate, but always equal, often mixing and clashing.

There remains an exceptionally strong and widely shared belief that the well being of citizens must be guaranteed by governments, and it is unlikely that this will ever change. But there is also an increasing awareness that the range of governments has broadened, and there are many more formidable competitors for tax funds than just social service programs. There remains the dominance of national security demands.

In fact, one of the great lessons we must learn is that the world of government has become almost unbelievably huge and complex and sophisticated, to the point that it has passed beyond "management." There is no such thing as "the government" in the old fashioned Constitutional sense. Governance in the United States is an enormous conglomeration of hundreds of thousands of governmental entities, across the whole spectrum of American life.

Hundreds of thousands. There is no way that any system of government is really controlling these entities in total. Efforts are made to control each unit in their own terms, but the conflicting interests involved in each are so complex and demanding that they exceed understanding, much less control. Nobody understands this extraordinary complexity – nobody.

Many countries have given absolute priority to economic development—even over social services—in the belief that in the long run, the added wealth of a stronger economy will generate the public revenues that make the delivery of social services possible. But there are new and ominous social threats that have grown in recent years that must now be dealt with—AIDS, drug abuse, terrorism, civil unrest and civil disobedience, ethnic and religious conflicts. Environmentalism has become a world force, capable of demanding a growing share of available money and social commitment in competition with older demands. Think of it this way: every political decision or action must somehow accommodate hundreds of basic conflicting interests, implacably defended and pressed.

If greater citizen self reliance is a critical need, there are at least some positive trends to strengthen this ability. What helps people to cope with the demands of their lives, and how to improve them? Much is quite properly made of the value of education, but in a moderate and stable country the whole framework of cultural values can contribute mightily to the buttressing of individual lives. Society is carried along by custom and habit, and most of this is good because it seems to happen that the best will be approved of and adopted by most of the people. People get along, cooperate, do their jobs, protect their children, pay their bills, honor their obligations and try and help each other.

The emergence of women is an extraordinary experience. More and more women are achieving the ability to manage their own affairs, and as their talents are given broader scope, they are adding more and more to the world's economic and social base. The same thing is happening to all citizens in countries where too much control and been usurped by elites. While it seems inevitable that "the rich get richer", it is not self evident that the poor get poorer.

Flowing through society are two other human tides:: a preference for stability, status quo and enertia and resistance against "change"; and then a striking enthusiasm among many for adventure; for bold action; to try something new – an appatite for challenging that status quo. Both are high cultural influences and both are culturally important and necessary.

And the acquisition of knowledge and skill is certainly not confined to the national system of formal education. In fact, by far the greated enrichment for learning is in the workplace. People take jobs and then must learn how to do them, thus acquiring a skill – as accountants, or carpenters, or truck drivers, or retail sales people, or waiters, or up the curve as managers and executives. And increasingly, these skills arfe portable and mobile. Fewer jobs are tied to fixed locations such as manufacturing factories. An accountant or car salesman or painter can take their skills almost anywhere. This in turn has opened up both income and profits.

These cultural flexibilities have been strongly reinforced by the greater upgrading of more elements of society: women yes, and also race and ethnic populations. Women and minorities are probably the most positive force in the country to stengthen the reliance on those elements of American culture that give it its greatest strength and value because they are likely its greatest beneficiaries. It is very rewarding to understand that more people are finding ways to liberate themselves, enhance their own position in society, and right some of the wrongs of the past. The trend toward growing complexity of governance has made it critical that there will be a growing ability of citizens to penetrate the power base. In the last analysis, despite some lurches and staggers, and some failures and mistakes, the American society and economy has competently carried successfully forward. We possess both the talent and the money to govern the country successfully. The issue is really if we have the good sense and the courage.

It is an additional tragedy that, in perhaps more than a hundred countries around the world suffering from serious debilitating conflicts of war, revolutions, insurrections and heavy citizen/government clashes these cultural reinforcements are essentially being destroyed along with a stable economy and vital public services such as health care, education and transportation. It is probable however that if and when destroyed countries begin to recover, these societal reinforcements will be among the first to reassert themselves, because that is the most human thing to do.

THE NATURE OF AMERICAN GOVERNMENTS

S OME FORM OF GOVERNANCE has existed among humans from the dawn of time, beginning with the coherence of families to the bonding of clans, on to a long and complex process by which power in human affairs evolved to become more concentrated and deliberately projected. Clans became tribes, and tribes became nations. The more or less democratic forms of clan chieftains and tribal councils became parliaments and almost inevitably, these systems concentrated power and control in the hands of often dictatorial leaders. Power became the legitimate instrument of the State – the power to decide, to create facilities and services, and to develop sub systems for performance and control. The power included the ability to extract resources from the country and to decide how to deploy them. It remains generally legitimate that government power can create and maintain a military to protect the nation; or to create and maintain a system of police and courts and systems of laws for the domestic safety and security of the nation's citizens. In developing nations where private enterprises were not sufficiently developed, the government has been a legitimate option for the creation or expansion of critical elements of the economy. The government is generally accepted as a force to limit crime or terror or other unacceptable citizen conduct. These roles of government are needed and constructive – until they become excessive and oppressive.

But it is inevitable and immutable that the tides of change are always flowing, and as the world changes, and becomes far more complex, different demands are placed on people and their governments. Individual people adapt because they are forced to do so to live with the new realities. Human institutions both public and private have a certain degree of ability to choose their fate, and they have responded to change in a wide variety of ways. But every government ever created, for the last 10,000 years has possessed critical characteristics which oppose change. Government leadership has almost always been in the hands of relatively small and highly centrist ruling elite. Such governments are strongly inclined to produce a powerful oppressive leader; they stoutly resist change because it might produce a loss of power and control. Thus, they cannot abide opposition or even criticism, however modest. Few people realize that any government can, if it wishes to do so, involve itself in virtually anything and everything in the country. Why and how governments do this is endlessly complex and muddled and conflicting; endlessly arrogant and often dangerous.

In a very real sense, the norm for governments has been authority from the top down, even in the face of a fair degree of social coherence, as for example the enduring strength of tribes, clans, regions and beliefs. But centrism is the father of preferment, which is the father of corruption. What is missing is the sense of the need for the government to be accountable or to be efficient and productive. It is far more difficult to forge a government based on unity, cooperation and mutual support among people.

There are universities full of people who are studying the most worthy and noble modern theories of governance, but it is important to study governance on the dark side. One great failure is the far too human gap between pompous intellectual utterance and the enormous difficulty of actually getting anything done. So much of the decision making in governments is emotional and not essentially rational, and many of these motives are destructive – an urge for power, a greedy desire to get very rich, a cult of corrupt alliances, hatred of something or someone. Meanwhile, the general population is largely passive, feeling powerless and intimidated by oppression. The government itself will often create and exacerbate conflicts between elements of society; if people can be taught to hate each other, they may hate government less.

But the world has always found itself trying to deal with a wide variety of human dysfunctions. There is a whole range of eternal conflicts between people in families, clans, tribes, villages, regions, races and religions. There are further equally eternal conflicts between men and women, old vs. young, rural vs. urban, rich and poor, race, religion, and many, many others. Then there are our modern conflicts deliberately created: between political parties; between Communists and democrats; State Socialism vs. individualism; and the totally incomprehensible 1400 year Islamic history of Sunni vs. Shia. In fact, governments – at least good and effective governments – are perhaps the most difficult thing thing that human beings are called upon collectively to do. What people need to understand is that running a government involves not only local politics but also a command of the worlds of economic development, social services, public infrastructure, finance, national culture, environment, foreign relations, and powerful human yearnings for well being, peace, stability and even "progress". Governance has become a world of incomprehensible complexity and irreconcilable conflict. It is extraordinarily difficult to find people who can deal with such complexity, or to design institutions to assure adequate control.

In relatively well run countries like the United States, there is a reasonable recognition that the government does really important and necessary things, and does most of them reasonably well. There may be little difference between the levels of performance by public organizations and private ones. But many people feel that their government has gotten out of hand; is running amok and exceeding its reasonable roles. As the nature of governments becomes more authoritarian, the view from the bottom up becomes more fearful, involving feelings of increasing risk, and a growing sense of constriction of freedom of action. There remains the fond hope, mostly expressed by the advocates or representative democracy, that governance will ascend to a level of cooperation, persuasion, mutual respect, and the application of power through common sense and moderation.

But the modern world remains full of bad governments – corrupt, uncaring, incompetent, wasteful, unjust, oppressive and dictatorial. Bad governments always produce counter reactions from citizens. Those counter reactions may range from legitimate political opposition or to vigorous resistance to the government's policies and actions, all the way to armed conflict, insurrection and even civil war. Public resistance to bad governments may be seen as justified and deserves to succeed at some level but there is much simple human inertia, and stubborn resistance to "change" The issue becomes when such opposition can reach some fundamental characteristics of rightless and reality. Many in the U. S. believe they see portents of increasing "badness".

The main motives of national oppressors seem to blend the urge for power, advancement of some cause, and/or serious greed; but also hopefully in most countries some sense of responsibility to advance the welfare of the country and its people. But tyrannies are all too often successful, and oppressive regimes are remarkably complex and resistant to pressure and change. Tyrants are often motivated by strange combinations of perverse psychology, questionable rationalizations, and flawed visions of reality. In many cases, the success of an insurgency produces a "I am the liberator" leader who then uses that justification to perpetuate outrages against the people who have supposedly been "liberated" In other words, tyrants are often replaced by new tyrants. There are other forms of perverse psychology: a high capacity to ignore reality, the grip of some powerful prejudice, the dominant desire to control. Once in power, there is an almost overwhelming attitude to anchor power so that it is beyond challenge. And of course, in the worst case situations, dozens of governments have pushed far beyond "unfair" to the point of being actively oppressive and dangerous. Many top down governments have indeed become tyrannical, abusive, murderous and deadly, and even the average citizens are in constant fear for their own lives, their families, their property, their well-being, and their freedom.

Finally there is the fearful admission of the exist of genuine evil. It is simply true that some situations can be explained only by recognizing that a tyrant is absolutely evil and is driven by the urge to inflict pain and to do irreparable harm. This is not artificial tactics; is is basically basic inexplicable horror.

The American government has managed mostly to avoid these malfunctions. It now finds itself dealing with four great tides, each of which creates a set of demands that must be satisfied and then must be financed:

1. The provision of basic elements of government; a directing organization of government leadership and management of crucial activities; the provision of public services; a legal/judicial/court/

police system; a military establishment for defense of the country; and a nationaal system for currency and banking.

2. The demands of special interests vs. the general public interest.
3. The tides of population increase, national growth, the reality of change, the shift of populations to cities, and the hightening of sociatal sophistication.
4. Mounting national divisiveness and political and social stalemate.

The tide, especially since WWII, has been for governance to assume a broader and deeper role in American society. Not only are there more people, but their perception of the responsibilities of government has changed. Thus, not only are there more children, but it is now universally assumed that they have a **right** to education at least through secondary grades, and increasingly, the sense that a university education should also become a right, and possibly free. It is no longer enough to have adequate sources of health care available. It is now believed that health care must be provided for all people, even if that means that more of the cost must be borne by governments. Two lane roads become eight lane highways. Hundreds of airports have spung up. Millions of acres have become national lands and their care and maintenance publically financed. The elderly must be cared for, often at public expense. The unemployed must be publically supported – and on and on.

The modern American economy has slowly evolved into a far more complex and often disturbing set of relationships between the government and private business. Public money is provided to private organizations in hundreds of strange and mysterious ways through the tax system, the public budget, and the structure of regulations.

In sum, as governance has become broader and more sophisticated, it has inevitably become far more expensive. It is very important to understand this reality: the potential system at all levels will be fed and lubricated by its ability to spend. It is wonderfully rewarding politically to be the provider of some public good or service. It seems infinitely painful for politicians to say no. As a consequence, government has simply burgeoned. It is an engine that can move in only one direction. There is little effective constraint and little ability to refuse or reform. Nor is this expansion a response to any coherent plan or sense of defined purpose or sense of limitation.

All of this must be funded. Each of the hundreds and hundreds of public programs must be financed. The Catalog of Federal Domestic Assistance now lists more than 1000 federal grant programs. Each of these programs requires a government organization and staffs and delivery mechanisms, creating a whole a second range of costs in addition to the costs of the programs themselves. And the fact that the government operates at a deficit means that there is an additional cost through the financing of enormous government debt.

Then there are two additional tides. America is so alluring that it attracts immigrants from all over the world. There are now about 40 million people who immigrated to this country, legally and illegally, during the last 2-3 decades. In the short term, they are costly. It is hoped and expected that in the long term they will be productive. Then, since WWII, America has been the most extensive participant in international relationships, and there again, there are major demands for financial support for an urgent and growing range of assistance demands in every part of the world. With the new wave of national conflicts and terrorist oppression, this need can truly become the perverbial bottomless pit.

Thus, the size and range of the government seems destined to continue to expand and to challenge the acceptance of the American public. Increasingly, many people are willing and able to construct a counter power base which can offer some protection from mandated government from the top down, and provide a base for negotiations with a very demanding centrist regime. Local governments are able to argue their own interests versus the centrist control. Private companies are automatically a counter force against government oppression, but on the other hand, private special interest groups can bargain their support of the regime in exchange for protection and preferment. The military, the police, and lately the intelligence services always form their own power centers. Corruption can be used to strike deals between the crooked parties.

The bottom up world has two further levels of functioning. In the first, there will be people who oppose a regime, but do not try to overthrow it. Instead, they insert themselves into elements of the establishment, hoping to mitigate its excesses, and to push forward moderating positions and ideas. This is the essence of the current stance of the two American political parties.This is an extraordinarily long term approach, but it is often the one that works. Governments do moderate themselves. Other people simply decide that the safe course is just to "go along to get along", hoping to dodge any stray bullets on the way. But many people are willing and able to construct a counter power base which can offer some protection and provide a base for negotiations with the holders of power.

Some of the patterns of governance are so horrible that they surpass rational understanding. The more one studies the roles of bad governments, the more one is forced to accept the fact of human evil. After all of the excuses are examined and rejected, and motivations are explained, and not believed, there remains a horrible number of human actions that are inhuman and insane, and utterly beyond rational explanation. The United States constitutional system, and the positive attitudes of the great majority of the population have succeeded in protecting the country against such horrors.

Governments are always "top down"; people are "bottom up". Governments are necessarily about the exercise of power. National leaders are almost by definition centrists in character, and most of the philosophies that have been developed about how to run a government are highly centrist as well, ranging from the pharaohs as gods, to the divine right of kings, to Communism, State Socialism or the Islamic Caliphate. Even representative democracy, in modern times, has a strong tendency to justify the supposed need for more and more direction from the top. The ultimate level of bottom up activity is armed resistance to the regime: street protests, anti-government actions, attacks on government officials and facilities, insurrections, or civil war. These forms of action are excruciatingly difficult and dangerous. In some cases, regimes of crooks and scoundrels are overthrown, only to be replaced by a new group of crooks and scoundrels. But the glory is that many such drastic bottom up surges have triumphed.

Beyond the governments that are merely bad are the governments decend to the level of human evil. After all of the excuses are examined and rejected, and motivations explained and not believed, there remains a horrible number of human actions that are inhuman and insane, and utterly beyond rational explanation. Many of these actions are perpetrated by individuals or small groups, but these actions can inflict unbelievable death and destruction. Terror groups like Boko Haram in Nigeria, or al-Qaeda or ISIS may posture that they are saving people from corrupt and inept governments, but they cannot conceivably offer any explanation that justifies the nature of the hellish attacks against defenseless people and the deliberate slaughter of innocents, including even the smallest of children. Americans need to understand how fortunate they are because our governance and society have largely been able to avoid sinking into these bottomless pits.

GOVERNMENTS RIGHT AND WRONG

★ ═ ★ ═ ★

How do we judge whether our government is "right" or "wrong"? By what standards or criteria do citizens make that judgment? If we are to judge whether government institutions and leaders are corrupt or pathological we need to employ some framework for that judgment. A bad government is not necessarily corrupt or pathological. A government may be bad for the following reasons:

* Honest Error: Governing is very complex and almost always characterized by direct conflict of interests over every issue. It is possible therefore for politicians or government officials simply to be honestly mistaken. This situation is neither corrupt nor pathological.

* Incompetence: Even when the government is right in its policies or management choices, it may fail because of incompetence including poor leadership, the lack of adequate skills, knowledge, or understanding, the lack of adequate public funding, deep and unreconciled public divisiveness or external forces beyond its control such as world economic recession.

* Pathology: A government may be truly pathological because of perverse policies and practices, leadership lacking courage and moral conviction, or leadership that is excessively dictatorial, or merely corrupt. This may include misdirected financing and delivery of public services, the failure to adhere to constitutions, the perversion of the rule of law, and the deliberate neglect of the best interests of the nation as a whole. Governments may deliberately limit access to their internal machinations to reduce opposition or cover up corruption. And most perversely, governments may deliberately choose to mismanage their

affairs – by a willful failure to identify and prevent failure modes and letting "fail safe" systems such as auditors and inspectors deliberately fail. A government is pathological when it knows it shows repeated and persistent incompetence or error, yet it does not apply adequate effort to correct these known problems. Similarly, there may be stubborn adherence to failed doctrinal policies, despite strong evidence of their failure, or the unwillingness to recognize the need for change and respond to it. Many a government goes wrong when they wallow in incompetence and inertia.

HOW TO DEFINE GOOD AND BAD LAWS

Since anything and everything can and is locked into law, it is very important to decide how broad and interventionist the body of laws should be. Is it necessary and desirable that everything in society must be law defined, driven or limited? One school of thought has been that laws should be limited to areas which civil society cannot adequately handle for itself. Important arenas such as religion or individual thought and action, or social relationships within a community are left largely free of legal intervention. Another school defends the premise that most of what happens in society will evolve properly only when defined, directed and constrained by a broad, overarching body of legal structure. The tendency has been that, as societies develop from the primitive to the complex and as the numbers and diversity of the population increase, most societies have little choice but to extrapolate the body of laws to deal with the complexities and conflicts that modern societies create. But there is the further necessity to choose between good and bad law, and indeed to evolve some framework for defining goodness and badness. The following is an attempt to discuss such a framework.

THE NATURE OF LAWS

A law may be good if it reflects and adopts the best values of the society itself, and rejects the worst values. Such laws will reinforce what is good but -what is more difficult to define - - what is destructive or dysfunctional. Laws should reflect what is generally regarded as acceptable social standards of fairness and equity. These social standards may arise from social and cultural mores, religious principles, and widely held views about what is just and equitable. They may capture enduring community preferences, and even a sense of what succeeds or fails.

Also, one of the greatest public concerns is the sense of outrage when laws are seen as inequitable and unfair, and when they deliberately create greater inequity in society or set out to abuse the interests of minorities. Other vague but telling phrases are used to describe bad laws, such as unethical, intolerant, undemocratic, improper, of dubious intent, socially undesirable, inappropriate, or just plain "wrong". Pathological leaders have proved time and again that they can turn the rule of law upside down. Here are some of the perverse laws that pathological regimes employ, and some of them have a grip on American governance:

1. To block the electoral system which provides for free elections; to forbid political parties and block the political efforts of everybody but the government itself.
2. Operating the tax system to reward friends and deprive enemies, and then cynicallly to forgive the tax debts of regime supporters and friends.
3. To control information sources so completely that criticism of the government is impossible, and to try is very dangerous.
4. Control the creation and functioning of organizations in the country including businesses, economic organizations, or social activist groups.
5. Giving preference or limitation to specific ethnic, religious or tribal groups for access to public services or resources.
6. Assign key government appointments to loyalists without regard to ability or rationality.
7. Dispose of public assets such as land, buildings, mineral rights of valuable concessions in corrupt, illegal and destructive ways.
8. Maintain a corrupt control over the deployment of public funds through government contracts, grants, bank lending and tax policies.

9. Subsidize inefficient and loss-making state owned enterprises, in large part to conceal both economic and political failure.

10. To retain failed organizations, programs and policies, even where their failure is obvious, congenital and destructive.

11. Pursue a policy of redundant employment in government agencies and state owned enterprises to conceal the true level of unemployment.

12. Deny real independence to judges and public prosecutors, thus limiting the availibility of real justice.

13. "Selectively" enforce public regulations, again to help supporters and punish opponents.

14. Use the police and the military to suppress almost any form of civil activity.

15. Extend excessive power to government intelligence services, giving them unlimited access to any information about private organizations and people.

16. Pervert the election system so that elections can easily be "stolen".

LIMITING THE RANGE OF LAW.

Another important criterion centers around the idea that laws should reflect only those actual needs in society that require political intervention—as opposed to the idea that laws should encompass everything. There are several reasons for this sense of wanting to limit the scope of laws. First, universal law means universal government, and there remains a deep seated resistance in the United States to such an idea. Second, it is presumed, or at least hoped, that laws will be liberating, useful, enabling and facilitative. But there is plenty of evidence that in reality, many are inhibiting, controlling and constraining, even if justified by an acceptable public purpose. Each law further creates the necessity for enforcement, which may require the reduction of individual or group freedom of choice and action. Third, the aggregate of all laws can (and usually is) so complex that it defies understanding, even by the people who must administer them.

It is possible to design a system of governance so complex that it cannot be governed, and such complexity is the enemy of democratic understanding. And experience has proved that what the people really want is often very different than what politicians think is good for them. It is useful therefore to argue that government laws should be kept as simple as possible, and within the range of what people can understand if they try. A target should be to define the "least" government that is consistent with national need and intent. As collateral to this reasoning, the more complex and confusing a body of laws become, the more possibilities are created for misuse and corruption. Therefore, laws should be written to meet the general public good and this standard should always be held up against legislation proposed merely for the advantage of some special elite or specific special interest.

The process of reform has to start at the top with the drafting of national laws. There should be constant pressure to define in law if possible that which is not authorized, or is specifically forbidden, or is defined as illegal. Even policy statements that do not convey specific authority can still be used to commit to national goals and preferred actions. The point is that any means of preventing pathology from being locked into law is of enormous value. Any limitation of political excess of power is worth fighting for. Even if these laws are ignored or violated, they still serve as anchors which opponents of a regime can use to justify attacks on tyrants.

Similarly, politicians love to draft broad noble sounding legislative language which seems to promise a government solution to all ills. But reality often is that the broader and more open ended the legislative language, the more power it conveys, and the more vulnerable it is to pathological interpretation. There is usually too great a gap between legislative flights of fancy and the harsher world of implementation. Even in wealthy and stable countries, there is increasing disenchantment over legislative promises not kept. In authoritarian states, wide open legislative mandates are often deliberately sought, since each represents a form of legislative abdication. It transfers all power to the executive and leaves the legislature with no basis for curbing that executive power. Once such wide authority is obtained by the executive, it is extremely difficult to take back, and legislative bodies, having conceded too much, become largely irrelevant.

It is therefore exceedingly important that legislative bodies must be pressed, by whatever forces in the country can be brought to bear, to retain their ability to act as a counter force to the usurpation of power by the executive. Legislatures need to protect their own authority, first by having the courage to resist pressures to corrupt the laws, and then through their own internal control of the law drafting process. The American two house legislature appears to be superior to a single house because it creates some checks and balances between the two, making it more difficult for executives to collect power. It is also valuable to create a separation between the drafting of laws and the approval of appropriations of the money to implement the law. As an adjunct of this reasoning, legislative bodies should resist any authority of the government to generate revenue that is not officially controlled through the legislative oversight process. Further, the legislature must guard the Constitution and important basic authorizing laws by making them harder to change, usually by requiring a 2/3 majority vote for change approval, or even requiring a Constitutional convention to ratify change. The Constitution and supporting legislation should clearly authorize the conduct of political parties, and preferably they should lay down the rules for honest elections in some detail if possible. Constitutional definition of proper elections would highlight the nature of such pathology and provide a stronger basis for opposition.

Also if possible, Constitutions or basic laws should provide mechanisms to prevent the abuse of presidential appointment powers. Patronage is one of the most powerful tools of authoritarian regimes, and it conveys four great advantages. First, it is used to make sure that key jobs – particularly those which involve control of money or the allocation of valuable resources – are filled by regime loyalists who will do as they are told. Second, political allies and supporters can be rewarded for past services. In many cases, these payoff jobs are in lesser positions such as "commissions" or "boards" with little or nothing to do. Third, some appointments will be protective. For example, if a law requires the appointment of an Inspector General in an agency, the threat of that office to the corrupt can be mitigated by the appointment of a loyalist or an incompetent to the post. Fourth, appointments can reach down below the crucial top positions. Unless the number and location of authorized positions is strictly controlled, the agency can be filled with numerous, largely meaningless jobs such as "special assistants", or "assistant deputies" or "deputy assistants", all of which provide comfortable salaries without the discomfort of doing any work.

LIMITING THE RANGE OF GOVERNMENT.

Laws about the structure and authority of the government itself are of particular concern. Many a hopeful new nation has drafted a constitution and an initial package of enabling statutes, only to find out later that these documents are so vague and inconclusive that they are not only useless but dangerous. Laws should be clear about their purpose, defining both powers to act and the limitations of those powers. Vague, open-ended statutes or regulations are highly vulnerable to misinterpretation, unwarranted extrapolations of power, abuses of authority, and the corrupt exercise of legitimate authority. Instead of vagueness, laws should provide the public with a clear explanation of why the law is necessary, what it will authorize, who it will benefit, and how it will be implemented. Many laws are "missions impossible"; they appear to enable a response to some public problem, but prove to be impossible to carry out. Almost every country has laws that mandate "the elimination of poverty", or "university education for all", or "a clean environment", yet in fact, neither the government nor society itself may be able fully to achieve such goals.

The public has a right to expect that governments will operate with reasonable efficiency, and that public programs will in fact deliver the goods or services expected of them. While there is little direct lobbying support for "government efficiency" there is certainly a willingness to see some public money invested in a stable and competent civil service, proper maintenance and repair of public facilities, efforts to improve performance and productivity, adaptation of the advantages of new technologies.

It is much the same with the institutions of the government. Most are given exceedingly broad legal charters, but then the political system proves incapable or unwilling to live up to its grand promises, or to prevent the abuse of such wide-open authority. In reality, it is probably wiser to write each law so that it limits authority only to that necessary to carry out the law's defined purpose, and to limit the ability to extrapolate political and bureaucratic authority into areas that the law did not contemplate.

If there is a defining philosophy for the drafting of laws it should be that the body of national laws should reflect as closely as possible the accepted social standards and mores of the civil community, and they should be written to be empowering, facilitative, and realistically achievable rather than restrictive, constraining, prejudicial and hopelessly impractical. This does not mean that laws cannot and should not be visionary, but governments should avoid creating unattainable expectations or making promises it cannot keep. There are similar problems with the cherished concept of "accountability". In the political science sense, this usually means accountability of the bureaucracy and of appointed officials upward to the political leadership of the executive and legislative branches of the government. But here again, what if this leadership is corrupt? Is it not pathological for corrupt leaders to demand blind loyalty as the only test of accountability? Corrupt organizations too are "accountable" but in ways that become dysfunctional since they reinforce the hand of such pathological leadership. Consider for example, the problem of an honest program official who has been ordered to do something that is inherently wrong. Is it proper for that official to be held "accountable" to bad leadership; or are there other values of the sense of accountability that apply?

In its broadest sense, accountability in the American government means many things, the most important being accountability to the general citizenry, and this accountability should run from top to bottom. Stated more firmly, accountability to the general citizenry – to "the country" – is ultimately more important than loyalty to the agency head, or the Congress or to "the government". It should also mean accountability to the longer term guiding principles of good governance; to the body of general laws and regulations; to one's personal and professional ethics; responsiveness to the wellbeing of one's organization and of the organization's workers.

Within the framework of a nation's political structure there is a second structure consisting of the agencies of the government – ministries, departments, bureaus, commissions, and their professional substructures. Like all organizations, these institutions may be skillful or incompetent or corrupt. When organizations are instruments of government, they should be held to a higher standard of probity and responsibility than may be typical of private institutions. In the best of governments, there is a common ethic of positive public service that should be reinforced by laws that set forth clear principles and policies and procedures as to how public service should be rendered. There should be no doubt as to what is legal or acceptable practice. This cannot be done without many areas of doubt, but as much as possible should be clear and unambiguous. Every public process should deal with the possibilities of corruption.

While private organizations can operate in private, in general, government organizations should not. There should be open government all the way from legislative policy formulation to the execution of ministerial process. It is not enough to make the functioning of the bureaucracy open, if the political process is concealed.

Of great importance is the need for a clear understanding of the obligation of the government to respond adequately to proved, important needs or threats. It is pathological to be inert—to fail to decide—or to be unable or unwilling to take action. Specifically, it can be judged pathological when it is clear that the government knows there is a problem/opportunity, and fails (at least to try) to act. The public is also entitled to a reasonable degree of governmental efficiency and effectiveness. Government agencies are after all not simply clerical paper pushing but are huge and sophisticated management problems requiring the use of systematic, integrated and comprehensive management policies and procedures. This in turn requires a well trained and educated civil service motivated by a spirit of honesty and serious effort from the top down. Not all things in government are politics, driven by political motives. At some point, the political structure should allow the professional managers to take over and apply their own form of skills. This should include some way for the career service to point out where the political context is wrong, or where political leaders are standing in the way of effective management results.

Finally, there is the growing recognition that the most important concept is that of "governance" which is broader and more fundamental than simply the role of the government structure itself. Thus, there is a critical need for a widely involved segment of the whole civil community that concerns itself with the validity of its government's actions. The government has two critical responsibilities to this community of concern: it must maintain its openness, and provide the kinds of public information that lets the public understand what is happening, and there must also be some mechanisms for the government to be criticized from the outside, and some willingness to respond to legitimate criticism of violations of stated mandates. The whole civic community should be able to turn to a legal system that is fair and honest and accessible when needed. Other forces external to government apparatus, such as a free press and public interest groups are powerful assurances that "governance" will be broader than just the government itself.

The rightness or wrongness of government can be tested by attempting to examine the context of how societies themselves judge "good or bad"; "acceptable or unacceptable". What people think is often based on what they believe. Societies have developed many doctrines – sets of fixed beliefs – that have internal coherence and which provide a comforting sense of stability and a means of responding to new ideas or dilemmas in society. These doctrines therefore can become the basis for defining the characteristics of our government and for suggesting answers to problems. At the very least, they become a means for understanding how the government is likely to react to the need for policy formulation. The following seem to be the most commonly used frameworks for making such judgments:

A. RELIGIOUS DOCTRINE

Predominantly religious states such as contemporary Iran are very rare, and such a state was deliberately prohibited in the framing of the U. S. system and Constitution, and like the predominant pattern in the world, we have become a secular state with very limited degrees of formal religious intervention or involvement. The long term trend has been to move away from states dominated by priesthoods (ancient Egypt or Catholic Spain) toward more secular forms of leadership of both government and society in which the authority of religious leadership is much retrenched. This is not seen as a rejection of religion, but only a resistance to religion in its ability to function at the political level. While religious doctrine may offer valuable frameworks of ethics and morality upon which governments can draw, religious zeal and the rigidity of religious doctrine are very difficult to cope with in the political context of negotiation and compromise. Even when religious leaders attempt to remain flexible, they may still see the world in terms of two parts of society—the faithful, and all others.

In the United States, the main concern has been "the separation of church and state"—a lesson learned from the older countries of Europe and the Middle East where involvement of religion in governments had been greater and more complex and intensive. Even now, it is not unusual for organized churches in other countries to have heavy involvement in political parties, important influence in government bodies, and active involvement in political campaigning. Religious involvement seems most constructive when it acts as a moral force in society, rather than as a basis for active political leadership.

Aside from the role of organized religion, is there a "morality" of governance? Is the American government guided by some religious thought expressing the nature of accepted moral principles? If so, are moral principles reflected in the official policies and actions of the government?

The answer seems to be "sometimes" and "somewhat". In earlier, simpler times almost every one of the rudimentary concepts that drove tribes and clans and villages were based on a fear of God, and the need to please or placate Him. Kings and emperors and pharoahs insisted that they ruled by divine right. Yet reality seems to show that obedience to god was often more rhetoric than fact, and leaders simply acted in their own self interest, clothed with religious rectitude. In fact, governments dominated by religion seem to be dysfunctional when bad leaders, pursuing horrible policies, insist that they are instructed by God whose will cannot be challenged. But St. Mathew said in the new testament "For we wrestle not against flesh and blood, but against municipalities, against power, against the rulers of darkness of this world, against wickedness in high places."

And yet, on the other side of this reality is the hope that a belief in God and the morality that is a vital component of every religion will permeate the minds and hearts of people and their rulers as a powerful force for good. Said another way, where people struggle against oppressive regimes, they most often do so by relying upon and advocating the enduring moral principles espoused by their religion. Many concepts of morality are judged good or bad for governments.

GOOD	BAD
1. Fairness and the lack of prejudice	1. Unfair, deliberately prejudiced
2. Being constructive and helpful	2. Negative and dysfunctional
3. Telling the truth	3. Lying as official policy
4. "Thou shalt not steal"	4. Government officials as crooks
5. Opposition to terrorism and crime	5. Government sponsored terrorism
6. Positive influences on society	6. Govts. Negative, oppressive
7. Civil equity	7. Deliberate divisiveness
8. Official honesty	8. Deliberate misinformation
9. Defense of freedom	9. Special interests, preferment
10. The Rule of Law	10. But – evil laws.

B. THE LAW VS. JUSTICE

Another eternal dispute, reflecting the extraordinary difficulty in developing a moral base for governance, is the apparently universal conflict between "the law" and "justice". Every government, both good and bad, has established a system of laws and their implementing regulations. These laws are supposedly society's attempt to establish what is good and acceptable versus what is bad and should be rejected. As argued elsewhere here, this body of laws and regulations can be misused, but the more fundamental argument posed here is that, despite the best of human efforts, the laws may not really define what the collective wisdom sees as right and just. Here are a few examples:

1. The Koran is almost universally accepted by Muslims as the unquestioned guide for the conduct of the Faithful; yet there is a widespread feeling that even this holy guidance is unfair to women in almost every facet of their lives; that it denys the authority of any government not totally based on the Koran as defined by religious leaders; and that it justifies killing non-Muslims and even Muslim apostates.

2. A very poor man may be driven to theft to feed and clothe his family; but "the law" sends him to prison and his family suffers.

3. In countless cases, it is said that the very rich can subvert the law through illegal means, and thus escape any justified punishment.

4. Huge companies maneuver to avoid any taxation, while the middle class pays through the nose.

5. There are hundreds of thousands of cases where the provisions of laws and regulations are blatantly ignored or perverted.

6. Corruption runs rampant, and efforts to control it are seen as inadequate, incompetent or deliberately ignored.

7. The deliberate action to avoid legitimate taxation often has the status of a national sport, enthusiastically played by millions of cheaters.

8. Known criminals cannot be convicted because of inadequacies of the criminal justice system.

In reality, these conflicts are very improper, but they are very human. Is it better to obey some government rule, or to feed your family? The recent American political campaign posed many such moralistic dilemmas: it it right for the rich to get even richer while the poor get poorer? Is it right to try to keep out poor and oppressed people fleeing from terrible dictatorships? How can we stand by and watch millions of people around the world getting killed and injured or forced to flee as refugees? Why do we underfund organizations that are trying to feed starving people? Why are the rights of blacks and women and people of transgender so poorly dealt with? Ultimately – why are our government leaders in Congress and the governments so weak and lacking for courage?

There are many other moral dilemmas beyond the above, and they seem to have been around forever in one form or another. Perhaps what they seem to show is that they are never solved because they are insoluable. At an equally murky level, the roles of government can be questioned around their basic intent. Fundamentally, in this country, it has been more or less assumed that the very existance of a functioning system of governance is positive and facilitative. But this assumption is shaky as richly experienced in the recent U. S. presidential election campaign which was widely seen as all about "can't" and "don't": about constraint and conflict and restriction, and both the protection against change and the urgent need for it. What people feel now is that they might get basic help or service from governments, but what they cannot expect is enablement or facilitation or innovation or friendly assistance. Increasingly, they think that what they see is ominous – top down control rather than bottom up sense – endless, often mindless extrapolation of government authority, and a bureaucracy that favors process over principle, and an arrogance where the government believes that only it knows what is right and should be done. Compliance with rules is "right"; creativity is not provided for.

But perhaps the most important change now emphasized is the public perception of these changes. Forty years ago, American governments were generally well respected, along with the civil service. But this perception has radically changed, and has become ominously worse. In 1972, when public opinion polls posed questions like "do you trust the government to do the right things?" or "how well is the government managing programs?" the public response was favorable at the level of 70% or more. But a similar poll conducted by the Zogby Organization in 2007 showed positive views down to about 47%, and negative views at an all time high. A similar poll conducted in May of 2011 by Hart Research Associates, for the Center for American Progress was even worse. The "confidence in government" was down to 35%, and the "no confidence" factor was at an all time high of 33%. Many polls now are not just about politics; they are increasinglly about management. Many newer polls are now asking questions that more clearly relate to the terrain of the government's executives and managers and not just its politicians; and these ratings make difficult reading. There are increasing concerns about programs that are wasteful or ineffective, contractors overcharging the government, smelly tax breaks, bribery, excessive military spending, government duplication and overlap, lack of technological advancement, and high cost/low value programs or programs that are obsolete.

The government has the reputation of not ever being able to change itself, yet this is very obviously wrong. We now have four new cabinet agencies, perhaps thirty whole new independent agencies, and another fifteen or twenty that have been substantially modified and upgraded. The federal government has actually even abolished 12-15 agencies! New programs have been initiated; program funds are being better targeted;

there have been countless efforts to cut costs, make better cost estimates, and control cost overruns. And yet, the public concerns are far from satisfied. The new fear is that America is somehow inventing it own version of the concepts of State Socialism, which are in general retreat in countries around the world. The ideals of universal health care and free university education remind us of the old Soviet socialist guarantees of supporting and defining the lives of people "from the cradle to the grave". It must be remembered that "cradle to the grave" really meant <u>control: control of people and their lives.</u> The answer to this kind of posed dilemma is basically a deeply moral one.

In the end, we will come to realize the implacable conflicts inherent in human kind. The world is never risk free; there cannot be created a risk free world. What can be done is for people to demand that their leadership does not exacerbate these conflicts for shoddy political advantage; that the nature of govenance should be more positive and supportive. We must somehow stop the government's preoccupation with "can't", or with "us vs. them". Human choice is the enemy of regulation. Governance can be shifted to laws, policies and regulations that are simpler, shorter and based more on principles of guidance and away from restrictions and prohibitions. If this were to happen, it would produce a desirable reduction of challenges and law suits over the enforcement of government's vast layer of control. People yearn to believe that "the rule of law" will define all that is good and proper, but the rule of law is not enough, since the laws themselves can be perverted or ignored.

C. POLITICAL DOCTRINE

Every state is a political state, and most have constructed a doctrinal framework articulating some broad and generalized form of governance. The most prominent political frameworks in use today are communism, state socialism, representative democracy and centrist authoritarianism. None of these frameworks are absolute, and they often overlap or are in conflict in some very confusing ways. But in each country the prevailing political framework is seen as a vital way to explain and justify the policies of the government to the people, and to provide a test of acceptability for each encountered public policy issue. Different versions of the predominant political doctrine may be constantly in conflict, but this is normally seen as healthy. Socialism vs. capitalism; the "right" vs. the "left"; Republicans vs. Democrats—all bring vigor and change, and keep the political doctrine from being too rigid. It is simply not possible for any government to invent a new political theory for every new issue. Therefore, political parties or interests are constantly negotiating the practical consequences of political doctrine, and the results are used to define what is right and wrong.

The United Nations has repeatedy sought to define a world-wide array of international development goals, which are in fact a compelling moral statement of what should be the ideal set of political doctrines. The Millenium Development Goals as defined anew in 2016 are as follows:

1. Eradicate extreme poverty and hunger
2. Achieve universal primary education
3. Promote gender equality and empower women
4. Reduce child mortality
5. Improve maternal health
6. Combat HIV/AIDS, malaria and other diseases
7. Ensure environmental sustainability
8. Develop a global partnership for development.

Obviously, it would be hard for anybody to object to any of these noble objectives, but they should be seen primarily as a somewhat pompous assertion of all that is seen as good and noble. Compliance by nations is voluntary, and it is certain that any degree of success will be claimed by the UN as the result of their goal setting. Meanwhile, other agonizingly serious problems have not been recognized. For example, 161 of the 196 countries of the world have enthusiastically endorsed the UN Convention Against Corruption, including almost all of the enthusiastically corrupt regimes in the world. Countries where starvation is desperate, or children are malnourished, or women are treated unequally are all dutiful signatories of the Millenium Goals.

CULTURAL IMPERATIVES AS DOCTRINE

Every society is really based on its culture, which is a combination of ethnic, religious, racial, tribal and social mores. Social coherence is imbedded in deeply felt concepts of survival and self-protection, identity, mutual support, and broad judgments about what is good and bad, and what needs support or resistance. The more forcefully these cultural mores are held, the more they tend to become doctrine that must be defended and not allowed to change. Cultural values must be honored by the government, whether they seem rational or not. Thus, "good" governments are those that find a way to accept theses values and incorporate them into policy.

One of the most powerful of these cultural mores is the sense of nationalism - the degree of national coherence and sense of nationhood beyond tribalism or narrow geographical identity. In a sense, nations are what tribes become—broader, more inclusive, more powerful, and with higher potential. Nations become more future oriented and more instrumental, and "what is good for the country" becomes a powerful determinant of what governments decide to do.

Most people have a strong willingness to be <u>responsible.</u> Flowing through society are two human tides: a preference for stability, status quo, and an inertia against "change"; and a striking enthusiasm among many for adventure; for bold action; for trying something new – an appetite for challenging uncertainty. This is not either/or. Both are high cultural influences and both are culturally important and necessary.

And the acquisitiion of knowledge and skill is certainly not confined to the national formal education system. In fact, by far the greatest environment for learning is really in the workplace. People take jobs and then must learn how to perform them, thus learning a skill – as accountants, or carpenters, or truck drivers, or retail sales people, or waiters, or up the curve as managers and executives. Increasingly, these skills are portable and mobile. Fewer jobs are tied to fixed locations such as manufacturing factories. A doctor or lawyer or car salesman or painter can take their skills almost anywhere. This in turn has opened people's lives.

GOVERNMENT CONCEPTS OF EQUALITY

Equality is argued first and foremost as a moral issue. Theologically, equality means that all people are born equal, with equal God-given potential. Government equality means that governments should treat people or classes of people or parts of the country the same in terms of the impact of laws, regulations and the availability of public programs. But the problems for governments (as well as for theologians) are that equality in this simpler sense does not reflect public reality. Governments seldom dispute the quality of human potential but they must decide a thousand ways in which they can facilitate or impede the manner in which people and institutions in society try to realize this potential, or the benefits from government they are allowed to receive.

Equality may also mean equality of opportunity and here the government's role is argued in three ways: one is that governments should as seldom as possible <u>prevent</u> opportunity; second, it may be argued that the government has a positive obligation to <u>create</u> opportunity; and third is the supposed obligation of governments to <u>assure</u> equality of opportunity.

Perhaps the more difficult definition to address is the concept of equality in terms of outcome. This argues that everybody's lives must be about equally successful and that no element of society should be allowed to succeed significantly better than another element. This is unrealistic, and it seems mostly an extrapolation (deliberate or inadvertent) of the equality of opportunity arguments. Not all elements of our society value the same things, nor are they all equally capable of reaching their potentials. Some societies are conflict prone. Some have degenerated into terrorist societies. Some are torn by deliberate, government-driven conflict. Thus, while human potential is God-given, reality is that societal potential varies widely as a function of history, resources, social mores, economic well-being, and the quality of our leadership. But surely, at least governments can position themselves as promoters and facilitators of the greatest levels of **opportunity.**

These cultural flexibilities have been strongly reinforced by the greater upgrading of more enabled elements of society: women and ethnic and racial populations especially. Women and minorities are probably the most positive force in the country to strengthen the reliance on the elements of

American culture that give it the greatest enoblement. It is an additional tragedy around the world that, in the 100 or more countries suffering from debilitating conflicts of wars, revolutions, insurrections and heavy citizen/government chashes, these cultural reinforcements can essentially be destroyed, along with the any stable economy and the deterioration of vital public services. It is probable however that, if and when destroyed countries begin to recover, these societal reinforcements will be among the first to reassert themselves, because that is the most human thing to do. In the United States for example, each year the American public donates an astonishing $390 billion to a broad range of philanthropic enterprises, and more than $314 billion of these funds come from individuals.

Many such values exist simultaneously and are often in conflict. Ways must be found by governments to treat each equitably relative to the other elements of society. Cultural imperatives are often in conflict with political motives. There is also a terrible tendency of politicians to use these conflicts to pit one element in society against another, or to deliberately slant political largesse to gain short term political advantage. In fact, the best role of governments is to play the mediator and produce balanced judgments in the broad public interest.

What are the characteristics of a truly civil society?

1. The concept of national equality of rights under government laws and processes. There is a great risk that governments may pathologically seek to pit one element of society against others for political gain. National equality rests primarily on the ability of civil society itself to honor this need, relying on a high degree of interpersonal trust and mutual responsibility. If such equality exists among the general public it becomes the greatest bulwark against a "divide and conquer" political mentality.

2. Equality must be accompanied by a strong sense of enlightened self interest among citizens and avoidance of dangerous over reliance on the government. In extraordinary ways, this sense of self interest can be accompanied by effective group interaction around mutual interests, outside of governments and often counter to government imperatives. Many governments will constitutionally declare their

citizens to be independent, but the real test is how dependent a citizen may be on the government, or the degree to which individuals can meet critical needs themselves. In the old Soviet system, few citizens were permitted to own their own homes, to invest in and develop their own businesses, or to accumulate any of the attributes of wealth that permitted them a real degree of independence. If the State failed to make good on its promises, as it often did, individuals and families had almost nothing of their own to fill the gap. One of the great dilemmas of the collapse of the Soviet Union was just this issue: if not the State, then what?

3. <u>Politics balanced by the power of the courts</u>. Courts must be given, and must defend, a high degree of independence, and must be protected against control by either a tyrannical regime or a captive legislature. The starting point for such independence is in a constitution defining a mandated court system including a supreme court, a stipulation of independence of functioning, and a clear statement of the illegality and impropriety of meddling with that independence. But even the bedrock of constitutional definition is not enough, and the courts themselves must defend their own independence, and "sell" the importance of that independence to the general public. The appointment of judges is a crucial vulnerability. Authoritarian regimes will be motivated to "stack" the courts with their own loyalists. Great courage on the part of judges, both individually and collectively, is needed to resist such control. Reformist governments, if able to come into power, should move first and fastest to liberate the judicial system at all levels as a first priority of reform. Courts are also perhaps the most critical element of any program for attacks on corruption, which rests primarily on illegal acts that investigators and prosecutors can address. The most critical element however is in those pathologies that have been made legal. These pathologies can be purged by election of a reformist government and the revitalization of honest legislatures, but many crucial dilemmas will end up in the courts which must be free to eliminate their specious legality.

4. <u>Politics challenged by the media</u>. For this to be real, the media must be granted independence from the government, and have a legal base defined by law including defined protections from almost any form of political or bureaucratic interference. Any state ownership of media organizations such as newspapers or TV stations should be suspect, even where there are independent media outlets as well. But the real issue is the vulnerability of the media to control by other means: threats and intimidation; suppression of media content, laws that limit the freedom of views that the media may express, denial of funding either by the government or by private resources, denial of access to important information sources, and corrupted leadership.

5. <u>The "balance of powers" doctrine</u>, involving the chief executive, the legislature, the courts, the bureaucracy, and the allocation of government powers to different levels of government. In many countries, the balance of powers extends into three other critical sets of relationships: the government vs. the private sector; and the civilian government vs. the military establishment; and the power of special interests vs. the general wellbeing. Again, the starting point should be a clear definition in a constitution as to the separation of powers, and if possible, a clear expression of how these powers should be "balanced" each with respect to the other. But a balance of power of some kind will happen, whether the constitution defines it or not. In the Soviet Union for example, the real power holders were the Communist Party, the military, and the intelligence organizations. In many countries, it is the elite, somewhat offset by the bulk of an unorganized opposition by "all other." Once a "balance of power" is established, it becomes exceedingly difficult to displace.

6. <u>Governance should be diffused between the central government and regional and local governments</u>. It is widely accepted among both scholars of government and its practitioners that the practical operational affairs of government should be conducted by those governments that are closest to the people and most responsive to

their needs and desires. It is probably also true that state/provincial taxes and municipal taxes are more acceptable to individuals than taxes paid to remote central governments. But the real case here is that decentralization of power to local governments reduces the power of the centrist government and the sins of omission or commission it commits.

7. <u>Maintenance of an effective law enforcement system that is politically neutral.</u> While the law enforcement institutions must be created and sustained by the government, they must be allowed to function within a carefully defined set of rules. The rule of law, while "not enough" is still critical, and it is vital that law enforcement be given an institutional framework sturdy enough to stand up to pathological interference or neglect. It seems demonstrable that options to government law enforcement are worse. It is possible for large organizations such as private corporations, industrial plants, and government organizations can create their own internal law enforcement with security guards and personal bodyguards, but they have little or no impact outside of the organization, and such expensive self protections are not available to the average citizen.

8. <u>Latitude for civil dissent</u>: governments have a legitimate right to attempt to sustain themselves, and politicians have the right to try and retain power, but there is an urgent need to balance the power of the government in this respect with a legal recognition of the right of citizens and groups to protest and criticize the actions of government, to demand types of change, to challenge corruption and perversity, and to demand fairness and equity from their governments. Part of this need is encompassed in the concept of "the rule of law" as it applies to the institutions of the government: clear definitions of power and authority defined in law; laws that themselves define the limits on the power of the government and spell out the criteria or ground rules for the exercise of power, and equitable rules for access to public programs. It is a clear evidence of danger when governments tend to mask their power by invoking

"the good of the State" as a general means to ward off criticism. Thus, the right of dissent goes beyond politics and should extend to all of the powers exercised by any incumbent regime.

E. LEGAL AND BUREAUCRATIC DOCTRINE

The evolution of governments has led to the formalization of policies and processes into laws, regulations, and ministerial structures with defined powers, and a complex set of definitions about what government should and should not do. These formalizations become doctrine. They are created by constitutions and formal laws, by court cases and legal precedent, and they are inherited from ancient common law, religious practice and maybe even common sense. They endure over long periods of time and are used to guide the great bulk of individual government decisions and actions. They are the means of directing the public and defining how they too should act. The whole national justice system is a classic example of a legalistic and procedural doctrine at work. Such doctrines can evolve and change, but it is intended that they change very slowly, and within a controlled process.

F. THE DOCTRINE OF "REASON" AND "COMMON SENSE"

How do governments really decide what to do? Most are in fact committed to the idea that the problems and dilemmas of governments can and should be decided through rational thought and action as opposed to simply "muddling through" (although muddling is very popular too). Governments should employ the tools of strategic planning, priority setting, setting targets for achievement, rational allocation of resources, and the managerial skills in the implementation of public activities. Political rationality may start from a doctrinal base, but it usually moves toward negotiation and compromise as the means of resolving short term conflicts and finding a basis for decisions. Bureaucratic rationality emphasizes the managerial skills of optimizing results based on what works, and works best. Management "doctrine" is getting things done within ground rules of fixed responsibility and authority. Every country, even the richest, is bound by practical limitations on resources, and by conflicting demands in society. None could survive if they did not fine some practical solutions even if they defy the doctrinal base of reference. Every country is highly dynamic and constantly changing, and no doctrine can defeat such change.

Part of this rational base is that of professional standards and ethics. Professions such as medicine, engineering, law and corporate leadership have evolved strong internal standards and ethics that are adopted and absorbed into the values systems of government management. There are also private sector standards and organizational or "movement" standards, as for example environmentalism or labor relations. Conforming to these professional standards lends strength to governments and becomes a working definition of "rightness".

One of the chief enemies of this concept of rationality is the concept of "attack by hyperbole". There are fools and deliberate liars who either stupidly or deliberately go beyond reality and use arguments like "If you favor abortion, you favor murdering babies"; or "if you burn coal, you are trying to destroy the planet"; or "if you want to cut Medicaid or Social Security, you are trying to starve the elderly"; or "to fight terrorism is to hate all Muslims".

G. ECONOMIC IMPERATIVES.

Finally, because most governments are critically involved in the workings of the national economy, the need for economic "rightness" has become compellingly important. Economic decisions are expected to be rational; the trick is to decide what such rationality is. The usual answer is that there is a body of widely accepted economic concepts and practices defined by economic theory and the practical experiences of successful government. These can become the framework for defining how a given government should act within the overall national economic system. In some governments, economic development dominates everything; in most countries however, economic development is modified by other political and social factors. One of the major differences in governments in the post World War II era has been that of state socialism versus the concepts of market based economics. Socialist states made economic decisions based on socialist doctrine, and created a cadre of socialist economists to forge and justify these policies. As noted Indian economist Jadish Bhagwati famously said "The central role of the economists and their responsibility for India's failings cannot therefore be lightly dismissed. It is not entirely wrong to agree with the cynical view that India's misfortune was to have brilliant economists. India has suffered because her splendid economists were both able and willing to rationalize every one of the outrageous policies that the government was adopting by ingeniously constructing models designed to give the desired answers".

In the 1990's, the imperatives of the emerging global economy and the failures of many socialist economic institutions and policies has led to a growing retrenchment from such doctrines and the triumph of free market doctrine. Governments are now being tested against these new doctrines of how to run an economy. The resulting economic change, while economically more rational, is forcing new convulsions in both the old political structures and alliances and in other social and cultural beliefs. The United States should congratulate itself that it was wise enough to avoid this rise and fall.

But whatever the nature of the economic system, economic affairs are the source of enormous power and authority in governments. This often explains why many countries are highly reluctant to relinquish any lever of economic control, since it also means a loss of political power, and a shifting of power outside of the government – to the private sector – which may then become stronger in pursuing of its relationships with the centrist government. In addition, it seems to be a repugnant fact of life that elements of the economic structure controlled by the government have been highly vulnerable to both corrupt and pathological practices. Any element of government that has a hand in the control of money or the allocation of resources has become a target for outside corrupters and an almost irresistible temptation for the internally corrupt.

H. THE DOCTRINE OF AUTHORITARIANISM

Despite all of the above, it is likely that the predominant doctrine in use in governments around the world, and the most widely employed form of government leadership is that of the centrist use of authoritarian power, which means that what is defined as right is defined by the holders of power. Rightness means anything that retains or expands their grip on the levers of power. Anybody that disagrees or opposes is wrong. Such governments remain political beasts and are not immune to cultural doctrine or even rational decision making, but public needs or rational choices can be denied if they challenge centrist power. Public officials may be appointed not mainly for their competence, but for their loyalty to the power leadership. Such governments are not wholly incompetent, but they do redefine the basis on which "success" is judged. Every government has the right to seek its own continuation, but these authoritarian governments beg the question of whether it is right for any such State to rule and survive "by any means", and to defy so much of what society really needs and wants. Again, it is vital to realize that the American system of "balance of power" governance, and the real ultimate strength of "bottom up" democracy has protected the United States from the worst forms of this pathology.

A highly controversial role is that of governments protecting the public from excesses in the private sector. The socialist political argument, still very much alive, has been that private companies were simply too greedy and would further their own interests even at some harm to the government and to people. Pure private sector advocates counter by saying that the government should stay out of their private affairs, and that government meddling can only hurt the development of private entities. Both of these extreme arguments are fallacious and unrealistic, and bear no resemblance to the modern world, especially in the United States. What has obviously emerged is somewhere in the middle of a spectrum between complete control and complete hands-off. In the United States, governments and private sector interests are locked in an enormously complex web of interrelationships. While there are countless sources of conflict between them, increasingly it is recognized that these relationships need not be adversarial, and the conflicts are reconcilable. The real objectives are to make these relationships as mutually productive as possible, and to maintain a high degree of stability and balance between them.

How then can the American government be judged in terms of whether it is good or bad? There is no single pattern of set of concepts than can be used to answer this question, but over time, several frameworks have been developed that can be used to judge governments. All of them are relevant and in current use in some complex combinations. They may seem too philosophical, but in fact, they are given life and vitality by the people who believe in them. They have emerged out of actual human experience and many ways of thinking about human affairs, and they have coalesced into doctrine—a body of principles and motives that are strongly held, and which are used as a guide or framework within which people want to live and make personal decisions. From these accepted doctrines, governments draw support, and they can be used to guide the policies and actions of governments. Such doctrines may be very rigid or they may be loose and undefined, and they may not easily translate into guidance for the dilemmas that modern governments face, and yet they may have decisive weight in setting the tone and direction of public policy.

FIRST: THE THREAT OF
PATHOLOGICAL GOVERNANCE

★ ═ ★ ═ ★

E VERY FORM OF GOVERNMENT ever invented has proved to be highly vulnerable to a wide range of what can be termed "pathological" behavior, defined as "conditions of abnormality and/or deviations from propriety or the assumed normal state of things." Pathological means diseased. When applied to governments, this concept means a government that is malfunctioning and abnormal – based on some definition of what is healthy and normal. One of the diseases of pathological governments is corruption. Here the test is primarily a legal one: corruption here is defined as an illegal act in violation of duty, induced by improper means. In government it involves deriving personal and private gain from the exercise of official duty, or acts by others to induce government officials to act illegally in violation of duty. But even if corruption could somehow miraculously be eliminated, it is the premise of this book that there is an extraordinary range of other ways in which governments are pathological.

Any given failure of governments may come about from honest error, insufficient understanding or mere incompetence, and such failures are not necessarily pathological. But there are some elements of governance that appear to distinguish pathological behavior: (Bingman, "Why Governments Go Wrong")

1. If laws are broken by public officials, especially through deliberate acts of corruption.
2. If the intent of a policy or action is pathological; that is, the deliberate sacrifice of the general well-being in favor of improper institutional advantage or self-interest.

3. Where, in the face of evidence of failure or impropriety, the leadership chooses to ignore the evidence.

4. Where the leadership is incapable or unwilling to admit and correct mistakes either to avoid negative political consequences or to conceal incompetence or corruption.

5. Where the rule of law is persistently and deliberately ignored, violated, or manipulated for perverse motives.

6. Where professional knowledge about "how to do it right" exists – but it is not utilized; where knowledge of best management practices are ignored. Incompetence may be exhibited by individuals and not be seen as pathological. After all, it is human to be a little ignorant, or dumb, or indecisive or lazy. But government institutions should be much closer to full competence since they can employ many talents or buy expert assistance.

7. If the body of regulations of the government has, either deliberately or incompetently, become oppressive, excessive and/or unfairly, ineptly or corruptly enforced.

8. Where the government refuses (deliberately or incompetently) to make clear how the powers of government are exercised, who is responsible for decisions, who benefits, and what the limits of government authority are.

9. Where corruption is widespread, and efforts to prevent or cure it are deliberately or incompetently inadequate.

10. Where the control of money – both revenues and expenditures – is deliberately or incompetently vague, inadequate or obscured and where adequate preventive measures for financial management have not been developed.

11. Where the resources to conduct a government program or activity are, either deliberately or incompetently blatantly inadequate for the task.

Incompetence may be exhibited by individuals and not be seen as pathological. After all, it is human to be a little ignorant or timid or indecisive or lazy. But government institutions should be much closer to working competence since they can employ many talents or buy expert assistance.

POLITICIANS VS. MANAGERS

PEOPLE HAVE ALWAYS SOUGHT to manage their own affairs effectively, and it is not unreasonable to expect governments to do the same. Management is one of the oldest of known disciplines – as old as politics or religion. People may try to find some magic management formula, but management is very situational, and one of its strengths is that it is endlessly flexible. In essence, what is meant by management can be boiled down to something like the following logic:

* Any kind of human activity will inherently involve options and uncertainties. Some choices will provide better results than others. Therefore, people want to develop ways to select the best options.
* To get what you want, positive actions are usually better than passive inaction. Therefore, it is better proactively to make choices and direct action than to just let things drift.
* Things change; things can go wrong. Therefore, managers need ways to recognize when this is happening to them, and must understand ways to to adjust their actions to reality and make the corrections needed in order to achieve their objectives.
* Most human activity is shared and collective. Therefore, ways must be found to make this sharing positive among the cooperating participants. Even cave men had to organize hunting expeditions, and starvation was the consequences of poor "hunt management". Or envision the enormous management skills needed to build the pyramids, or the great cathedrals. One of the first true management roles was that of assembling, equipping and directing armies or putting

ships at sea for long periods of time. Military commanders were among the first true executives.

But even in ancient times, the conflict between managers and politicians existed. Imagine the master builders of the pyramids. Even while they were probably glad to have the work, they must have questioned the "political" nonsense of enormous, costly structures just for tombs for the mighty. Pharaohs as politicians and Gods thought that pyramids were vital and they had apparently no trepidations about investing huge amounts of national wealth and human effort in their construction. On the other hand, the pyramid builders as managers could undoubtedly have suggested more "cost effective" ways to conceal the burial places of the pharaohs, such as sneaking out into the desert one night, digging a nice hole, putting pharaoh and his accoutrements in, and covering up the hole so nobody would notice it. Total cost: a couple of diggers and a couple of days. The slaves and forced laborers whose toil paid for pyramid extravagance would undoubtedly have sided with the managers and would have no trouble thinking of better ways to spend their lives and the national wealth.

The basics of management have evolved into one of the most highly sophisticated forms of human endeavor and have produced a class of professional executives and managers at a level of skill comparable to any other in society. Management has it own professional culture, disciplines, techniques, standards for success, and ethical ground rules. Management skills are not just used in business. Housewives manage their homes—they plan, schedule, budget and (try to) manage and direct their children's development. Individuals plan and manage their education, careers and finances. Churches, law offices, medical clinics and even kindergartens all seek to avoid chaos and incompetence through use of managerial skills. In short, management has become an essential in any modern society. Peter Drucker put it this way: "Our society has become, within an incredibly short fifty years, a society of institutions. It has become a pluralist society in which every major social task has been entrusted to large organizations— from producing economic goods and services to health care; from social security and welfare to education; from the search for new knowledge to the protection of the environment. The institution, in turn, is itself an organ of society and exists only to contribute a needed result to society, the economy, and the individual. Organizations are never defined by what they do; let alone how they do it. They are defined by their contribution."

"If the institutions of our pluralist society do not perform in responsible autonomy, we will not have individualism and a society in which there is a chance for people to fulfill themselves. We will instead impose on ourselves a complete regimentation in which no one will be allowed autonomy. We will have Stalinism rather than participatory democracy. The alternative to autonomous institutions that function and perform is not freedom. It is totalitarian tyranny. But it is managers and management that makes institutions perform. Performing, responsible management is the alternative to tyranny and our only protection against it."

"While management is a discipline—that is, an organized body of knowledge and as such applicable everywhere—it is also a "culture". It is not value-free science. Management is a social function and embedded in a culture — a society—a tradition of values, customs, and beliefs, and in governmental and political systems. Management is—and should be—culture conditioned, but in turn, management and managers shape culture and society."

Politicians however might not believe such an analysis, and they have their own criteria for deciding how to think and act. The success or failure of governments almost always reflects this difference between political and managerial thinking. The following attempts to summarize these differences in the key areas of governance, and offer some forms of reform.

1. A Constitutional amendment could be passed, either to require a national balanced budget, or to limit debt to some fixed percentage tied to the Gross Domestic Product (GDP). Some states have such balanced budget amendments, but it did not stop spending as long as income from taxation was rising. Then, when their economies turned weak and income dropped, the balanced budget amendment became a serious problem, states ran deficits, borrowed money, or cut services.

2. A more limited form of such a limitation is to require a balanced budget by law, with a provision that the amount limit cannot be changed for a set number of years. An even more limited

version would be to enact a budget cap for any given year, with the provision that any appropriation that would exceed the cap would have to be accompanied by some equal reduction elsewhere in the budget. Such a cap could be on the whole budget or on a specific range of programs. The U. S. government enacted such a system in the 1990s, requiring any increase in a budget line item to be offset by a comparable decrease elsewhere. Germany is trying a "debt brake" which requires the structural budget to stay below 0.35% of GDP, starting in 2016. This system is weak because the political reality is such that special interests work to breach the cap for their own interests, and it is a problem to get the political leadership to legislate it. The sum of special interest politics results in the legislature simply raising the cap to cover the added costs; the Congress has had to raise the supposed debt ceiling 74 times in the last 50 years.

3. Even more fundamentally, governments can change their whole major philosophy – from one of "what can the government do for you" to one of "self reliance; take care of yourself". This change of philosophy would have to apply not only to individuals but to organizations. It would be a direct challenge to and refutation of the philosophy of government by special interest because it would tell every special interest "do not lobby the government for money or aid; take care of yourself". If intelligently applied, the government would still be widely involved in national affairs, but more limited to the "truly needed" acid test of government involvement.

4. Another new attitude might be possible; to stop asking "what new government programs can we create?" and to start asking "is this really a government responsibility?" Almost every serious study of the nature of American political policy gets hung up on this point. Literally hundreds of federal government programs are widely seen as having moved the government into activities where it makes no sense whatever for it to be involved. If necessity or priority are not relevant, what is? All too often, it is that giving money away

is such a valuable political ploy that it simply cannot be resisted. It creates a "feel good" reaction, and buys many a vote. It should be possible to find a way to set tighter and sharper limitations to the range of public programs based on **real need** and not just on self serving special interests. It is wrong to think of all budget items as valid or deserving. More of them should be challenged based on some measurable determination of need and the necessity for government intervention. Priority setting resurrected as a government skill would lead to a sensible unburdening of public budgets, and perhaps even guide government support to the truly needy and not so much to the rich and self interested.

5. Another critical policy issue: even when a pubic program is valid and justified, there is the further determination as to precisely who or what organization should be eligible. One legitimate argument centers around the criteria for eligibility for some public program. Should Medicare or Social Security be "means" tested?

6. And perhaps the most basic issue of all – philosophically and politically and even morally – is whether American citizens fundamentally want to be self reliant and self supporting, or even given the legitimate roles of governments, do citizens want a communal world where they are content to rely heavily on the support of the government? Self provided health insurance – or Medicare – or Medicaid – or free universal health care? Free elementary education – but free university education? Well, nothing is ever really free!

Every government since time immemorial has engaged in serious forms of deliberate misinformation, concealment, skewing, misdirection, artful dodging, "spin" and downright lying. Yet, however governments may maneuver, until recently the basic policy was that people could not lie to the government, and the government would not lie to the people.

Many governments have departed from this policy, beginning really with Nazi Germany's Ministry of Public Enlightenment in WWII, and including the Department of Agitation and Propaganda of the Soviet Union.

The Chinese Communist Party changed the name of their huge Central Propaganda Department to that of the Central Publicity Department for public visibility purposes, but the outpourings of misinformation never wavered. North Korea's Propaganda and Agitation Department of the Workers Party is a massive generator of books, messages, films, TV shows, internet postings, posters, and even music and poetry, almost none of which have any connection to the truth or reality.

There is no longer, in most official circles, such a thing as abstract truth. What is deemed "true" is that which the government says is true, and it is usually that which benefits the regime. What is false then is anything that harms or contradicts the regime. This policy has been flatly asserted by many governments as rightious and correct. People who still think in terms of some abstract right and wrong are said to deny reality. The United States has been fortunate in avoiding the more extreme ranges of this perversion, but a new challenge is now emerging. The enormous surge of social media has created an unbelievable great river of public communication, much of it aimed at governments right or wrong. But this surge is, at its worst, hugely false. It is the broad population itself that has abandoned the old policy of honoring absolute truth and falseness. Lies, deliberate and inadvertant flood the media and the new social media systems, and uninvited fake news has become a new kind of threat. People are often unable to know what is true or real, or to know what the government's policies really are, or whether they are good or bad. New meaning has been given to the old saying "There are lies, damned lies and government policy". But what constitutes "lying"?

* Major propaganda campaigns, either positive or negative
* SPIN!
* Flat out lies, issued as official government statement
* Meaningless ideological platitudes
* False promises, known to be false
* Propaganda which overstates value and understates problems
* Deliberate manipulation of attitudes and emotions
* Delay tactics: "we are working on that", or "we have appointed a committee"
* Silence

* Deliberate misinformation
* Denial: "who, me?" "some other person", "SOD!'
"* Hyperole: e. g. "If you favor abortion, you favor murdering babies"; or
   "If you favor oil drilling, you are trying to destroy the earth".

But this is terribly distructive and dangerous, and it is vitally important for governments and the media to prevent or harness this new world of lies and fakery. It has been U. S. policy to protect the right of free speech, but we must learn how to defend this policy while policing the government and the public interest against the development of official falsehood, or even trickier, the falsehoods promulgated by weird but legitimate personal utterances.

Financial inequality is another of the ancient facts of life. All people are born equal in the eyes of the law, but in the U. S. there are no laws that demand that they are must be equally rich or poor. Yet this policy has been prevalent in half of governments of the world as justified by the principles and policies of state socialism, which were rejected here in the 20's and 30's, and again after WW II.

Most people recognize that disparities in wealth and income exist, and that this is generally accepted. The remaining public policy debate occurs when these disparities are so great that they are outrageous and offensive. Why should some people live on $15,000 per year, while others get $15 million? Wouldn't it be a great idea to increase the taxes on the ultra rich and use the money to help the poor?

For a long time, the U. S. tax system has tried to do just that, but the public reaction now is increasingly that the intent of tax policy has been perverted, and increasingly and unfairly, "the rich got richer and the poor got poorer", and increasingly, this great disparity should not be tolerated.

The last presidential election campaign witnessed a surge of "democratic socialism" advocating that the government should far more assertively tax the very rich far more heavily and that the money thus captured would be sufficient to pay without pain for a new wave of social benefits such as free university level education, and universal publically funded health care.

But most Americans are neither very rich or very poor. They are somewhere in the economic middle, and they are deeply suspicious. Economists point out that even if all of the money was taken away from the "top 1%" of the very rich, the money could not really cover the costs of free social services, and thus the middle class would once again end up being stuck with the check. These dark suspicions are unfolding in a period where the national economy is broadly changing: a declining manufacturing sector, the surge of competition from cheap goods from overseas, and a general reduction of "muscle" jobs vs. "brain" jobs. The real expectation is that as the nature of the American economy changes, the American public will somehow keep up. It may be that the range and nature of public social services will be augmented, as they have been over the last 50 years.

THE THREAT OF SPECIAL
INTEREST POLITICS

=====★≡★≡★=====

O NE OF THE MOST important tides running in governments today is
that of the universal presence and power of special interest politics. In
the United States, Americans have grown up with the somewhat innocent
belief that all groups that represent specific interests are "good" because
they are presumed to be a form of democratic freedom of expression,
and they help safeguard the public against an indifferent or wrong-
headed government. But special interest politics have become far more
sophisticated and, in most countries including the U. S., far more ominous,
and nobody particularly knows what to do about it since most political
systems are ideally suited for it.

It is necessary to distinguish between special interests and "special
interest politics". In essence, everybody is involved in special interests,
some of them in conflict with others. Thus, a family could be concerned
about improving the school system but oppose performance evaluation
for teachers; be members of a union but vote Republican; worry about the
environment but create trash and consume enormous amounts of energy;
support a political party but not vote. They can be advocates of more public
infrastructure and lobby for more highways and public services and still
oppose any increase in the public budget. Many special interests center on
powerful ideas – environmentalism or women's rights or the well-being of
minorities in society. It is therefore natural and normal for people to think
and act around their special interests.

At the same time, since politics is so vastly extended and interventionist,
a growing proportion of the population now feels threatened by our
governments. Yet they want help in protecting their critical interests in

the government arena, and in advancing causes in which they believe. People are remarkably willing to invest time, effort, and stress because they think these interests are important. People's reactions can become both assertive and defensive. They are assertive in pressing for the success of their cause or group, but defensive if they feel that their cause is being threatened or ignored. Neither of these attitudes is likely to be wholly rational; much will be emotional or uninformed. The "special interest" mentality is single minded rather than balanced and refuses to deal with government problems in their whole impact.

Special interests tend to organize themselves so that they have collective influence and a more powerful voice. They will therefore tend to become more formal and bureaucratized, and much more assertive. Professional staffs are hired, recruiting stepped up, funds marshaled, a political agenda decided upon, and lobbying begun to search for allies or resist opponents. This leverage can initially be in the nature of information, education or persuasion, but as these groups press harder, they tend to phase over into "special interest politics" where they actively seek to change laws and regulations to favor their interests, or to capture funds and preferment to aid their cause.

From the political point of view, politicians respond to special intererst politics as a powerful means for garnering political support, or at least to avoid active opposition to their politicial agenda. Once these concessions are gained, they tend to be "forever" and vigorously defended. Subsequent retreat from such concessions is not only regarded as a defeat for the benefited interest group, but probably also as a "betrayal" by the political leadership. Governments therefore clash with, and collude with special interest political interests.

Special interest politics in most countries are very aggressive and heavily pointed toward the government and what concessions can be obtained – a new program, a subsidy, a tax break, a favorable policy or the overlooking of some wrongdoing. In many cases, including in the United States, there is a professional special interest bureaucracy that exists to lobby the government. These people have to gain something out of the political system from time to time in order to justify their work. And it must be perceived that the "something" that the government grants may be something that it was otherwise not inclined to provide. In other words, the ideal outcome for a special interest bureaucracy is to appear to have wrung concessions or resources from a reluctant government.

A special interest concept has been developed around the idea of "state capture" which has been defined as the actions of individuals, groups or firms both in the public and private sectors to influence and dominate the formation of laws, regulations, decrees, and other government policies to their own advantage. This may be as a result of illicit and non-transparent provision of private benefits to public officials, or simply that their political influence becomes overpowering.

There are many different forms of the problem. Distinctions can be drawn between the types of institutions subject to capture – the legislature, the executive, the judiciary, or regulatory agencies, or public service delivery organizations like power plants or transport agencies. And there are many types of actors engaged in the capturing – private firms, political leaders, or narrow interest groups. Yet all forms of state capture are directed toward extracting benefits from the state for a narrow range of individuals, firms or sectors by usurping the basic legal and regulatory framework with potentially enormous losses for society at large. They thrive where economic power is highly concentrated, countervailing social interests are weak, and the formal channels of political influence and interest intermediation are underdeveloped

But the more ominous cases are those in which the influence of special interests is secret and carefully concealed, and deliberately intended as the absolute antithesis of "representative democracy". The history of countries all over the world is filled with this kind of "special interest" politics: the perverse collusion between corrupt officials and countless individuals and groups who are seeking to wrest wealth and power from a fumbling government. What has emerged in every country therefore is a special interest political system based on the following elements:

1. A very broad range of national interests in the hands of the government, with the political system in charge of the decision-making apparatus, and capable of allocating huge resources with some degree of discretion, ranging up to 100% in dictatorships. The more public programs there are, the more special interest

groups will be created, and the more intense special interest politics will become, seeking not just money, but power.

2. The system takes place at two levels: first, there will be forms of public debate such as legislative hearings, public utterances, press releases, and endless study commissions. Then there is a second "back room" political process of negotiation and agreement, not visible to the public, which is usually where the real threats and promises are employed. The public operations of government are deliberately designed to be essentially bland assurances, to deflect the public concerns and avoid efforts to penetrate the back room process.

3. Government's own procedures and program delivery systems which are both massive and ubiquitous are both necessary and valuable, but they can become vehicles to deliver political preference to special interests. The most important are the public tax system, various forms of government regulations, selectively applied; items in the public budget; the award of government contracts; import and export controls, and of course, simple under-the-table corrupt payments. Both politicians and career civil servants are involved. One of the telltale signs of special interest government is when these delivery mechanisms become so extensive and so technically complex that they defy common understanding, thus giving the people in charge endless opportunities to punish or reward.

It is important to recognize this fact**: Special interest politics is enormously successful.** The very broad public participation in so many forms of special interest gives them so much political credibility that political opposition seems almost unworthy. But while the "general public interest" is very broad and diffuse, special interest politics is usually very specific, and has a cutting edge that makes it easy to penetrate the political system and find backers to carry the freight. Organized special interest politics involves money, tactics and political clout specifically designed to bring pressure to bear at some key point in the political system.

For the overt forms of special interest politics, the agenda is to maneuver for a trading of interests. The special interest group will demand its agenda of advantages; political leaders will seek to trade such concessions for political support and campaign contributions, or at least for the absence of active political opposition. Government agencies will trade concessions in program funds and/or favorable regulations for restraint in pressure, or support of the agency's goals and objectives. For the this kind of special interest, the agenda is the art of the "back room deal".

In Washington, there are now hundreds of offices of registered lobbyists, containing everything from huge staffs in opulent office accomodations down to guys with cell phones. Even beyond that, there are many organizations and individuals who are trying to leverage the government in some way. The halls of Congress and the corridors of government agencies are crowded with eager throngs of professional pleaders. The nooks and crannies of laws and regulations, budgets, tax codes and administrative procedures quietly show the results of their efforts. It is probably next to impossible to identify and list all of these people and all of their nooks and crannies, but it is one of the major elements of this book to emphasize the overwhelming power that special interest politics has gained over the American political system, so it is important to show the reader a useful listing of the kinds of lobbying influences that govern in Washington.

One specific example shows the nature of such special interest alliances. As reported by Mark Zupan in his book "Inside Job", there has been a special relationship between public unions and state/local government politicians. To quote Zupan, "A critical sector of the U. S. economy increasingly usurped by government insiders is K-12 education which has become more monopolized due to the growing teacher unionization as well as a consolidation of school districts. Such education has become less accountable to the public interest. The growth of union power in public K-12 education mirrors what occurred for state and local government workers in general." He also reflects the serious concern that, in substantive terms, benefits to unions have often been at the expense of educational systems effectiveness. Teacher unions have a long, very visible record of political action to promote their own interests. The two leading unions, the American Federation of Unions (AFT) and the National Education Association (NTA) have political unfluence unrivaled by any other group, and they are among the top donors of funds, mostly to Democratic Party candidates, in presidential, local government and school board elections. They have long been heavily represented in the delegates at political conventions at all levels of government. Teachers have tenure and are very hard to fire, and they are strongly opposed to the idea of more precise teacher performance evaluation, and the whole idea of private charter schools as an option beside government furnished schools.

Imagine that you are Donald Trump – or Barak Obama. What interests could you count on to charge out strongly, either for or against, any policy or program initiative you wish to undertake?

1. Democrats vs. Republicans
2. States, counties, cities, units of local government.
3. Hundreds of race based groups: African Americans, Hispanics, Muslims, Asiatics, and "whites", and a wide range of conflicts within these groups themselves.
4. Dozens of religion based groups: Christians of many disciplines; Muslims, Jews, Hindus – and the same kind of wide ranging differences within each.
5. Rural/small town interests
6. Literally thousands of industrial and commercial companies in every element and level of the U. S. economy, carrying a wide range of conflicts, attitudes and advocacies.
7. Labor unions, both public and private, which have become among the most important financial contributors to politicians and political campaigns of any element of American society.
8. Hundreds of groups intensely committed to environmental threats, global warming, energy generation and natural resources utilization.
9. Gender groups: mostly women, and in an increasingly sophisticated range of public concerns.
10. The huge "health care" world, with organizations ranging from basic scientific research and down through the whole medical profession and medical plant and equipment to a very high level of interest and concern on the part of millions and millions of people who are both individuals and patients – and also tax payers.

11. The elderly, with a high order of public sympathy and support (after all, eventually, they are us.)

It is usually the ambition of special interest politics to get concessions locked into statute or regulation, since they know that it is infinitely harder to change a law or regulation than to get it enacted in the first place. Thus, these concessions tend to be "forever", with each special interest stoutly defending and protecting them. Special interest groups tend to be implacable, insatiable and immutable – and often insufferable. A listing, in no particular order, of the special interests that generally support the U. S. Democratic Party serves to illustrate the near impossiblity of political concensus:

Democratic Party officials and staff
Urban interests
Farm families and small communities
The elderly, and the retiree establishment
The African American establishment
The environmentalist establishment
Anti-war, anti-military interests
Socialist and "semi-socialist" liberals
Conservationists
Anti-police elements
Unions
Moderate anti-extremists
Black Lives Matter
Those who just want "change"
Animal rights groups
Teachers and teacher unions and organizations
Anti-Republican groups
Anti-Trump groups
Feminists
Consumer rights groups
University liberal interests
Litigation lawyers
The unemployed

SNAP (food stamp) defenders
Welfare recipients
Medicare defenders
Medicaid defenders
Government employees at all levels
Anti-nuclear groups
Home owner/financer interests
Renewable energy interests
The Civil Rights establishment
Religious groups

These groups and interests are generally seen as beneficiaries of the policies and activities of the Democratic Party and their elected offficials, and of course, a similar list could be shown for the Republican Party. For both parties, the demands from these groups, separately and in concert create an almost intolerable pressure. This kind of list has a crucial importance. It helps people to understand something of this intolerable pressure, and it begs the question of how all of these institutions apply that pressure. All of them live by making demands upon governments, and their general philosophy is the demand for "more": more money, more benefits, more preferment. These interests almost always cloak themselves in the garb of public benefit, and indeed some interests such as womens rights, or African American rights, or support for the poor and elderly have broad public bases and support. But ultimately, most will press their own advantage, not as disinterested supporters but as clients with expectations, rather than advocates of the best interest of the general public.

Why do politicians agree so easily? Special interest politics is not just campaign contribution money or short term political support. It is more importantly about the forging of longer term alliances for mutual advantage. The special interest group will continue to provide support as long as the politician continues to deliver. And once a politician is committed publicly to a position, it would be embarrassing to abandon that position, even for just cause, for fear of being perceived as weak or inconsistent, but also for fear that it will outrage special interest backers.

George F. Will, in an article in the Washington Post on November 19, 2017, laments the near fatal impact of a special interest alliance which he characterizes as "the blue model" which he describes as "the iron alliance of the Democratic Party and government workers unions." Under this long term alliance, "unfunded state and local government retirement debt is more than $260 billion and rising. Unfunded pension liabilities for the nation's highest paid government workers are $130 billion and are expected to increase for at least through the next decade. The state is approaching a death spiral: departing people and businesses suppress growth; the legislature responds by raising taxes; the exodus accelerates. The "blue model" is bankrupting cities and states from Connecticut to California."

According to the Federal Election Commission (FEC), of the top 100 contributiors to political campaigns, 25 are unions; of the top 25, 13 are unions. The larget contributor in the FECs data base is the Service Employees International Union, having contributed $ 222 million. The next largest contributor is a private Political Action Committee (PAC) on the west coast called ActBlue which has collected and distributed $149 million, all to Democrats and liberal organizations. The next is another union: The American Federation of State/County/Municipal Employees, contributing $93 million. The National Education Association is next with $92 million, and the American Federation of Teachers is # 6 at $69 million. # 5 is Fahr LLC, another PAC run by Thomas Fahr Stayer, a notable Democrat Party supporter, who has contributed $75 million.

The Democrates love to cite the money contributed to Republican Party causes by the Koch brothers. In fact, the Kochs are 50th on the FEC list at $28 million. But in addition to ActBlue and Fahr cited above, Soros Fund Management is far more generous then the Kochs, having contributed $44 million to the Democratic Party. In general, in contrast to the unions and dedicated supporters who contribute only to the Democratic Party, most corporations contribute to both parties, just in case, but with an edge to the Republicans.

This is a classic example of how special interests create powerful and sophisticated linkages among themselves in order to provide mutual leverage. Education and labor groups not only support a liberal government, but will frequently be allies over specific policy issues. Business groups, industry associations, and small business owners will form alliances to support government economic development policies and tax relief issues. Many of these alliances are semi-permanent, but can also be temporary and transient, shifting like a kaleidoscope, depending on the issues under consideration.

In the last analysis, special interest politics, as with all politics, is first and foremost about power and money. While most special interests construct an edifice of public purpose for their position, few make any pretense of seeking for a balance of judgments about the broad public interest, nor are they concerned about the success of the government itself, or the ethics of governance. Special interests can be positive and constructive, but their performance, especially in developing countries, is seriously in doubt.

REFORM OF GOVERNMENT
STRUCTURE AND MANAGEMENT

WITHIN THE FRAMEWORK OF a nation's political structure there is a second structure consisting of the agencies of the government - departments, agencies, bureaus, commissions, and their professional substructures. Like all organizations, these institutions may be skillful or incompetent or corrupt. Because these are instruments of government, they should be held to a higher standard of probity and clearer responsibility than may be typical of private institutions. In the best of governments, there is a common ethic of positive public service that should be reinforced by laws that set forth clear principles and policies and procedures as to how public service should be rendered. There should be no doubt as to what is legal or acceptable practice. This cannot be done without many areas of doubt, but as much as possible they should be clear and unambiguous. Every public process should deal with the possibilities of corruption.

Finally, it needs to be restated that the most compelling concept is that of "governance" which is broader and more fundamental than simply the role of the government structure itself, and this reflects the fact that there is a critical need for a widely involved segment of the whole civil community that concerns itself with the validity of its government's actions. The leaders of governments in turn must recognize that their obligation is not just for the government, and certainly not just for their political party, but for that whole broad range of citizens and their imperatives.

The government has two critical responsibilities to this community of concern: it must maintain its openness, and provide the kinds of public information that lets the public understand what is happening. And there must also be some mechanisms for the government to be criticized from the outside, and some willingness to respond to legitimate criticism. The whole civic community should be able to turn to a legal system that is fair and honest and accessible when needed. Other forces external to government apparatus, such as a free press and a wide range of public interest groups are powerful assurances that "governance" will be broader than just the government itself. While private organizations can be "private", governments should not. There should be openness of government all the way from legislative policy formulation to the execution of ministerial process. It is not enough to make the managerial functioning of the bureaucracy open, if the political process is concealed.

Of great importance is the need for a clear understanding of the obligation of the government to respond adequately to proved, important needs or threats. It is pathological to be inert—to fail to decide—or to be unable or unwilling to take action. Specifically, it can be judged pathological when it is clear that the government knows there is a problem/opportunity, and fails (at least try) to act. The public is also entitled to a reasonable degree of governmental efficiency and effectiveness. Government agencies are after all not simply clerical paper pushing but are huge and sophisticated management problems requiring the use of systematic, integrated and comprehensive management policies and procedures. This in turn requires a well trained and educated civil service motivated by a spirit of honesty and serious effort from the top down. Not all things in government are politics, driven by political motives. At some point, the political structure should allow the professional managers to take over and apply their own form of skills. This should include some way for the career service to point out where the political context is wrong, or where political leaders are standing in the way of effective management results.

If one could stand back and somehow view the whole range of even the federal government at work, they would be astonished and fascinated. The great daily ebb and flow of government operations includes thousands of important things. It is therefore not surprising that some of these activities are badly done, and increasingly, the media is sensitive to reporting on these failings. **The following reports were gleaned from just <u>one week of the Washington Post</u>, in November of**

2016, portraying problems, not of politics but of operations of the Federal government:

1. Concern over the lack of Federal government leadership and coordination from Federal agencies.
2. Concerns about the slowness of government organizations to develop procedures for protective money handling of all kinds.
3. The slowness of hospital staffs to develop their own response mechanisms, absent Federal guidelines.
4. Discussion of new protections for whistleblowers at the Department of Veteran's Affairs (DVA), citing the long term and widespread patterns of agency retaliation against them in the past.
5. Discussion of the whole DVA record of failure to provide rapid provision of medical care, and the fact that there are 30 ongoing investigations of this problem.
6. Reporting of a whole long series of scandals surrounding false record keeping, and lies about the backlogs of DVA patients.
7. A report reiterating the whole widespread pattern of management failures in the initial implementation of the Affordable Care Act.
8. An article recording many examples of agency denials of information, misrepresentation of facts, failure even to collect basic management information, and slow response to addressing problems.
9. Reports of the low morale at the Department of Homeland Security; 75% of employees say "senior leaders can't generate positive motivation; innovation is discouraged"; there is arbitrary treatment of employees; "this is not a good place to work"; failure to recruit some needed skills; lack of employed training opportunities; exodus of top people and others; protracted vacancies. DHS is in last place in the government "Best Places to Work" survey.
10. Another article on the whole broad problems of recent border crossings, and the lack of effectiveness of our border control management.
11. Another article on the whole problem of the misfeasance of Secret Service people.

12. A critique of the whole "overkill" of airport security procedures. Reports of how even this security can be defeated.

13. An article on the failure of Department of Defense (DOD) procurement management to prevent the illegal procurement of unauthorized weapons silencers. Cases are cited of lying, deceit, misrepresentation of facts, and unwarranted secrecy by hiding behind "national security". The buying agency people cited false assertions of law enforcement powers; officials suspiciously burned documents; there are allegations of nepotism in the selection of a contractor.

14. An article that cites dozens of examples of the improper seizure of private property by the police. Then allegations that the property or money for which they are sold is improperly used by the police or other elements of government.

15. Report that the DOD scrapped $486 million worth of aircraft used in the Afghan campaign and sold them for scrap for just $32,000. The sense of the article was that effective management could surely have found a better and less wasteful way to dispose of these aircraft.

16. Another article that cites reports that these aircraft were largely unusable because of "problems of performance, maintenance, lack of spare parts"; in other words, DOD management made a mistake in buying them in the first place, and did not know what they were doing.

17. An article referring to the fact that serious recommendations for DOD cost savings and cost effectiveness measures advanced by former Secretary Robert Gates had simply been deliberately ignored.

18. Discussion of a report citing the fact that 30 % of Federal "reverse auctions" were useless because they did not induce any competition. There was general criticism of alleged excessive and improper use of sole source procurement.

19. Reference to an alleged preferment for one contractor by a Department of Veterans Affairs (DVA) procurement official.

20. Report of unreported "transaction fees" hidden in certain contract services or other government operations.

21. Reference to Secret Service misconduct in Cartagena, Columbia in 2012, asserting that undue pressure was brought to bear that caused officials to hide facts that might have been "embarrassing to the Administration".

22. Report of a Supreme Court case regarding treatment of whistleblowers; the case argues the long history of agency negative and vengeful attitudes, and the use of questionable practices dealing with whistleblowers.

23. Reference to a public opinion poll that shows that 77% of Americans do not trust their national government.

24. Reference to the widespread practices in agencies of "cutting deals" with special interests, usually in the back room in secret meetings. There was passing reference about the fact that Congress also has a lot of unreported back room dealings with special interest groups.

25. Discussion of the failures of the DOD in the supposed training of the Iraqi Army, which then collapsed under pressure.

26. Reference to the incompetence displayed by the leadership of the Secret Service, where the old guard "closed the ranks" to protect the guilty.

27. Discussion of the need to do a total revamp of the Federal security clearance system.

28. Discussion of the overly expensive veterans health care eligibility criteria.

29. Report that Alan Gross, an Agency for International Development (AID) contractor, was convicted for illegally taking prohibited electronic equipment to Cuba. The report criticized AID officials for not properly briefing or supervising the contractor. (Gross has recently been released from prison and returned to the U. S.)

30. A report discussing the mismanagement by the Army of the Guantanamo Bay facility.

31. Discussion of the poor management of the treatment of prisoners in Federal prisons and the lack of needed due process.

32. An article discussing the shortcomings of Secret Service personnel who allowed a man to enter the White House with a knife.

33. Another long article about the management problems of the initiation and subsequent administration of the Affordable Care Act.

34. A long article about mismanagement in the Internal Revenue Service (IRS), and misconduct by agency officials.

35. Reference to excessive expenditures by Federal agencies on conferences, travel, and entertainment.

36. An article about the failure of the United States Geological Service (USGS) to adequately map most of the state of Alaska.

37. An article about how large nursing home chains regularly overbill the Federal government, and the failure of government officials to catch these swindles.

38. Report of the fact that the former mayor of Charlotte N. C. has been sent to prison for improperly billing the Federal government for services never performed, and the failure of Federal officials to catch the swindles.

39. A long article about extensive failures of medical and health care practitioners, and how these practices go undetected by government overseers.

40. One of a series of article about "the Ferguson Affair", and the need for a fundamental and massive reconsideration of the functioning of law enforcement organizations and systems.

41. An article citing bad laws that produce bad management:

    -Implacable budget excess, failure to set rational budget priorities, failure to achieve budget cost effectiveness.
    -The failure to deal with the huge and growing public debt.
    -The compelling need for immigration reform
    -The compelling need for tax system reform
    -The growing problems of the decay of public infrastructure; the need to save the highway trust fund.
    -Government subsidies to rich people and businesses

42. A summary of the Oxford University study of government contracting: 258 major projects in 20 countries. Over 70% of

contracts experience cost overruns: rail projects = 44.7%; bridge projects = 33.8%; road projects = 20.4%. The report also cites the widespread need for major public subsidy of such projects after activation, and a needed element of determining ultimate public cost. The report summarizes the negative motivations of contractors – to understate the cost in their bids; to solicit political interference in the selection process; to overcharge during performance; to conceal facts from government overseers.

43. A long article outlining huge backlogs of applications for government services in several Federal agencies: a horrible 990,000 claims pending appeals in the Social Security Administration, requiring an average of 422 days; a backlog of 526,000 claims in the infamous Dept. of Veterans Affairs (957 days); and a backlog of 606,000 applications pending in Patent Office (800 days). The article also documents a record of petty, outdated and overly complicated rules and regulations, many of which have not been updated for decades.

THE MALFUNCTIONING FEDERAL GOVERNMENT

In a similar vein, Senator James Lankford has made a career and a reputation for digging out examples where the federal government has been wasteful or mistaken or incompetent. He has published two documents entitled "Federal Fumbles: 100 Ways the Government Dropped the Ball", and they make sad reading. It is understood that many sources deny and justify the activities he condemns, yet the point remains: there are hundreds of policies and practices of the federal government that are challengeable. Here are a few examples drawn from these Senate publications:

* The National Science Foundation (NSF) has let more than $500,000 in grants to study "the connection between religion, politics and cemeteries in 12th-century Iceland". In addition, NSF also spent $200,000 to study "500 year old fish bones in Tanzania." Further, NSF has paid more than $2 million to find out whether climate change has impacted China;s giant pandas."

* Federal government agencies spends $80 billion a year on computer services, but $ 55 billion of that money is spent on "services that do not use more efficient solutions". Thus, the federal government is actually investing less and less on new technologies that would provide enhanced capabilities and decrease the costs of operation and maintenance."
* The Department of Agriculture paid what were titled "Value Added Producer Grants" totalling more than $ 44 million to billion dollar companies such as Sunsweet and Ocean Spray and other billion dollar companies which are prefectly able to grow their own sales.
* At a far more serious level, the managers of the Medicaid program have themselves admitted that, in 2012, they allowed improper payments totalling $19.2 Billion! The response? In 2015, improper payments had risen to $29.1 Billion. The response? It is now estimated that improper payments will reach more than $ 38 billion by 2017. In addition, improper payments are also out of control in the Medicare Program, totalling $41.1 Billion in 2016, and it is estimated that the total for all government programs exceeds $135 Billion each year. The loss of valuable funds is serious enough in itself, but the second and perhaps more serious dilemma is how it is possible for these improper payments to continue to be made year after year after year.
* The Veterans Administration enthusiastically launched a major project in 2011 to upgrade its information systems into a more efficient computerized system. Six years later in 2017, the agency miserably admitted the failure of this project, despite the expenditure of more than $1.1 billion and the muddled involvement of 138 contractors and sub-contractors. Now? The Veterans Administration has enthusiastically launched a major project to upgrade its information systems, using a new main contractor, and planning the expenditure of — $ 10 billion!
* It is not enough that we have serious problems in the U. S. government. The Department of Defense (DOD) is managing to waste a huge fortune on the government of Afghanistan. As reported by Langford for example, "As part of the U. S. reconstruction efforts in Afghanistan, the Air Force awarded a $48.7 million contract in 2009 to build a new headquarters for the Afghan Ministry of Defense. As planning and construction progressed, the completion schedule slipped several times,

and the cost was escalated to $ 107.3 million. Then, in 2014, a further $48 million was added, and the building was finally completed, only $ 106 million over the original estimate." In another case, in 2010, DOD spent $36 million on the design and construction of a command and control center. In 2013, an Inspector General report found that the facility was not even being used, and it was deemed obviously unnecessary. Further, DOD funded the construcction of a large power plant, yet a 2015 audit points out that the facility is "severely underutilized", producing less than 1 percent of its production capacity.

* Another "Afghanistan" blunder is the remarkable case of a program run by the DOD Task Force for Business and Stability Operations (TFBSO). Unbelievably, from 2011 to 2014, TFBSO spend **nearly $43 million** in order to construct a CNG automotive filling station! The mind boggles. It is difficult even to envisage how such a huge sum could even be wasted. Had TGBSO bothered to check it would have found that there was no natural gas distribution capability in the country, and few cars were even able to use natural gas.

* Other U. S. federal government agencies contributed to the total mismanagement of U. S. aid to the Afghanistan governmemt. In 2008, the Agency for International Development paid for the construction of an industrial park, designed to provide to hold many businesses and provide employment for about 900 jobs. Six year later it was found that only two businesses had started up in the park, employing just 22 workers. In attempting to figure out why the failure, the auditors found that neither USAID or the Afghan government could produce documents dealing with contractor selection or oversight.

* The State Department somehow decided that it was responsible for the environment in Morocco, and thus it gave a $250 thousand grant to the Moroccan government to encourage its "green movement". Morocco is a country of more than 33 million people, with a fully competent government, an active environmental protection agenda, and membership in the environmental programs of international organizations. Thus, Morocco is perfectly well able to support its own programs, and there is therefore no rational reason for the U. S. government to give them any money. An ominous question: if the State

Department can give money away to Morocco, what about the other 195 governments in the world?

* Similarly, the State Department seems to believe that it is responsible for the governance of the Gaza Strip under Hamas. A recent report submitted by the Inspector General (IG) of the United States Agency for International Development (USAID) shows that, as of early 2015, the agency had obligated $762.5 million and spent more than $600 million to support 437 projects in Gaza and the West Bank. But the IG report showed that some of the roads built with these funds were in serious disrepair; that pumps at a water reservoir have malfunctioned and have not been repaired after three years; that a medical diagnostic center could not open because diagnostic equipment was never provided; and that schools and health clinics funded by USAID have been underutized or in some instances, never put to use. USAID should have known that the government in the Gaza Strip was wholly incapable of assuring effective use of these facilities.

* The State Department and the Department of Health and Human Services combined to provide a U. S. government attack on the newly threatening Ebola epidemic, and more than $5.4 billion of emergency spending was authorized for this purpose to finance the construction of 11 treatment centers in west Africa. But a New York Times investigation in 2015 reported that, after spending hundreds of millions, and involving the support of thousands of military personnel, only 28 Ebola patients were actually treated! These findings were supported by another investigation, this time by the Washington Post, that reported that some of these treatment facilities had actually never treated a patient. Question: where did all of that money for centers actually go?

* The Department of Housing and Urban Development Inspector General issued a report stating that more than 25,000 families receive subsidized housing payments despite the fact that they are not qualified.

* The State Department has established a fund for ambassadors to promote cultural development in foreign countries. Using these funds, State has paid $700,000 to preserve a Buddhist temple in Vietnam, document Bengali folk music in India, preserve weaving traditions in Bangladesh, rebuild an historic log house in Russia, and preserve the ancient

dialects of S. America. Such projects can and should be undertaken by the countries themselves, and are not a rational expenditure for U. S. tax funds.

* The Social Security Administration (SSA) has paid funds to 6.5 million people who are said to be over more than 110 years old. In fact, other data suggests the more realistic number of 40 such very elderly people. This strange assessment simply highlights the long and unsavory record of SSA in failing to guard the proper distribution of its billions and billions of funds.

* The Justice Department indicted an attorney, a doctor, and a retired administrative law judge on charges of defrauding SSA out of $600 million over the course of eight years. These frauds were professionally managed and executed. The attorney falsified records and then bribed doctors to sign off on the false statements that his clients were disabled. When the claims were filed, their approval was guaranteed when the attorney bribed the judge to approve the claims. Of 1284 claims submitted, the judge approved of 1280; and SSA management simply did not seem to recognize the threats.

* The Inspector General of the Treasury Department issued a report that at least 1.7 million taxpayers who claimed a federal tax credit targeted at college education, had provided no proof that a person had actually attended any academic institution. Further, another 361,000 students were paid despite the fact that they were not properly enrolled. More than 3.6 million tax payers received more than $5.6 billion in potentially erroneous education credits.

* The Internal Revenue Service (IRS) has maintained its record as having the government's highest rate of improper payments. For example, the Earned Income Tax Credit designed as an anti-poverty measure has an estimated error rate of up to 28%, and it is estimated that a total of improper payments of $134 billion over the last ten years, including $17.7 billion in 2015.

* But the Department of Agriculture (USDA) is challenging IRS for the title of worst improper payer. In FY 2015 USDA disclosed a total of $6.3 billion in improper payments from 18 of its 300 department programs, or an improper payment rate of almost 6%. The Food and

Nutrition Service leads the way with an improper payment rate of just under 23%.

* The Environmental Protection Agency has paid $29.1 million to conduct studies about the possible effect of fracking techniques for the extraction of gas and oil sources – despite the fact that many states conducted valid studies of their own, which did not find a connection between hydraulic fracturing and any underground water contamination.

* The National Nuclear Security Administration (NNSA), part of the Energy Department, initiated in 2002 a program to dispose of excess weapons plutonium at a cost of $ 1 billion. By 2014, not all of the plutonium has been disposed of, the cost of the project has reached $7.7 billion, and the end is not yet in sight.

* The Congress has usurped much of the decision-making for the National Park Service. This has meant the expansions of Federal government land ownership, but meanwhile the NPS and other federal land management agencies lost the ability to care for the lands they already control, due to lack of funding. The result of this intervention has been creation of a huge deferred maintenance problem estimated to now need about $20 billion to fix, including $11.5 billion on NPS alone. Failing 70 year old sewer lines in Yosemite National Park has been dumping raw sewage into the park river for nearly a decade, and some of this outflow is threatening precious 2,000 year old sequioa trees in the park.

* The federal government owns more than 900,000 buildings totalling more than three billion square feet of space. Most of these buildings are well used and managed, but an estimated 77,700 properties are appraised to be unused or underutilized. This is not only bad property management, but it is costly. In 2010, a study found that it has cost $1.67 billion to maintain these properties. Why not run a sale?

* The federal government has 42 different programs in several agencies to fund transportation for people of low income to receive medical care. The laudable purpose of these grants is marred by the waste of funds. In similar duplication mess, the federal government currently operates more than 100 separate mental health programs in eight different government agencies, spending more than$ 5 billion. In this case, the Congress has made no effort to curb this duplication,

but it did establish the Substance Abuse and Mental Health Services Administration to "coordinate" these programs, but GAO has reported that such coordination "has been largely absent".

* When the Department of Homeland Security was created in 2002, it combined 22 agencies, with 22 different human resources systems, which was immediately recognized as dysfunctional. Therefore, the Human Resources Information Technology Program was established to integrate and modernize these systems. A total of 15 areas were marked for improvement, and 77 projects were defined. But GAO recently issued a report stating that – after 15 years — "DHS has made very limited progress in addressing the 15 areas of improvement and the 77 projects" despite the fact that at least $180 million has been appropriated by Congress supposedly specifically for these projects. This dilemma shows two concerns: the enormous complexity of government organizations and activities; and the seeming inability of human managers to deal successfully with this complexity.

Similarly, DHS has taken 11 years to overhaul management systems and information technology in the U. S Citizenship and Immigration Services. After 11 years, this overhaul is still under way, behind schedule and seriously over budget. Initially, it was planned to complete the project by 2014 at a cost of $2.1 billion Now, the date of completion has been shoved back to 2019, and the cost is now estimated to be on the upside of $3 billion.

None of these reports are about "politics" per se; they are about management which is primarily in the hands of the professional civil service. It is also recognized that these are newspaper reports and not "evidence", and that many of the circumstances discussed are debatable. But it is obvious that there are hundreds of such examples, and they must surely raise the question of how effectively the Federal government is now managing its operations and administration. At the very least, this turgid list helps to remind the reader how extraordinary and utterly complex the business of government has become.

Forty years ago, the government was generally well respected, along with the civil service. But this perception has radically changed, and has become ominously worse. In 1972, when public opinion polls posed questions like "do you trust the government to do the right things?" or "how well is the government managing programs?" the public response was favorable at the level of 70 percent or more. But a similar poll conducted by the Zogby Organization in 2007 showed positive views down to about 47 percent, and negative views are at an all time high.

A similar poll conducted in May of 2011 by Hart Research Associates, for the Center for American Progress was even worse. The "confidence in government" was down to 35 percent, and the "no confidence" factor was at an all time high of 33 percent. Many polls now are not about politics; they are about management. Many newer polls are now asking questions that more clearly relate to the terrain of the government's executives and managers, and these ratings make difficult reading. There are increasing concerns about programs that are wasteful or ineffective, contractors overcharging the government, smelly tax breaks, bribery, excessive military spending, government duplication and overlap, lack of technological advancement, and high cost/low value programs that are obsolete. In essence, there is an increasing concern that what we call "the government" is really far beyond any coherent manageable single entity, and has become a huge, vastly complex and totally confusing interrelated mass of conflicting interests and demands.

REGULATORY REFORM

═══════════★═★═★═══════════

T HE ESSENCE OF REGULATION is to force people and institutions to change the way they act and think. Thus, enforcement is a vital part of any regulatory authority in many ways, the crucial part. But it is very hard to decide when such enforcement goes beyond reason and becomes an instrument of oppression. Regulation tends to become an end in itself. There is such a thing as "the regulatory mind" where the tendency to believe that each body of regulation needs to to be broadened and deepened; to be extrapolated in application; and to be pushed down into second and third levels of detail. Many oppressive regulations are unwarranted extrapolations of a basically sound statute. Regulations may be a form of legislative abdication or at least shifting of some of the legislative role to the agency regulators — because legislative bodies did not have the front-end understanding of the whole consequence of the creation of a regulatory policy, nor the technical expertise to legislate specifics. But according to Philip K. Howard in his book"The Rule of Nobody", "The law (for regulation) is seen as a tool for self-interest, not as a beacon of fairness. The first flaw of the cherished philosophy of moral neutrality is that neutrality is impossible."

Why do Governments regulate? There are, of course many legitimate reasons. Some such as the following are for economic policy reasons (Bingman, "Why Governments Go Wrong"):

1. To promote economic "efficiency": i.e. to preserve market competition, to prevent excess profits, or to promote fair prices for value received.
2. To induce competition in any given market.

3. To control entry into a market place: controlling the issuance of licenses to do business; setting minimum standards of business or individual professional performance.
4. To require disclosure of economic information such as ownership, financial assets, level of debt, or legal challenges.
5. To prevent unacceptable public risks: examples include information about stock issues or financial risks (e.g. the savings and loan disaster).
6. To provide national uniformity of certain ground rules (e.g. conflicts of regulatory authority between the federal government and the states).
7. To limit competition in certain sectors (i.e. public utilities, maritime transport)
8. To redistribute income (i.e. minimum wage, labor protection)
9. To allocate scarce resources (e.g. Federal Communications Commission allocation of broadcast rights; access to natural resources on public lands).
10. To control economic outcomes (e.g. banking stability; home mortgage security; performance standards; anti-trust controls, etc.).

Other regulations are for social policy reasons:

1. To provide national or specific standards to assure equity, fairness and equality in issues of race, gender, ethnicity, cultural beliefs.
2. To preserve and enforce public/private rights (i.e. voting, civil rights, health and safety protections).
3. To prevent injustice (e.g. cheating, misrepresentation, failure to perform under contracts, freedom from civic or government abuse of authority, etc.).
4. To prevent or control anti-social behavior (e.g. sexual harassment).
5. To redistribute public power and prevent the abuse of power (requirements for public participation in government decisions; appeals against government actions, etc.).

In examining this listing of the legitimate purposes of regulation, it is unsettling but illuminating to recognize how each power can be perverted and made either pathological or corrupt or both. Regulation has become one of the most powerful tools by which governments enforce their will, and in countless couuntries around the world, regulations are in fact powerful tools for oppression. The power to regulate can be given to almost every government agency at all levels, and it is used to redirect institutional and individual behavior by defining what is prohibited and what is "allowed". The proliferation of regulations is so great in some countries, nobody including those who write them and enforce them understands them all, much less understanding their consequences, which can be enormous.

The problems of destructive regulation are ubiquitous. Regulations can be used to force organizations to pay their workers more money, with no recognition of the economic realties of the organization. For example, a minimum wage regulation may be set so high that many smaller businesses can't comply and are driven out of business or forced into the informal economy. Labor standards may require such exceedingly expensive compensation for released workers that companies avoid hiring them in the first place. In one African country for instance, night and weekend work are forbidden, and the minimum wage is 82% of the average value-added per worker. To discharge an employee an employer must first retrain him, place him in another job and pay him a lump sum equivalent to a year and one half of his regular wages. Similarly, bureaucratic complexity makes the creation of new businesses extraordinarily costly and time consuming. According to the Economist: "In Congo it takes 215 days, costs close to nine times the average annual income per person, and firms must start with a minimum paid-up capital of more than a third of that preposterous fee. These rules are generally regarded as stupid and pointless.

There is virtually no serious intellectual reasoning that helps to define the limits of regulation. Almost nothing in society and life is unregulated, and nobody can say when it should stop and at what level. The Federal Register is now approaching 100,000 pages. The Code of Federal Regulations now has more than 178,000 pages. Regulations are now not only far more numerous, but they are longer, much more complex, more detailed and longer in preparation and approval.

The basic questions are the hardest to answer. How safe is safe? How safe is safe enough? What, in society, should be left essentially unregulated?

When and why does regulation become excessive and pathological? For the regulatory mind, the answer seems to be Never!

Another hard question is how far the imperatives of governance and the need to execute public policy should be permitted to overpower the rights of individuals and of institutions. Most people favor control of private sector institutions, at least with respect to public health and safety, but are often not aware of the many powerful but subtle means by which their own individual rights are also constrained.

Governments have proved universally and notoriously unable to regulate themselves. Laws intended to protect the public are often drawn too broadly and given too much room for perverse interpretation and the abuse of power. Political leaders can and do violate even well defined regulations. Many regulations contain the power to allocate valuable resources, and this has proved to be an enormous source of corruption. Each regulatory authority defined in some enabling statute has precipitated enormous volumes of second and third level regulations generated by the responsible regulatory agency, so voluminous and complicated that nobody can understand them all, and bureaucrats may play the game of "selective" application of the regulations they choose to enforce. Most regulations are highly technical and complex, and it very difficult to find a basis for challenging those that are seen as unnecessary or perverse. This is the major source of power for the government interpreters of these regulations, and of potential corruption in governments. In many developing countries, salaries are low and police, customs officers, building inspectors, tax officials and contracting officers may cynically regard corrupt income from the interpretation of regulations as an "alternative form" of compensation.

PROBLEMS OF REGULATORY ENFORCEMENT

Even in moderate and respected governments, enforcement can be a very corrosive role since it is used to make people or institutions do things that they may not want to do, and the more intrusive the regulations, the more likely it is that they will be resisted by both people and institutions. Ultimately, excessive regulation can breed suspicion of government itself. Political ambition or an excess of regulatory zeal may produce regulations that are managerial "missions impossible" – dreams or hopes of perfection rather than practical rules that are capable of being achieved. In countries with multiple layers of government such as the U. S., there are serious problems of duplication and even conflict of regulatory power and authority, and overpowering examples of the tyranny of intensly bureaucratic enforcement of the power to regulate. In this regard, it is worth while to repeat in detail a damning commentary from George Will, reported in the Washington Post on June 25, 2017: "It took nine years just for permitting of a San Diego desalination plant. Five years and 20,000 pages of environmental assessments and permitting and regulatory materials were consumed before beginning to raise the roadway on New Jersey's Bayonne Bridge, as project which had virtually no environmental impact (it uses existing foundations and "rights of way"). Fourteen years were devoted to the Port of Savannah, which has been an ongoing process for almost 30 years. While faux environmentalists ligitate against modernizing of the U. S. electrical grid, transmission lines waste 6 percent of the electricity they transmit, which is equal to the output of 200 average size coal burning power plants. In 2011, shippers using inland waterway systems of canals, dams, and locks still endured delays amounting to 25 years. In 2012, the Treasury Department estimated that traffic congestion wasted 1.9 billion gallons of gasoline annually. Analysis shows that a six year delay in starting construction of public projects costs the nation over $3.7 trillion. America could modernize its infrastructure at half the cost, while dramatically enhancing environmental benefits, with a two year approval process."

There are not any agreed upon definitions or even intellectual limits on the theoretical power of governments to regulate, and there is a tendency of regulators to expand and extrapolate the range and depth of their regulations. Abuses of regulatory power have created a growing feeling that governments can and do go too far, and there are no effective means to limit the expansion of such power. Regulation is intensely bureaucratic: complicated, technical hard to understand, and often lacking adequate justification for their creation. Enforcement is usually costly and time consuming, requiring long time delays, and excessive paperwork. And regulations, once imposed can prove to be highly rigid, difficult to change, protected by their special interest backers, and almost immortal.

One of the risks associated with government regulation is that the regulated industries learn to "play the game" better than their government supervisors, and in effect, capture the regulatory apparatus, by fair means or foul. Then, regulations can be softened or avoided, enforcement can be fended off, oversight can be made friendlier, and price or cost control regulations mysteriously turned to the advantage of the regulated.

But most of the time, the power of the government is so strong that a pathological regime can easily use regulation as a form of tyranny designed deliberately to enhance the power of an authoritarian regime, and provide the basis for reward of one's friends and punish one's enemies. It must constantly be remembered that the old Socialist promise to support people "from the cradle to the grave", really turned out to mean controlling people from the cradle to the grave. It has also proved all too possible to avoid the consequences of regulations that would quash corruption such as prohibitions against bribery, influence peddling, money laundering, concealment of assets, extortion, malfeasance, misfeasance, and others.

The counter reaction to excessive regulation has led to a new interest in what effective alternatives to regulation could be used, including the following:

1. Societies may want deliberately to decide more carefully that there should be some functions in society that need not be regulated (religion? personal privacy?). The basic question is whether there are elements of society that can be trusted to conduct their activities with only general community oversight and not official government regulatory oversight. The attitude of an authoritarian regime? We trust nobody.

2. The public can be protected by public education instead of, or in partial implementation of, situations justifying control. Voluntary controls are feasible in many areas and should be tried before government application of controls. Despite experiences like Enron, Parmalat or Credit Lyonnais, most corporations exercise voluntary use of independent auditors to provide public assurance of legality and probity as a vital element of business conduct.

3. Professional standards are a widely used and highly effective means of assuring publicly acceptable outcomes. Doctors are strongly motivated to observe professional ethics in the treatment of patients. Professional engineers are motivated to build bridges or dams that will not collapse. Teachers and university professors usually want to teach the truth. Professional managers have personal reputations at stake, and in many cases, managerial experience and judgment are superior to hard regulatory mandates. In their book "Public Policymaking by Private Organizations", Fritschler, Rudder, Choi), they state "private groups such as the American Bar Association, or Underwriters Laboratories, or the National Association of Home Builders, make and enforce rules that function like government's laws and regulations.

4. Instruments other than regulation may be employed. The tax system can be used to design rewards or penalties to achieve acceptable outcomes in lieu of regulation. There may also be rewards/penalties available through fiscal allocation.

Regulations are tough to deal with because they are so complicated and technical. This means that there is little public understanding of them. At best, this can be mitigated by careful public education and explanation. At worst, public ignorance is deliberate and highly prized by the holders of power. Governments can select from an almost unlimited variety of tools in the regulatory tool kit: price regulation, import/export limitations; quotas, tariffs; granting or withholding of licenses and permits; health and safety regulations for every segment of the economy; franchising and licensing; controls for anti-trust, anti-monopoly and anti-cartel mechanisms; and control of the right to do business. It can be seen that regulations, limitless in their scope, obscure in their technical detail, open to extrapolation and interpretation, and selective in their application are the ideal tools for government centrists, whether they be democratic representatives, socialists, dictators, or tyrants.

Overregulation is common, and it can be deliberate and political. oliticians find it easier to write broad regulatory authority; it gives them endless opportunities to control a power base that makes everybody else pleaders for something. Overregulation simply gives officials more points of leverage to broker their own power, and their very volume and complexity creates the basis for "selective" regulation where officials can choose what to enforce and how, and in the process, regulators can become petty, tyrannical, mean spirited and, especially, corrupt. If policy is the arena of the big tyrant, regulation is the arena of the petty tyrant.

Regulatory statutes when enacted are usually followed by a "lock-in" of clientele interests, and regulatory statutes are enormously difficult to changeespecially if change involves a shift in power. Thus, a regulation may be "forever." This should suggest that regulatory statutes should be carefully drawn, but many are not. The attitude of most politicians seems to be the urge to draft a vague general law conveying sweeping powers and with no sense of limitation. This then provides a platform for forcing outsiders to come to them to negotiate the consequences. The results of these protracted negotiations are then "sealed" into the basic law, which tends to accrete immutable detail.

In most governments, the tendency in regulation is highly centrist. That is, where there are regional and municipal governments, it is their desire to have some regulatory authority of their own, to accommodate regulation to local circumstances. But the centrist government argues "if it is right to enforce a regulation, it is right that it be enforced all over the country with little latitude for variation." It has long been reasoned that the political capital is best expended in passing a single national law, than in permitting regulatory variations to exist at lower levels of government.

EXAMPLE: REGULATION VS. MARKET COMPETITION

The promotion of competition in market places is a concept much admired by economists, but often viewed by politicians with fear and loathing. Two major trends in the economic policies of governments following WW II were actively opposed to market competition. In the Soviet Union, in Soviet bloc countries, and in other socialist states, the "market" meant the private sector, which was viewed with suspicion by governments, and was excluded from many of the most important sectors of the economy in favor of state control or heavy regulation. Also, in many developing countries, a natural desire to encourage and support the development of local economic producers, in both the public and privates sectors, led to extensive commitment to a policy of "import substitution" which tried to develop local sources to replace goods or services that came from outside of the country. To implement these policies, a wide range of regulations were developed. In order to control the entry of foreign goods into a country, governments developed a formidable array of regulatory controls. In some cases, foreign imports were simply banned. In a somewhat more sophisticated version, all imports were banned except those that the local economy really could not live without, such as machine tools or certain kinds of metal products for production facilities, medical supplies not locally produced, or supplemental supplies of things that the local economy could not produce in sufficient quantities. In other cases, imports were allowed, but they were subjected to various forms of entry controls such as quotas limiting the quantity of items allowed into the country, or high tariffs as taxes on imports – sometimes set deliberately so high that importation was simply infeasible.

This approach remains an evergreen for politicians who can be on both sides of the import argument, and this evergreen is alive and well in the American political scene. With quotas or tariffs, governments have been able to say that imports are allowed; for internal consumption, it is pointed out that the real effect was that importation was effectively denied. A similar outcome has been achieved by the use of technical specifications relating to public health or safety, which can be effectively "gamed" to favor what local enterprises produced, and foreigners did not.

The volume and value of contracts issued by governments has been an extremely important component of the total economy. It is therefore not surprising that regulations controlling the deployment of government contracts are also very important and highly sensitive. It is not coincidental that one of the most serious arenas of government corruption in the world – bribery, kickbacks, and bid rigging, over billing, and downright theft – has been in the murky world of government contracting.

One area in which economists and politicians seemed to have been on the same wavelength was the need for full disclosure of economic risks, and information about the financial strengths and weaknesses of economic enterprises. For economists, disclosure is seen as a prerequisite for rational economic decision making. For politicians, disclosure is seen as critical to the protection of the public from unknown risks. Yet the facts seem to be that disclosure which is so popular in theory has been largely neglected in practice, because, among the corrupt, disclosure is deadly. Governments themselves and their SOEs are notorious for the ominous secrecy of their information.

REGULATION OF SOCIAL RISK

Regulations tend to fall into two broad categories – economic and social. Economic regulation is universal because it relates so significantly to the broader issues of economic development. Social services regulation has had its greatest impact in developed nations, especially the United States and Europe, and the European Union is now very strongly asserting its influence in unifying and extending social services protections. In addition to the more traditional health and safety regulation, a powerful new wave of environmental and conservation concerns have triggered the proliferation of regulations in these arenas. Social services regulations tend to have high public acceptance and support, and are relatively free of corrupt practices. But there are many nations, mostly developing countries, where these protections are not nearly adequate. In part, this is due to the fact that many of the developing countries are barely surviving, and have trouble finding funds for more than the bare essentials of life. In part, social services themselves tend to lag behind the demands of economic development that preoccupy poorer countries. There is a significant correlation between national wealth and the ability to afford social services programs. Where a country is marginally able for example, to afford an adequate national health care capability, it is marginally able to enforce laws mandating universal health care, and regulations that seek to enforce levels of service that cannot be afforded.

Environmental protections are often neglected not only because of their costs and the complexities of their enforcement but because they are regarded as creating negative inhibitions to some form of industrial or commercial development. But industrial waste may be dumped into lakes and rivers because it is deemed too expensive to dispose of them properly. Power companies pollute the air with effluents from their smoke stacks because they do not want to bear the costs of cleaner but more expensive fuels. It is not unusual therefore to find that the legal or regulatory base is handsomely enunciated and defended in broad fine sounding commitments but falls far short of achieving such promises. Each regulation requires often very complex and expensive enforcement which has seldom been fully achieved, since it is far easier to write a regulation than it is to see to it that it is enforced. In some countries, the political and bureaucratic thrill of creating regulatory mandates has produced absolutely ridiculous situation where thousands of detailed regulations are on the books. This allows those in charge to "select" those regulations they choose to enforce, an opportunity seldom missed by the corrupt. Even where government ministries are trying to act responsibly, they have often lacked the numbers of trained staff to reach all of the people and institutions required to live under regulatory mandates, and it has proved relatively easy to ignore such mandates, or to get around them. In the United States, the official Code of Federal Regulations, with 50 huge chapters, now contains an overwhelming 178,000 pages.

The lack of adequate staff is often pathological in the sense that the shortage is deliberate in order to limit enforcement, and as a false fiscal saving. Regulations written for political visibility prove impossible to implement. Inspectors, who are generally underpaid and overworked, often find it easier to decide when and how to enforce by the simple process of soliciting bribes to assure inaction. "Speed bribes" are paid to overworked officials in order to get approvals or clearances put at the head of the queue. There are thousands of cases where construction inspectors are bribed to turn a blind eye to serious violations of construction standards, and often buildings, roads, or bridges rapidly deteriorate or even collapse as a consequence. Doctors in state hospitals may face hopeless patient loads, and decide to provide medical service first to those who are willing and able to pay extra. Corporations that build facilities in places where they can take advantage of cheap labor often collude with governments to keep the cost of labor down. This may lead to neglect in the development of health and safety protections in the work place, or the ever popular "selective" enforcement of such regulations. All of these dilemmas can be resolved, but it requires a high priority effort by the government to make change happen, but a paucity of knowledge and experience exists about how to redraft legislation, rework regulations, and undertake the administrative burden of dealing with hundreds of thousands of cases for the privatization of land and property disposals.

THE NEED FOR GREATER FORESIGHT: PLANNING AND PRIORITY SETTING

★═★═★

THE COMMON SENSE HUMAN being or family probably plans better than the average government. Most private institutions (businesses, churches, universities, associations, hospitals) plan better than most governments. Why?

In large part, because politicians tend to resist formal planning. They much prefer to use case-by-case short term negotiation and compromise within the political system. Thus they making people come to them to beg (or buy) a political decision. It has often been asked "Why doesn't the U. S. government have some kind of "national plan" to guide our courses of action? But politicians have a hard time even focusing beyond a relatively small set of immediate problems. They see foresightedness as irrelevant since it is difficult, confusing, and not seen as politically rewarding. The time frame for political thinking is usually five years or less, most often one year, and often just the time until the next election. In most political systems, this is probably "rational" since it is extremely hard to build any operable consensus around even immediate issues, much less for uncertain events years into the future.

It is a serious question as to whether something like a National Plan for American governance is desirable or even possible in political terms. One of the great "case studies" for central national planning was the Soviet Union. In the USSR, national planning was universal, detailed, and enforced. It relied on a central planning agency that produced a broad ranging Plan which incorporated national, regional and cultural goals, allocations of national resources, and directions for the functioning of both economic and social means of implementation. The Plan was the control, and the

Plan was the product of the political dictatorship of the Communist Party, and thus more political rather than managerial. But the experience of the Soviet Union proved that such a control Plan was ultimately not only ineffective but seriously dysfunctional. It was ineffective because it was rigid and defensive. To question the Plan was to question the will of the political leadership, which was dangerous. The Plan was often wrong. It mandated unreality, and was blind to the forces of change as pointed out by state managers, economists, and citizen interest groups. It set standards and goals for institutional performance that could not be met, and it forced the managers of such institutions to subvert the Plan by lying or cheating in order to prevent disastrous real world consequences. Similar failures were experienced in most Socialist countries including, China, Vietnam, Cuba, N. Korea and others.

Fortunately, the United States has never had such a National Plan, for various reasons. First, such a plan would most likely be formulated by the President and the Executive Branch of government, but the Congress was always deeply suspicious of allowing such an Executive Branch plan any degree of credibility. Plans, if approved, could harden into decisions that had escaped the give and take of political negotiation. Plans became "tests" where people could later demand to know why the commitments in the Plan had not been achieved. It was also felt that planning was a very uncertain art beyond a few short years. But most importantly, it was very apparent that the development of the United States, both economically and socially, tended to progress at very high levels of achievement without such plans, in sharp contrast to the stagnation in most "planned" economies such as the Soviet Union, and the Soviet style governments in Eastern Europe and elsewhere.

Planning however has a far higher value at the managerial level. Managers need and rely on planning as a vital tool of management, and it is part of the professional ethic and training—and indeed of the realities of managerial experience. For the manager, planning is seen as a way to anticipate the future and get ready for it—either to take advantage of rising opportunities or to anticipate and avoid problems. Planning gives a sense of direction and purpose which acts to focus the organization and its people. It defines how and where to optimize resources and concentrate talent. It gives an institution's people a sense of direction, and helps to eliminate uncertainty, confusion, duplication and overlap of efforts. Such planning is a tool used in both the public and the private sectors. Government agencies are perfectly able to use planning in the management of public programs, and it is widely advocated by such international institutions as the World Bank, the International Monetary Fund, the United Nations and development agencies as a vital form of improvement for developing countries.

Of course, like everything else, planning has its downsides. There are two general levels of planning—strategic and operational. In government, strategic planning is widely shared between political leadership and agency management, since strategic planning which defines goals, decisions about the allocation of resources, and the authorities to be given to the organizations of the government are necessarily political in nature. Operational planning is primarily managerial since it involves second level decisions within the framework of approved strategies to set short term objective, priorities, management authorities and processes, and the day-today operations of program management. Increasingly, it is expected that, when the performance of public programs is evaluated, such evaluations will be against the officially approved plans.

Strategic planning is very difficult, and it starts with efforts to define current and future purposes and goals for achievement, or risks to be avoided. In the private sector, such strategic thinking tends to be fact based and analytical. In the public sector the real test for the use of planning and goal setting in political environments has to do with the ability of the political leadership to control both the planning itself, and subsequent plan implementation.

It is also true that corporate planning tends to be more realistic about money. Corporate strategies usually are limited by the ability of the corporation to generate future revenues. Failure to generate revenue modulates corporate plans if stock holders don't get dividends and growth, and bank loans can't be covered. Political thinking on the other hand has been based on the belief that, since government programs are "right", they will justify whatever level of taxation is required to finance them. This view led to a highly expansive growth in public program promises and commitments in governments all over the world, with governments unable and even unwilling to calculate the cost of delivering on these commitments.

The absence of fiscal foresight is highly damaging. Even in rich developed countries such as the U. S., Japan, France and others, once expensive public programs are launched there is a tendency for the political system constantly to broaden and deepen them further and thus make them ever more expensive. And once fully elaborated, such programs are almost impossible to abandon or even retrench. The net consequence has been to create intensive pressure for greater government taxation even to the point where the effectiveness of the national economy is threatened. There are realistic limits to the amount of money that a government can extract from its national economy. This was true even in the Soviet style command and control governments with their unlimited power to allocate resources. As government extraction increases, so too does resistance to taxation until some uneasy point of equilibrium is reached. But this point is usually far short of the revenues that governments would need to meet its uninhibited political promises.

If governments were more willing to face up to doing foresight strategic planning, they might learn more about the sobering realities of what they can and cannot do, or can't afford. Further, such foresight might also permit a clearer identification of real national threats and imperatives, and a better concentration on realistic priorities for funding. The inability/unwillingness of political leadership to attempt this course dooms many governments to endless misdirection and inadequacies, and the public trauma which follows.

But even if future needs are foreseen, they tend to be so extensive that they will exceed predicted available resources. Common sense dictates that governments therefore need to develop strong capacities to set priorities so that limited resources are committed to programs of the greatest need and payoff. The combination of political and bureaucratic leadership and assertive special interest groups tend to define everything as high priority and to deny that anything can be relinquished or delayed. Many priorities are enunciated in policy. In periods of available money, the tendency is to expand with more programs added and existing programs enlarged. In bad money years, the tendency is to delay or cut uniformly across all programs, rather than to eliminate or reduce, based on some rational understanding of priorities. Nothing is ever low priority, subject to retrenchment.

How do politicians think about priorities? Bigger is better; more is better than less, more money is better than less money; special interests are more critical than general public interest; expensive is better than cheap; new construction is better than maintenance and repair; adding new clientele is better than creating individual self independence. Cutback management is unpopular and always seen as temporary until the flow of taxes can be revitalized. This political context dictates the lack of political interest in what planning can reveal. Why even bother to think about the future when you are never willing or able to act on that knowledge? Politicians stick to what they do best—short term negotiation and horse trading within the political decision making system they own, rather than attempting to deal with a future real world that is beyond their control. Business thinks everyone is a potential customer, and politicians think everyone is a potential supporter. While business may fight to increase market share, for politicians, the only "market share" that counts is 51% of the votes in the next election. While business people can be ambitious, most of their success will be linked to their institutions. Politicians have almost no interest in the operational institutions of government.

Politicians tend to use what might be called the "political/rational" model for decision making which has the following characteristics:

1. Political motives and imperatives are seldom "managerial". Management considerations are largely ignored. Costs tend to be ignored as well or deliberately downplayed because they are unpopular subjects.
2. There is not necessarily any logically derived "right" answer; or politicians feel that an answer derived from logic or management sense is not necessarily the politically desirable or feasible answer.
3. The real vehicle for decision making is negotiation and compromise within the framework of the political system. The outcome of these negotiations defines "rightness".
4. Politics is defined as the art of the possible. Any answer may satisfy the political pressure. In general, public pressures for decisions

can be so contradictory that they offset each other and can be comfortably ignored.

5. The political system lacks the ability to produce wide ranging consensus; thus partial solutions are most common and are usually aimed only at relieving the immediate pressure. Legislative bodies in particular have trouble facing up to hard issues and the need for big decisions. Politicians love acts of creation or expansion; they seldom can handle acts of retrenchment.

6. The "lock-in" of special interests around existing policies tend to prevent even rational change.

7. Increasingly, lying is acceptable government policy. The government feels entitled to withhold information from the public; to generate and publish skewed and manipulated data; to "spin" public decisions and attitudes; to generate deliberate misinformation, and encourage confusion and conflict.

In Japan, the government issued national Plans for decades, but they were advisory only, and were meant to guide the actions of corporations, political entities, and individual citizens in certain directions. These were not direct government national Plans, but were the responsibility of special planning commissions with membership from outside of the government, staffed and supported by professionals from the Japanese government. To a remarkable degree, this guidance did effectively channel national effort. But despite the independent nature of the planning commissions, with often distinguished members from all walks of Japanese life, the commissions mirrored official policy, and were relatively uncomfortable with strange or innovative ideas. Ultimately, such Plans were also dysfunctional because of this rigidity. Many other countries, especially those with centrist socialist governments were similarly committed to some form of national planning. All seem to have suffered similar problems of rigidity and inability to cope with fast changing national circumstances.

REFORM OF PROGRAM EVALUATION

Every government is responsible for a wide range of public programs—education, health care, public transportation, national security, taxation, foreign policy, economic development, and many others. Each of these programs will contain many related activities and projects, and all are complex, difficult to administer, and not guaranteed to succeed. It would therefore seem sensible and logical to develop the means to evaluate each activity and government project to determine whether it is being done well or poorly, and is achieving its stated purposes. Yet managers and politicians may take radically different views on how to evaluate programs—or whether to evaluate them at all.

The managerial attitude about program evaluation is generally straightforward; of course you evaluate your program. You must know what is working or failing so that failures can be eliminated and performance results enhanced. Evaluation is both a part of the professional ethics of management, and the route to greater success. Even managers who are making mistakes and might wish to cover them up in the short run know that eventually their mistakes will be found out and they will be made to pay for them

In general, politicians on the other hand do not like program evaluation even if they do it themselves. Their concern is this: what if the evaluation shows that the program is (a) useless; (b) too expensive; (c) poorly designed; (d) poorly managed; (e) corrupt; or (f) all of the above? This "exposure" is seen and negative and destructive since it can lead to client and constituent disappointment. Politicians who visibly backed failing programs fear that people will blame them. This is especially true since their political opposition will happily point out these failures as often as possible.

Even among professional managers however, evaluation is often viewed darkly. Many managers reject it simply because the results may be negative, and their reputations may suffer, or that people may actually expect them to do something about perceived negative results. In governments, there is the added negative that managers may believe that poor evaluations will either be ignored by politicians, and are thus a waste of time; or that they will get the manager in trouble at the political level, and are thus better off not attempted.

In most cases, politicians have their own different forms of evaluation, based on the views of constituents and client organizations on which they rely, and which they seem to trust more than the evaluations coming from the career bureaucracy. But this kind of political feedback often represents mainly the views of special interest groups which tend to be largely self-serving and not necessarily balanced or informed. Nor is it true that the political system is willing to act on such evaluation knowledge. Even when it can be (professionally) established that a program is obsolete, not needed, too costly, or of little value, one cannot expect the political leadership to act on this knowledge if it appears to be politically embarrassing, difficult, or untimely. Thus, one of the most common perceptions about governments around the world is that they are unable or unwilling to clean up their own messes and inefficiencies.

Thus, program evaluation which is so vital and realistic in the private sector, is far less useful in the political environment. Similarly, the political reluctance to demand evaluation, or even to permit it, creates other problems. Lacking effective program evaluation, poor professional management is often not recognized, and therefore is obviously not corrected. Lack of evaluation leads to significant wastage of public funds because nobody wants to acknowledge failures and certainly nobody wants to admit waste when they are not prepared to eliminate it. Ineptness and corruption are cousins, and very hard to differentiate so lack of evaluation ripens the opportunities for corruption. The most cynical critics of government, seeing these symptoms, conclude that governments are hopeless, and that their role in society must be curtailed. Some critics, also very cynical, conclude that democratic governments were never supposed to be efficient and that such waste and mismanagement is a small price to pay for what governments provide. The middle ground is that governments are really only as effective as their political leadership, and thus politicians must learn to face up to the consequences of program evaluations, or failed plans, or changing circumstances. Professional government managers will never be truly success driven or performance driven or cost effective if such management motives are held in contempt by the political leadership.

Every government should create a frank and revealing system of performance evaluation and accept the risk that some evaluation results will be negative and require tough political decisions. Any such system or systems must be accepted and approved by the political leadership, who must then live up to this obligation, and stop undercutting it. The evaluations should be conducted continuously and made public so that the negatives can't be hidden or ignored. Evaluation can be conducted within the agency through such resources as auditors, inspectors, or program evaluation staffs. To some extent, evaluations can be externally conducted and be as dispassionate as possible. Such evaluations may come from scholars or from reasonably neutral public interest groups. If the evaluations are neutral and frank there may still ample opportunity for the political leadership to put their political "spin" on them, but the worst form of self delusion is to distort the findings of the evaluations themselves. The political sensitivity to program evaluation must be freed up and sharpened, and this can best be done through a wider distribution of evaluation findings beyond the self-interests of the bureaucracies and related special interests, and this is a role that the media loves to undertake.

DEMAND ANALYSIS

Business thinks everyone is a potential customer, and politicians think everyone is a potential supporter. While business may fight to increase market share, for politicians, the only "market share" that counts is 51% of the votes in the next election. While business people can be ambitious, most of their success will be linked to their institutions. Politicians have almost no interest in the operational institutions of government, and they see public programs as resources to be politically allocated.

Political leaders face policy and management decisions with a mind set which is radically different than that of managers. Managers tend to learn and apply a rational decision-making model applying the following steps more or less in sequence:

1. First, identify the problem to be solved, or the need to be met.
2. Define the problem more closely, and set priorities for evaluation
3. Identify alternatives and analyze each in terms of feasibility, value, risk, advantages and disadvantages, costs and benefits, winners and losers, second order impacts and timing.
4. Select the best alternative — the one with the highest benefits, lowest costs, least risk, and the highest number of beneficiaries.
5. Decide, or persuade the decision makers with reason and logic
6. Implement the policy
7. Evaluate performance

8. Feed back the results of the evaluation, and decide whether modifications are needed.

Certainly, politicians will use this rational model too, but it is not how they generally reason. Instead, they have what might be called the "political/rational" model for decision making which has the following characteristics:

1. Political motives and imperatives are seldom "managerial". Management considerations are largely ignored. Costs tend to be ignored as well or deliberately downplayed because they are unpopular subjects.
2. There is not necessarily any logically derived "right" answer; or politicians feel that an answer derived from logic or management sense is not necessarily the politically desirable or feasible answer.
3. The real vehicle for decision making is negotiation and compromise within the framework of the political system. The outcome of these negotiations defines "rightness".
4. Politics is defined as the art of the possible. Any answer may satisfy the political pressure. In general, public pressures for decisions can be so contradictory that they offset each other and can be ignored. Every view is given political weight, even if irrational and dysfunctional. Thus, bad decisions may dominate.
5. The political system lacks the ability to produce wide ranging consensus especially in the longer term. Thus short term partial solutions are most common and are usually aimed only at relieving the political immediate pressure. Legislative bodies in particular have trouble facing up to hard issues and the need for big decisions. Politicians love acts of creation or expansion; they seldom can handle acts of retrenchment.
6. The "lock-in" of special interests around existing policies tend to prevent even rational change.

In broad terms, politics is about power and the retention of power, and management is about effectiveness and institutional and financial achievement. This difference can be illustrated in a discussion of program evaluation.

PROGRAM EVALUATION

Every government is responsible for a wide range of public programs — education, health care, public transportation, national security, taxation, foreign policy, economic development, and many others. Each of these programs will contain many related activities and projects, and all are complex, difficult to administer, and not guaranteed to succeed. It would therefore seem sensible and logical to develop the means to evaluate each activity and project to determine whether it is being done well or poorly, and is achieving its stated purposes. Yet managers and politicians may take radically different views on how to evaluate programs — or whether to evaluate them at all.

The managerial attitude about program evaluation is generally straightforward; of course you evaluate your program. You must know what is working or failing so that failures can be eliminated and performance results enhanced. Evaluation is both a part of the professional ethics of management, and the route to greater success. Even managers who are making mistakes and might wish to cover them up in the short run know that eventually their mistakes will be found out and they will be made to pay for them

In general, politicians on the other hand do not like program evaluation even if they do it themselves. Their concern is this: what if the evaluation shows that the program is (a) useless; (b) too expensive; (c) poorly designed; (d) poorly managed; (e) corrupt; or (f) all of the above? This "exposure" is seen and negative and destructive since it can lead to client and constituent disappointment. Politicians who visibly backed failing programs fear that people will blame them. This is especially true since the political opposition will happily point out these failures as often as possible.

Professional program evaluation is therefore seen as a management tool, based on management principles and practices. Politicians find this approach uncomfortable, since they prefer the route of negotiation and compromise — the political system which they control. Dispassion is not valued or even believed in. Obviously, corrupt officials will automatically oppose and sabotage any evaluation of their performance. In many bad governments around the world, auditors, inspectors, investigators and other evaluators are deliberately under staffed, underpaid, undermined and poorly supported.

Even among professional managers however, evaluation is often viewed darkly. Many managers reject it simply because the results may be negative, and their reputations may suffer, or that people may actually expect them to do something about perceived negative results. In governments, there is the added negative that operational managers may believe that poor evaluations will either be ignored by politicians, and are thus a waste of time; or that they will get the manager in trouble at the political level, and are thus better off not attempted.

FEEDBACK AND REASSESSMENT

Every evaluation creates the potential for a learning process in which the results of the evaluation, when reported to top management or to the political leadership, permits a realistic identification of problems and failures and the development of and corrections and improvements. Almost all managers develop their own evaluation and feedback cycles, and most are willing to use such information for their own advantage. The real issue is whether managers are willing to share their feedback knowledge with others, particularly political superiors. Wise corporate executives or upper political leaders should not permit managers to conceal failures or shortcomings, but should insist on knowing any bad news as soon as possible so that corrective actions can be taken. But this makes the assumption that leaders are in fact motivated to make corrections. Especially in political systems, there is a definite lack of enthusiasm for knowing the bad news, and little zeal for investing political capital in revamping programs, even when they are apparent failures. Managers of government programs are very reluctant to report such problems since they are certain to generate public criticism — often seen as unfair or politically self serving. This is especially true in political environments where program managers have little latitude to correct problems even if identified. Think for example of doctors, nurses and hospital administrators in the old USSR who had to try and explain why the central government in Moscow could find no money for health care; or teachers who must explain why there are no text books; or engineers who had no explanations about why roads are falling apart. The problem is certainly not lack of evaluation; such sins of omission and commission were glaringly obvious to everybody. The failure lies in the fact that those who can take action are oblivious to the messages – often deliberately.

In most cases, politicians have their own network of evaluation, based on the views of constituents and client organizations on which they rely, and which they seem to trust more than the evaluations coming from the career bureaucracy. But this kind of political feedback often represents mainly the views of special interest groups which tend to be largely self-serving and not necessarily balanced or informed. Thus, there is a major difference in how managers and politicians view the value of "feedback."

Nor is it true that the political system is willing to act on such evaluation knowledge. Even when it can be (professionally) established that a program is obsolete, not needed, too costly, or of little value, one cannot expect the political leadership to act on this knowledge if it appears to be politically embarrassing, difficult, or untimely. Thus, one of the most common perceptions about governments around the world is that they are unable or unwilling to clean up their own messes and inefficiencies.

Feedback can and should result in internal management reforms but even when undertaken, it tends to be too little, too late, or very limited in scope. Where any significant element of a program is questioned the concern is usually taken out of the hands of the professional managers and drawn back into the political arena where it can be carefully controlled:

* If the problem can be "lost", it will be.
* If it can be blamed on the bureaucrats, it will be.
* If it can be blamed on the political opposition, it will be.
* If it can be "spun" it will be.
* If the failure is politically damaging, damage control will be employed.
* If changes are unavoidable, the minimum level of change will be undertaken.

Many changes stemming from program failures are made to culminate in politically popular "solutions". This is how politicians often decide to spend more money, or commit more effort on failing programs. Frankness about shortcomings never has been a political virtue.

As a result, program evaluation which is so vital and realistic in the private sector, is viewed with revulsion in the political environment. The only evaluation which is tolerable is that which announces success. Politicians have great difficulty admitting problems with programs which they have advocated and publicly supported, and which earn them the support of important special interests or clients. These special interests become part of the problem because they tend to be frozen into their own attitudes, often arguing that failure is the result of the government not trying hard enough or spending enough money on their favored programs.

Similarly, the political reluctance to mandate evaluation, or even to permit it, creates other problems. Poor professional management is often not recognized, and therefore is obviously not corrected. Lack of evaluation leads to significant wastage of public funds because nobody wants to acknowledge failures and certainly nobody wants to admit waste when they are not prepared to eliminate it. Ineptness and corruption are cousins, and very hard to differentiate so lack of evaluation provides ripe opportunities for corruption.

The most cynical critics of government, seeing these symptoms, conclude that governments are hopeless, and that their role in society must be curtailed. Other critics, also very cynical, conclude that democratic governments were never supposed to be efficient and that such waste and mismanagement is a small price to pay for what governments provide. The middle ground is that governments are really only as effective as their political leadership permits them to be, and thus politicians must learn to face up to the consequences of program evaluations, or failed plans, or changing circumstances. Professional government managers will never be truly success driven or performance driven or cost effective if such management motives are held in contempt by the political leadership.

Every government should create a frank and revealing system of performance evaluation and accept the risk that some evaluation results will be negative and require tough political decisions. This is merely plain old human common sense. Any such system or systems can be and must be accepted and approved by the political leadership, who must live up to this obligation and stop undercutting it. The evaluations should be made public so that the negatives can't be hidden or ignored. To some extent, evaluations must be externally conducted and be as dispassionate as possible. Such evaluations may come from scholars or from reasonably neutral public interest groups, but specifically <u>not</u> from political interest groups with their own fish to fry. If the evaluations are neutral and frank there may still ample opportunity for the political leadership to put their political "spin" on them, but the worst form of self delusion is to distort the findings of the evaluations themselves.

The political sensitivity to program evaluation must be freed up and sharpened, and this can best be done through a wider distribution of evaluation findings beyond the self-interests of the bureaucracies and related special interests, and this is a role that the media loves to undertake.

THE KEYSTONE: REFORM OF ECONOMIC DEVELOPMENT AND THE TAX SYSTEM

═══════════════════★═★═★═══════════════════

T HE BASIC STRUCTURE OF the American economy is a vital element of the need for government reform. In addition to the earlier national adjustments such as the shift from a rural to an urban economy, and government assumption of a broader agenda of social services provision, recent trends in the United States typify the major adjustments that have been happening in its economy and in most developed countries around the world.

The United States, more than almost any other country, is a "consumer economy"; that is, the greatest leverage in the economy is consumer preference and demand and not industrial development or public sector strategies. In most developing countries the opposite is true. Economic development is usually driven from the top down, and the drive is toward industrial development, and is almost indifferent to consumer interests.

In the U. S. there has been a shift from manufacturing and industrial operations to a service sector economy. More than 70% of U. S. employment is in the service sector, which also provides most of the growth in jobs. The U. S. leads the world in this shift, which has many important consequences. Despite perceptions to the contrary, the service economy is very profitable and "value added" and not just kids flipping burgers. It requires large numbers of well educated people because it includes education, banking, government, insurance, communications, media and others – all high value sectors with high intellectual demands. It is certainly not confined to lower value jobs such as manufacturiing, construction, crafts, transportation, or retailing which have dominated in the past. But computers and better communications and other technologies are changing that, and there is a new trend in economic development pointed at enhancing the productivity of the service sector. Here again, the U. S. leads the world. In addition, world competition, especially from Japan which caused deterioration in the U. S. manufacturing sector has now sparked a recent trend for these nations to reexamine and revitalize their own perceptions of what a successful economy looks like.

REFORM OF THE TAX SYSTEM

In its simplest terms, a national tax system is designed to raise revenues to finance the government; but as it has evolved, the American tax system has grown increasingly complicated and its purposes have been greatly expanded.

To begin with, the American tax system reflects the multi-level nature of the governments themselves so that government taxes are collected at the federal, state, county and city levels. This is a reasonable reflection of the fact that each level has its own jurisdictional authority and a specific array of projects and activities for which it is reponsible. In many countries, taxes are far more centralized at the national level, and the centrist elites that run such countries are reluctant to permit local governments to have too much independent taxing authority, because they see that as a relinqishement of their own power.

The predominant type of tax is that on income, and individuals, companies and even charitable or voluntary organizations are subject to this form of tax. Income taxes evoke two kinds of reaction. The first is the normal one of resentment – the feeling that it is not fair for the government to take away "our" money. This feeling is universal and understandable, but usually not actionable unless and until the drain of money is so great that it inhibits necessary and desirable actions by individuals and organizations. And indeed, one of the most ancient and enduring enmities of human kind is the hatred of the tax collectors and the government that hires them.

But the majority of people and even companies also feel that second motive, that paying taxes is a necessary and desirable civic duty, and the recognition that the government will probably use the money to finance an important and vital range of public goods and services. In America, this expectation is largely realized, and despite lurching and wallowing and complaining and whining, taxes are (usually) paid and services are (usually) delivered. Those who understand how often this connection is broken in other countries become more appreciative of how well the American system works.

In the overall sense, the American population is divided into two income tax layers: the layer that pay income taxes and the layer that does not. And then it is argued that those who do pay taxes are also divided into two layers: the layer that pays too little and the layer that pays too much. George Will (Washington Post, Oct 10, 2017) provides some fascinating figures: "forty-five percent of American housholds pay no income tax, either because they earn too little, or because they qualify for enough exemptions and credits to erase their liability. Sixty percent pay nothing or less than 5 percent of their income. The bottom 50% of earners supply less than 3 percent of income tax revenues." Wills also refers to the "existing 4 million word tax code" and doubts that the 429 page tax system reform legislation recently signed by President Trump is about to produce any "simplification".

But an understanding of the tax program as revenue producer is only the beginning of understanding the full significance of the American tax system. It has moved beyond revenue and is now being used for three other purposes; it can force the reallocation of wealth; it can reward or punish; and it can promote or inhibit the nature of economic activities. The supposed main purpose of reallocation is to take more money from those of high income and to avoid taking it from those of lower income. The American system seems to have gotten this reallocation approach about half right. As high as 44% of the people of lowest income generally escape income taxes altogether, but the top highest income people seem to have been endlessly clever in escaping too onerous a tax burden, as recent presidential candidate Bernie Sanders pointed out so enthusiastically. Then, the level of taxation across the whole range of incomes must be regarded as a reallocation issue. Low taxes mean that income stays with the earner. High taxes mean that the income is tranferred – to the government. But in the end, this is a dilemma far broader than just the nature of the tax system; it is an issue challenging the nature of the economy, the interpretation of what really promotes the development of the economy, and even the degree to which the American public might feel that, in the end, Bernie Sanders may be right.

Opposing excessive government tax rates is a game that everybody can play. This has become one of the classic debates in modern American society; when does the resistance to the level of taxation overpower the support for the goods and services that governments provide? This debate is pursued at a second level; does the government properly and productively use the money it rakes in, or is too much of it wasted or misdirected? Here too, the history is long and very confused. The debate over the proper roles of government automatically invokes the accompanying debate over how these roles are funded. The long term trend seems to have been to accept great willingness to expand the government and its costs, and to accept the tax burden this demands. But within this general framework, special arrangements abound, and they all seem utterly confusing, and many seem prejudiced and self serving. Here are some of the most significant.

1. The fuel tax

For more than 60 years, both federal a local governments have imposed a special tax on the sale of auto fuel, with the funds credited to a special trust fund to finance the national highway system and related state or urban roads, streets and mass transit. This can claim to be one of the most successful tax programs in modern government history because it has led to the creation of a network that has tied the country together. But the national population has greatly increased, the number of trucks and autos has skyrocketed, the roadways are showing increasing wear, and there is now an obvious need either to increase the amount of this tax, or to find other sources of revenue. The fear now is that the political leadership at all government leves lacks the will or the courage to bite this bullet.

2. The Social Security tax

This tax was created in 1935 as a valuable response to the plight of the elderly in a Depression driven economy. It was clear from the start that income from Social Security payouts was never intended as a full funding of individual retirement costs, but was to be a supplement and safety net added to the funds saved by each individual. Over the years, the government have struggled to deal with the demands of a far larger population of retirees, with the inflation in the economy, the rising costs of living, and with a populist political tendency to buy popularity with public money by increasing payment levels. In the end, this tax is treated sacred, and somehow it retains its high human value.

3. Medicare taxes

Mainly, this is a tax on employment income. Each employee is required to pay 1.45% of wages and salaries as a tax, and the employer is required to match this with a matching 1.45%. In addition, in 2013, an additional surtax of .9% was levied on employee wages and salaries. Self employed persons must pay both of these taxes, or a total of 2.9%. Huge amounts of money are involved, but the rising costs of health care, and the shifts of a large cadre of people from employment to retirement seems to threaten the stability and adequacy of this system.

4. Import/Export taxes

It is probably true that these taxes are less important as revenue producers than they are as tools to manipulate economic activity. Import taxes are widely used by governments around the world to fend off foreign goods or services that compete with domestic producers. In many state socialist countries a policy of Import Substitution initiatives (ISI) became a crucial element of economic policy.

There are two moderate versions of ISI policy – a "domestic content" policy and a "mandated exporting" policy. In many countries, foreign direct investment (FDI) was deliberately limited. Whole sectors of a national economy were not open for foreign investment, and in most cases, foreign investment was limited to minority holdings of local enterprises. Domestic content policy loosened up control of an economy to the extent that it permitted FDI, but the goods and services produced still could not exceed some arbitrary percentage of the total, usually 50%. The purpose of such a policy is to force foreign investors to partner with domestic enterprises and use locally produced raw materials, fabricated parts or subassemblies, and domestic labor. This policy is almost purely political and is widely used; it is even popular in the U. S., as witnessed by Buy American policies enacted into some laws and regulations. Opposition to foreign investment generally comes from labor unions, populist politicians, and locally subsidized or protected industries. Mandated export policies are also based on the political urge to assist domestic industry, but at least they were more positive and constructive. The usual approach is to use government mechanisms such as tax waivers for export earnings, fast depreciation of assets used in exporting, preferences in the granting of export licenses, waiver or reduction of export fees, and even government help in searching for overseas markets.

All of these centrist government policies proved to have value only in the short run and only in cases where a country private sector was very weak. But all proved to be pathological in the longer term. Import substitution had the effect of depriving national consumers of superior foreign products in favor of what all too often proved to be inferior local products. Domestic content regulations were almost always quickly abandoned simply because they seriously inhibited the willingness of foreign investors to invest in a country where the government officially forced them to combine with obsolete or inefficient local enterprises. It also appears true that when such a domestic content involvement is mandated, the venture begins perversely to act more like a "protected industry" and less like a dynamic private enterprise. Most will lobby to retain and enhance their subsidies, and there is a high risk that, unless the government is very skilled, they will subsidize enterprises that are never capable of making it on their own and will survive only as long as the government props them up. Export encouragement has often failed because the government's policy makers proved to have an almost pathetic lack of grasp of the markets their subsidized enterprises were trying to enter.

A basic prerequisite for foreign direct investors is the need for reasonable tax levels. Taxes that are too high drive investors away. It is equally important for investors to feel that taxes will be stable and will not be arbitrarily changed either to usurp profits or to threaten the value of the investment. But taxes are an old and complicated game even in the United States, and some investors are attracted by the possibilities of "gaming" the tax system to their own advantage, and governments would be well advised to be sophisticated enough to protect their own interests. To defend itself against such gaming, the government must exercise honest control over its own tax laws to forgo tax breaks for favored friends and tax subsidies for profit making organizations that are fully capable of fending for themselves.

Many countries retain the simplistic view that foreign direct investment can be captured primarily in order to take advantage of their cheap labor. This may well be true in the short run, and in industrial arenas were employee skills can be minimal, and early foreign investors may take advantage of low labor costs. But it is certainly not true in the long run because amost all elements of the economy are becoming much more complex and they require a more educated workforce and not just cheap labor. Governments are delinquent if they do not invest heavily in the education of large numbers of its young people. The economy of America has shifted radically away from earlier simpler forms to an economy that is more service/consumer based, and the national education system is sufficiently extensive and capable to meet new talent demands. Failure to do this would reduce the potential for more profitable and value added investments in the future. One of the biggest concerns expressed for example about the influx of illegal immigrants into the U. S. is that most of these people are underskilled and are fit only to hold the kinds of jobs that no longer exist in sufficient numbers. Yet there are many arenas of the economy that are searching for employees, and the immigrant/refugee population may be a valuable worker source after all.

Finally, investors are becoming aware of, and highly sensitive to the impact of corruption as a prime criterion for selecting places to invest. In fact, it seems that many governments are far slower in coming to the same realization than investors. Since there is competition for investment money, and investors can go anywhere they want, corrupt countries may simply be ignored, and local governments may not be wise enough to know why. Who now would look to invest in anything in Venezuela or Sudan or Syria? Most companies have learned cynically to accept widespread corruption, speak of it as a part of doing business, and chalk off its costs to "business expense." But increasingly, the evolution of the global economy includes growing pressure to resist financing corruption and instead demand that governments clean up their acts. Despite a worrisome pattern of problems, the U. S. remains relatively free from official corruption. Right now, FDI is a sellers market, and there are tides that are running that will make this even truer in the future. Governments are also learning that what the private sector wants is less government intervention in economic control – they want the government to "get out of the way" and let the market economy function efficiently.

What is growing is the realization that taxing exports is generally dysfunctional, and the better course of action is to use government policy actually to create incentives to encourage the ability of American companies to sell overseas. The U. S. government does so through the Export/Import Bank, the Commerce Department, and ever enthusiastically through the Department of Agriculture.

Another form of taxation widely being debated is the Value Added Tax (VAT). This tax is essentially a tax on consumption rather than income, and it has been widely adopted in other countries. It is seen as a replacement for the income tax, or at least a supplement to a substantially reduced income tax system. It is argued that such a tax would be far easier to collect since it would be "built in" to the money collection systems of producers, and not in the form of complex income tax paperwork prepared by millions of confused and unhappy individuals. At the same time, there are two major objections to such a tax. First and foremost, it is regressive; it impacts most on individuals at the lower levels of income. A poor person and a billionaire pay the same tax. Then, companies protest, because they fear that the VAT is an expense that would have to be recovered either by higher prices for their customers, or by lower profits for its managers and stockholders. Finally, state or local governments that have already imposed sales taxes on consumer products and much else, fear that these local taxes would be driven out by an overbearing federal tax imposition.

A second and very recent new tax proposal would be the imposition of a carbon tax, which would be levied against any source of energy use that adds carbon to the atmosphere. Here, the objective is clearly the enforcement of a government policy and not primarily the raising of revenue. Its advocates argue that this is a "win-win" idea – the environment is protected and government gets rich. The counter argument of course is that the burden of an added tax (level not yet defined) would, in the short run, simply get passed off to the users of the energy source, and in the long run, would inhibit the development of manufacturing and energy supply to cope with future national population expansion, and new and more demanding technologies. Part of this counter argument is that new technology will also include the development of new and more effective means to reduce carbon emissions, and this would be a "positive" solution as opposed to a tax "negative". Additional debates are simmering at a lower level about new taxes of a punitive nature such as a tax on marijuana sales or even on soft drinks with high sugar content, but public resistance to these ideas have a new tone where the public doubts that such taxes would really cut usage, and they are increasingly resented as oppression and arrogance, and about the desire of governments to meddle endlessly in people;s lives.

At a second level below the broad role of defining what taxes to impose is another set of issues dealing with how the tax system is really administered. At this level, a whole new array of gaming and manipulation is in play. The laws and regulations define and elaborate hundreds of different taxes – arcane, complex, legalistic, deliberately or inadvertantly obscure, inexplicable, controversial, contradictory, often outrageous and often obsolete. This is the chosen playground of countless politicians, corporate executives, foundation directors and a vast army of tax lawyers happily and profitably harvesting the benefits of this field of governance. Here are some of the sub plots that the tax system offers.

Tax expenditures: this is a tool for goverance at it's most patronizing. "Expenditure" really means "taxes we <u>could</u> have collected, but we are generous and we won't". Thus, the government acts as if it <u>had</u> collected the tax but had then given it back. The classic example is that the government does not collect a tax on home mortgages paid by people, and this particular sophistry has been going on for more than 70 years. The U. S. Department of the Treasury defines it as defined by law as "revenue losses attributable to provisions of the Federal tax laws which allow a special exclusion, exemption, or deduction from gross income or which provide a special credit, a preferential rate of tax, or a deferral of tax liability." Given this latitude, tax expenditures may be used as an alternative to other government policy instruments such as spending within the Federal budget, or some form or regulatory relief. The largest tax expenditures are:

* Exclusion of employer contributions for medical insurance premiums and medical care. ($2.74 billion)
* Exclusion of net imputed rental income ($1.0 billion)
* Capital gains, except for agriculture, timber, iron ore, coal ($1.0 billion)
* Deductability of mortgage interest on owner-occupied homes ($948 million).

The tax expenditure for mortgage interest deduction might allow the taxpayer to switch from itemizing deductions to taking the standard deduction if they would be better off. In sum a taxpayer may benefit from deductions from mortgage interest, charitable donations and state/local government tax expenditures to considerable advantage.

Tax waivers: Waivers are often sophisticated maneuvers; a game any number can play, and it seems that almost everyone does. In a sense, this is the most interesting, but also the most disturbing feature of the entire utterly confusing tax system. In essence, Congress will pass a law enabling the collection of some form of tax, but the same law may permit some often undefined latitude in how the tax is collected. In some cases, the tax may be waived or simply not collected. In other cases, only a reduced percentage of the tax is collected and the rest is foregone. Or the government may assert that the tax can be collected, but then the payer is somehow exempted. In some unpopular cases, taxes may be imposed where not otherwise applicable, as a form of government punishment.

It doesn't take much imagination to recognize that this is a fertile field for sophisticated maneuver. This is the home for the skilled manipulator. Every corporation, foundation, association or individual – or crook – seems to have set out to obtain some form of this advantage. The District of Columbia and environs is simply full of lobbyists, lawyers, representatives, and friends of the politicians and agency officials, working all the angles and pressing all the buttons. This is the very home and target and playground for our national problem of the primacy of special interest politics. At the second, or third, or fifth level of hundreds of laws and regulations there are thousands of little obscure, arcane paragraphs and sentences which open up the trap door of some tax collection machine. Often, these maneuvers represent bribes offered and taken. But most of the time, theft is not necessary, and craft and guile are sufficient. If there is a legitimate and compelling need for "tax reform" this is surely the place.

7. <u>Corporate taxes:</u> Corporations in America are the strength and the life blood of our economy, and they range from huge international conglomerates, down to corner hot dog stands. In theory, almost nobody agrees that these companies should not have to pay taxes, so the real arguments center around what they pay for and how much. These arguments in turn butt up against two additional debates of absolutely crucial importance. The first argument suggests that it is probable that a corporation paying a tax will simply fold this cost into the prices it charges its customers, or as back pressure against what it must pay to suppliers, or the wages and benefits it must supply to its employees. If customers and suppliers can successfully resist corporate pressure, this will be argued back against the government imposition of taxes in the first place.

The second momentous argument is that corporations are the key to national economic development – that the economy will not grow and innovate and produce greater national wealth unless corporations lead the charge. It follows then, it is asserted, that if government taxes are too stringent, this would inhibit the desire and the ability of the private sector to enhance the economy. This in turn will have the effect of reducing the profits that the government taxes to generate its own revenues. Referring again to the experience of other countries with State Owned Enteprises (SOE), in the end, SOEs proved not to be such efficient instruments of economic development, but instead became instruments of political purpose, even for the primary purpose of financing vital public programs. Because they are political instruments, their operations are proving heavily inhibited by ceaseless elements of political intervention in their supposedly superior economic operations. In economic policy terms, SOEs were equipped by their governments with a formidable range of advantages:

1. Capital for creation and development, supplied by the government at little or no cost. Private companies must either generate investment money themselves or borrow it and pay interest.

2. Governments can, by law and regulation, effectively block out private companies from certain markets, and reserve them for their SOEs. In some cases, SOEs have been given absolute monopoly control of a market against either domestic or foreign competition.

3. Governments can control national price structures so that SOEs get to purch ase the equipment and services they need at heavy discounts against reality. In some cases, prices forced on some suppliers are set below their actual costs. These price subsidies may actually be applied between two SOEs, as when a manufacturing enterprise gets its power below its costs from an SOE power enterprise.

4. Facing the other way, the government can set the prices for their SOE goods and services at the highest possible level to maximize income and increase what people are forced to pay.

5. In a similar way, when a SOE produces shoddy and unreliable products as a means to hold down costs or because of poor management, the public has to learn to live with inferiority.

The lesson to be learned in the U. S. out of these almost universal world experiences is not only that state enterprises are risky but, more importantly, that it would be to the great advantage of every government to become far more suportive and stimulative for private enterprise. As argued earlier, government regulations that constrain, or taxes that confiscate should be avoided at all cost.

This however has been a constant dilemma in the U. S. for almost 200 years. Taxes, yes, but not "too much". Regulation, yes, but not beyond common sense. Encouragement, yes, but not unneeded subsidy.

And in a sense, this is at the heart of the American national political debate. President Trump and the Republican Party generally believe that corporate taxes should be cut as a means to encourage economic expansion, entrepreneurship and technological innovation. The Democrat Party, through its leaders and spokespersons argue that, for a large percentage of corporations, their profits are already excessive, and that true economic development would come through placing – or leaving – more money in the hands of the poor and middle class. All of those little paragraphs in laws and regulations need to be reformed, but they would not have any compellling impact on these broader issues of the impact of the tax system on the American economy.

Another utterly fascinating tax battlefield centers around the question of which level of government gets to collect what taxes and for what purpose. In one direction, there are many public programs which are shared between governments at several levels. Others may be mandated by federal law but with performance solely at the local level. In other cases, the politicians and managers of local government programs think it would be a good idea to get the federal government to pick up at least part of the cost of some program.

An example is that of the great national network of highways, roads and streets, and of the vehicles that run over them. The U. S. government has, over the last 60 years, developed this vital network of interstate highways, knitting the country together as never before. This network is supplemented by additional roads that are state owned and operated, but partially funded by the federal government because they are designed to link the interstate system with local roads. Then, as in every state, there is a system of highways and roads strictly to meet state demands, and these are state funded, and this network can be of critical value to rural and small town areas where there are long distances between remote homes and scarce public facilities such as schools and hospitals. Finallly, small towns and big metropolitican areas alike all need extensive and often very complicated nets of streets.

Paying for this huge and complex system features three eternal struggles. First is the need to obtain the funds to build this infrastructure in the first place. Second is the infighting over which level of government pays for what. Third is the ominous and increasing concern about the deterioration and decline of these roads, streets and bridges, and the need to come up with a whole new funding strategy for "maintenance and repair". The inexorable incease in national population and the vast increase in the number of cars and trucks on the road, and the number of destinations has overtaken existing capabilities. From the federal level, the political preference is that the feds finance only the interstate system and closely related state roads. Local officials seem to want two things: avoidance of demands for state delivery of more capability without accompanying funding (the dreaded "unfunded mandate"), but perversely, stout lobbying in Washington to solicit federal funding even for infrastructure responsibilities that are clearly the responsibilities of the state.

This transportation example illustrates the utter complexity of intergovernmental financing across practically the whole spectrum of American public programs. Even the military establishment, which is clearly a national government responsibility still, in some cases, imposes cost burdens on local governments.

In State Socialist governments, the tax system was built on a whole different level of justification. It was argued that only the State and not the private sector must be in full control of the national economy; that private interests could not be trusted to protect the wellbeing of citizens, and that private companies could not be permitted to seize too great a proportion of national wealth. Thus, the state assumed command of national economies on the premise that it would take care of all citizens "from the cradle to the grave".

Perhaps the most "socialist" of the uses of the tax system is what has become known as the "GINI" factor named after an earlier Italian statistician, as an economist's measure of the degree of difference between the highest income and wealth and the lowest, and as Bernie Sanders asserted endlessly in the most recent presidential election campaign, the huge disparity between incomes of the very rich (the "top 1%") and the very poor is seen as evil. In general, the split of the American population is seen as about the following:

The poor (less than $ 30 thousand of income per year): 20%
Lower middle class ($30-50 thousand): 18%
Middle class (($50-100 thousand): 32%
Upper middle class ($100-350 thousand): 28%
The rich (more than $350 thousand): 1.8%

The premise then stated is that the greater the GINI spread the worse it is, and that governments have the moral and civic responsibility to "do something about it", presumably by substantially increasing the taxes collected from the rich, which would permit governments to reduce taxes on – not the poor – but on the middle class. The poor must be excused from income taxes entirely, and indeed some 44% of the low income people are now excluded from income taxes. The problem once again hinges on the nature of politics in Washington and state capitols where the rich are also the powerful; and their special interest has always been successfully defended.

HUMAN RESOURCES DEVELOPMENT

The shift from manufacturing to services has been accompanied by several critical human resources based shifts. College training is now almost mandatory and there is increasing intent to make college education more relevant to the workplace demands of the changing economy. Those with less education or relevant technical skills are falling into a "second tier" level in the economy. Unions are declining; organized labor now constitutes less than 9% of the workforce. Individuals with professional skills are now negotiating directly one-on-one with employers, and unions have seemed unable to connect with newer industries or to attract the growing numbers of minorities and immigrants in the country. The service sector remains to some degree "bi-level" – a top level of professionals, and a second level in lower skilled lower paying jobs. These low level jobs have helped absorb the influx of more than 40 million immigrants, but there is a lack of adequate bridges from the low level jobs to the more profitable positions. The obvious answer is education, at least for the next generation, with the understanding that education extends beyond college and also includes on-the-job development of a wide range of skills. Finally, workers are now more mobile and less tied to fixed manufacturing sites. This enhances the likelihood of finding a better job somewhere and increases worker bargaining power.

Part of this shift in the patterns in the workforce has been the decline of organized labor. As the numbers of workers has increased, the role and membership of unions has decreased. Historically, unions have been strong in manufacturing, transportation, crafts, and retailing and services. Despite the general impression, encouraged by some politicians, the manufacturing sector of the economy has grown, not declined. Total manufacturing output increased by 30% between 1990 and 2004, It is really regarded as negative largely because it has decreased as a percentage of the total national economy. Growth has been achieved in almost every sector of the economy, and yet the unions continue to decline. Part of the reason lies in the fact that corporations recognize that the cost of wages and fringe benefits is usually the largest single category of business expense and they are constantly looking for ways to reduce those costs by using automation and hiring fewer workers. This is especially true for small and middle sized businesses where labor costs are crucial, and it is these smaller businesses that are the primary sources of new job creation. Thus, it is usually to their advantage to employ as few workers as possible, and this fact in turn puts a downward pressure on wages and benefits.

In some cases, the introduction of automation and other new technologies has reduced the need for human labor especially in the automation of manufacturing. In other cases, the import/export stance of a corporation will have crucial workforce impact. U. S. corporations that have fairly people-intensive activities will be drawn to overseas locations if labor costs are relatively cheaper. U. S. firms that are more technologically advanced tend to stay at home and to rely on their technological advantages. But U. S. firms will not export their activities just because of cheap labor since there are other critical factors to be considered. One of most important is the attitudes of the foreign governments. Only now are many governments growing out of a period of antagonism against foreign companies, often as the product of State Socialist policy. In many cases, the laws affecting private entrepreneurship are constraining, regulations on operations may be difficult and expensive, and government corruption is expensive, demeaning and, in the case of U. S. firms, probably illegal. Also, any company considering investment overseas will look for countries where the government is supportive and the workforce is educated and industrious.

But unions themselves have sometimes been their own worst enemies, and have long suffered from short sighted leadership. In some cases, this leadership has been disastrous – riddled with corruption and incompetence so bad that it has soured both union members and the public alike. In other cases, union policy has been faulty, failing to recognize the tides that have been flowing in the economy and the changes that unions needed to make to keep up with the tide. Unions remain implacably opposed to the exportation of any jobs overseas, and tend to blind themselves to the new jobs created by foreign investments in the U. S. Unions have to a large extent failed to expand the range of jobs that they seek to unionize. Whole categories of jobs (mostly professional, semi-professional and service related) are all but untouched by the labor movement. Unions have all too often failed to understand the critical trends of entry of women and minorities and even undocumented immigrants into the workforce and have generated little credibility with these workers.

Over the last three of four decades, the composition and purpose of American unions has undergone a remarkable change. The center of gravity of unionization has shifted away from manufacturing and services to that of the public sector. According to Mark A. Zupan in his book "Inside Job" by 2009, there were more members of public sector unions (7.9 million) than private sector unions (7.4 million), and the percentage of workers outside of agriculture had shrunk from 38% in the '50s to just 7% today. The absolute number of public employees now stands at just over 23 million, and big government employers such as DOD and the Postal Service are heavily unionized. And the federal government costs of labor have become a serious part of the budget. According to Zupan, "In 2010, the government paid $268 billion in pension and health care benefits to 10 million civilian and military retirees or their survivors. And the size and power of unions have grown at state, county and urban levels as well. It is estimated that the unfunded pension and health care liabilities for public employees now exceeds $10 trillion, and they are considered the second most serious financial problem facing governments, second only to the costs of Medicare and Medicaid.

The nature of unions has also undergone a crucial change. Unions, especially in the public sector seem less concerned with the traditional union emphasis on "wages, hours and working conditions" and far more on the exercise of special interest political influence. Part of this influence led to the establishment of the Department of Labor at the federal level, and of similar agencies at the local government level, and governments have now largely taken over the responsibility to assure worker protection and the adequacy of worker compensation. It is hard now to overestimate the power and impact of unions in this new manifestation.

This power can be pernicious, and Zupan discusses a compelling example in the unionization of primary/secondary education. Almost all states now allow school system employees to bargain collectively; in thirty states, collective bargaining is mandatory. School districts in most states have been consolidated, and this plus increasing teacher unionization to the level of 80% has moved a lot of control within education systems away from their official supervision, as well as from the influence of parents. Studies of pupil performance seldom show better results in unionized systems, and in fact, performance in many jurisdictions is actually somewhat worse. The two largest teachers unions, the American Federation of Teachers and the National Education Association are among the top financial contributors in the United States to elections at all levels. This financial support ranges from the election of school boards to presidential and legislative elections. Union members have long provided a very large share of the delegates to the national conventions of the Democratic Party. At the same time, there has been a growing concern that union political backing has helped them push for teacher protections such as tenure, seniority preference, more benefits and higher pay, while at the same time fending off teacher performance evaluation or the fining of any teacher even for proven cause. In some districts, more and more of the faculty is working in offices, instead of actually teaching students in classrooms.

Unions have the general reputation of opposition to new technology. In many cases such as manufacturing plant automation, they have been forced to come to terms with reality, and even unions now acknowledge that computers are a whole new industry with millions of job opportunities and a general enhancer of productivity in almost every occupation. Companies have grown more sophisticated in meeting worker needs, thus to some extent preempting the traditional strength of unions. Governments now have become the provider or guarantor of worker benefits and protections, further reducing the perceived value of unions, even where unions may have been the force that brought about the government's assistance. Finally, the public itself is more sophisticated about the nature of the economy and have come to recognize more that their consumer interests may be at odds with union resistance to lowering labor costs. Meanwhile, the cost of public employee salaries, benefits and retirement pension costs have played a central part in bringing the financies of many states and cities into such huge future indebtedness that many seem to face actual bankruptcy.

GOVERNMENT'S VITAL ROLE IN ECONOMIC DEVELOPMENT

T HE MOST IMPORTANT ROLE of governments in the world today is to deal with the state of their national economies. Of the 196 countries in the world, more than 100 are in some form of serious economic dilemma and most of the rest face major challenges to keep their economies up with the demands placed on them. After the fall of the U. S. S. R. the 15 nations that emerged and the countries of the former Soviet bloc in Eastern Europe are all struggling to abandon their soviet style governments and economies and accommodate to a "market tested economy" that few of them seem initially to understand. Most of the nations of Sub Saharan Africa have economies that are so weak that they are scarcely able to support even basic public services, especially when in the hands of tyrannical and incompetent governments mired in wars, rebellions and the incursions of terrorist war lords. In the Far East, state socialist governments, mainly China, India, and Vietnam, are also being forced to abandon much of their socialist economies and retreat slowly and reluctantly into some form of market economy. Armed conflicts in a score of countries are destroying what little economic advancement has been achieved.

Unfortunately, these realities come at a time when the more developed countries of the world are evolving into a complex new "globalization" world which widens the gap between developed and less developed economies. A large part of this greater complexity relates to the ability to absorb new technologies, and to shift the economy of a country away from low value economic activities to those that produce a higher rate of wealth generation, and America and the U. S. economy are at the heart of these new tides. Economies can be characterized as falling into the following groupings:

1. <u>Primary economic level</u> consisting mainly of agriculture, forestry, fishing, crafts, cottage industries, and much of the informal economy.
2. <u>Secondary level</u> involving mining, primary metals creation and fabrication, processing of metals, soft goods, manufacturing production and assembly operations, construction, chemicals processing, machinery fabrication.
3. <u>Tertiary level</u> featuring provision of utility services (gas, electricity, water), finance and banking, real estate, communications, transportation, distribution and wholesaling, health care, social services, education, retailing, information management, cleaning maintenance and disposal, sports, culture, recreation and, in a very big way, government.

There is a long term trend which tends to move developing economies from the primary level up the scale of economic development. In addition, many governments are pursuing deliberate strategies to move into the secondary or tertiary levels because these economic activities are far more wealth creating and "value added". The United States is among the most advanced in moving heavily into tertiary levels, and leaders in countries such as Japan and S. Korea for example, have come to perceive that their prevailing policy of encouraging manufacturing has perhaps been overtaken, and needs to be modified to push their economies into tertiary levels of activity along the lines of the American pattern.

Also, one of the consequences of this movement is that moving up the scale requires a higher degree of education and technical training, and the capacity to advance is highly influenced by the quality of education in the country and the ability of large numbers of people to function in a less structured work environment than usually found in primary or routine manufacturing work. Economic success now rests more on answering the question "What does the world want?", and less on the issue of "What can we produce?" Protectionism of domestic economic facilities is increasingly seen as costly and inefficient in world terms.

Governments tend to intervene in labor markets in many ways: broad economic policies aimed at enhancing economic development and thus creating jobs; regulatory interventions aimed at protecting worker interests, often in preference to employer interests; and in specific regulatory interventions aimed at guarding the actual work environment. The first – broad economic policies aimed at creating jobs – has been one of the great dilemmas of the 20th century.

It is not easy for government leaders, especially in former state socialist countries to understand these powerful economic trends, and it is a great strength of the American economy that the private sector which dominates our economy is far more agile and adaptive than governments locked in old laws and policies. The state socialist economic tide has turned, largely because state intervention proved unable to create full employment and realize the dream of a superior economic world for both workers and the public through wise and benevolent government control. A powerful example has been created by the recent fact that the government of Great Britain was finally forced to face up to the failure of its heavily Socialist economy. It retreated on many specific cherished Socialist policies and practices:

1. It has begun, out of shear necessity, to sell many of its State Owned Enterprises (SOE), the former highly touted hallmarks of the government owned and operated economy.

2. It has been selling off other government activities where possible such as the highly subsidized high speed rail service or even the student loan program, both to cut government cost burdens, but also to achieve an upgrade of operational efficiency, and to get more value for money.

3. It has been forced to recognize that, under state socialism, the British Civil Service, especially at the national level had become overblown and over populated. A three year freeze was placed on civil service pay and benefit increases. The total number of authorized positions has been cut back where possible. Serious reductions have been undertaken in benefits paid for retirees, and a later date established for retirement eligibility. The benefits are now computed on an "average salary" over a period of time, and

no longer on the final salary which is usually higher. The rates paid into the system by employees have been raised.

4. The Value Added Tax (VAT) has been increased.
5. Cuts have been made in the national welfare program. Eligibility has been made more limited. Benefits have been cut, and efforts have been made to reduce administrative costs, long time delays, and bureaucratic paper shuffling.
6. Cuts have been made to schools and universities. There has been a substantial retreat from the concept of "free" higher education (sorry Bernie Sanders!), and schools have been urged to find more of their own funding, especially by charging students. Part of this shift has been the reluctant recognition that under socialist policy, and despite socialist money, far too many colleges and universities had slumped into mediocracy and the loss of technical relevance.
7. The tax on capital gains has been raised.
8. More stringent limits have been placed on unemployment compensation, and greater efforts made to clear the roles of cheaters.
9. A serious 33% cut was imposed on a range of government discretionary programs.
10. There has been a reduction in the numbers of low income people who are required to pay any income taxes.

Thus, the British government was forced to the recognition that much of the State Socialist philosophy and policies had not been feasible, and the government finally and reluctantly was forced to fall back, knowing that they would face a surge of outrage and opposition from those who would see a reduction in their benefits. This British example once again reiterates the wisdom of U. S. interests in avoiding the whole socialist mess in the first place. Yet American governance unfolded along the same lines of broad expansion and complexity, and therefore is now experiencing the U. S. equivalent of the same problems that the British have just been able to face.

TARGETS FOR ECONOMIC REFORM

═══════════════★═★═★═══════════════

T HE GOVERNMENT MUST BE able actively and productively to develop the national economy and maintain a monetary policy that concentrates on control of inflation and the stability of the economy. Both the government and the private sector must be able to find money to borrow at reasonable rates. The value of the national currency must be maintained and not allowed to fluctuate excessively, and it must trade at a reasonable rate in the international money market.

The government's annual budgets are highly vulnerable to the political tendency for overspending, and therefore the political leadership must attempt more effectively to hold down total government spending. Over the long haul, budgets must be held to the levels that can be afforded without punitive taxes that drain too much money from the economy, and to the point where it hurts individual economic initiative and impairs the ability of companies to borrow needed funds. Fiscal policy must deal separately with capital expenditures for public infrastructure, funding for a reasonable "social safety net", and the normal day-to-day operations of the rest of the government.

There is a political tendency to be too generous in providing social services programs. In the U. S., this concern is what is now driving the public debate by asking if there is any feasible limit to the growth of Medicaid, and Medicare, and Social Security, and all of the other "humane" progams which are feared to be bottomless pits, destined to become more expensive every year. This view is cast against the unavoidable tendency to "solve" this demand by adding to our great mountain of long term debt. The views of noted economist Robert J. Samuelson are especially disturbing when he states: " Given the magnitude of existing and projected deficits, there is no plausible rate of economic growth that, even if attained, would balance the budget." The idea that a tax cut will "pay for itself" in economic growth seems to him to be "wishful thinking." "Nor can we afford the Democratic-liberal equivalent: Hands off of Social Security, and Medicare and Medicaid and other subsidies for the poor and the needy. But that's where the money is. If we tried to balance the budget without any cuts to "entitlements", the needed tax **increase** would be roughly 25%. Similarly, if we loaded all the spending cuts onto other programs, we'd have to eliminate the Pentagon, or we could abolish all domestic discretionary programs (the Federal Aviation Administration, school aid, federal courts, the FBI, the Centers for Disease Control and Prevention ….. and many more. Their collective spending is around $600 billion."

Samuelson states well the essence of the economic debate: "What is government for? What could be eliminated without much loss to the nation? Is the expanding welfare state shrinking our military in ways that make us more vulnerable? Older Americans are wealthier and healthier than ever. How should we remake retirement to reflect without shredding the safety net?" When will our governance be willing and able to answer these questions?

As a part of this dilemma, it is also increasingly apparent that it is impossible to continue to suffer from the inadequacies of the tax system. In some cases, taxes are too narrow and inequitable so that some potential payers are allowed to escape. Whole segments of the economy such as workers in the informal economy, or the very poor, may dodge at least income taxation entirely, and an estimated 44% of low income people pay no income tax. If tax collection and enforcement is weak then more payers manage to get off the hook. In the U. S., the federal government may demand that they control the collection of most taxes, but this threatens to deprive regional governments and cities of the ability to take advantage of their own tax sources which they assert they will spend more productively. This problem is of growing concern because one of the most important facts of life in the United States has been the major shift of people from rural/small town areas to cities. Cities are now the obvious future of the nation. It is therefore absolutely vital that cities and their supervising states must be free to generate and deploy their own adequate sources of money. And this is true in an environment where all government taxes are resented and there is growing resistance to heavier taxation, and a growth in the skills of tax evasion.

TRADE POLICIES

Usually there is a great deal of concern about the balance of trade in a given country. Separate but related policies are needed which set the environment for both national exports and national imports. A deficit of trade (i.e. more imports than exports) is usually seen as bad because it drains money out of our domestic economy. In order to improve the balance of trade, many countries including the United States try to restructure their economies to promote industries that can export. However, export becomes feasible not because of government policy but because of what people want to buy: there are many companies that can in fact be competitive in trade markets by offering goods that people actually want, at prices they can actually afford, and that compete favorably with what is available in other countries.

One of the prime justifications for major public ownership or management of production enterprises has been the policy of import substituting industrialization (ISI) — that is, a deliberate policy by governments to encourage domestic enterprises to produce the things that are being imported from outside of the country. A key element of ISI has been for the government to take over substantial control of banking or lending responsibilities because it can then direct the preferential or subsidy flow of lending, largely for capital investment, to the elements of the economy that it wants to develop.

But the whole pattern of ISI strategies has led to what is now perceived to be the sub-optimal investment of scarce funds both public and private. Such government ISI policies have been interventionist on a broad front. t is now increasingly apparent that the track record is one of serious disappointment in the validity of the ISI concept and in the performance of SOEs: chronic losses, inability to avoid import reliance, the high cost of sheltering both industries and labor, and a growing realization of the failure to capitalize on export development potentials. In many cases, countries have been frozen in their policies despite clear failures or lost opportunities. Challenges to failing policies have led to defensiveness or modest reforms instead of fundamental change. The continuation of this policy defensiveness could be sustained only by becoming excessively reliant on external lending, which simply ran up external debt and led to spasms of "structural readjustment" problems.

In general, while there are some success patterns to point to, the risks of government mismanagement are greatest when the forces of the government are not balanced by real leverage in the hands of the public in their roles as consumers, and also by a private sector that is strong enough to protect its own interests and provide competition to keep the public sector "honest.

AMERICAN BUDGETING PERVERSIONS.

At another level, the U. S. government is infamously known for a form of public budgeting widely known as "PORK", which is closely linked to another budget skill known as "EARMARKS", closely followed by the friendly process of "LOGROLLING". These are the tools of special interest politics. Pork means the ability of special interest politics to slip provisions in bills passed by legislatures which favor their own advantage, either in the form of money from government or in some form of favoritism or special advantage. Earmarks are funds set aside by legislators for specific organizations or activities favored by some politician: roads, or schools or clients or community development. Both of these are perverse in the sense that they substitute corrosive political preferment for rational or superior decisions. As a current 2017 example, as Congress strives mightily to pass a tax reform bill, there is a move to include in such a bill a provision that would open up about 800,000 acres of land in northeast Alaska to new oil drilling allowance; totally irrelevant, but advocated supposedly because it would provide some more jobs and income.

According to the Congressional Research Service, there were 4155 earmarks in 1991. By 2002, that number had increased to 10,631, and by 2005 it had surged to 11,772 items. These assaults on the federal budget had become so frequent and so easy and so expensive that even the U. S. Congress was driven to act. In 2011, a new law for an "earmark moritorium" was enacted, and the results were remarkable. It is estimated that earmarks now total around 150 per year. Yet those that pass are still very expensive. Citizens Against Government Waste has estimated that Congress has "snuck in" some $4.2 billion of questionable expenditures. A perfect example is the listing of organizations funded by the Department of Agriculture so called Market Access Program described below.

A CASE STUDY: AMERICAN AGRICULTURE

=★=★=★=

I N ALMOST EVERY COUNTRY, public policy remains locked in obsolete concepts of what the agriculture sector of the economy is. This lock-in is largely political and highly pathological. In many U. S. states for example, while the actual number of farmers has shrunk drastically, the "rural community" vote is still strong, and still depends heavily on government subsidies. In 1933, about 25% of the population lived on 6 million family farms. Today, just 2% of the population lives on such farms, but they still possess a mysterious political clout, in part because it is now the "small town" vote; and also perhaps because most of those farms have been consolidated and are owned by major, politically astute corporations.

In the United States, 65% of all families living on farms claim that they lost money or broke even on farming operations, and that they live by engaging in non-farming businesses and jobs. 55% to 65% of farm income comes from non-farm sources. Yet the incomes of rural families are not bad in the U. S. In a 1987 study it was estimated that the total farm and off-farm income of farm families has exceeded the median income of other American families every year since 1964, and this favorable pattern has continued to this day. Similar situations exist in most developed countries in Europe and in Japan where farmers have been able to profit from government subsidies, in some cases without doing much actual farming.

But government supports for farming have often proved to be subsidies for agribusiness. Chris Edwards, in his book "Downsizing Government" referred to a bloated farm bill as "the largest corporate welfare scam in history, with logrolling, which means that spending programs that make no economic sense get passed. Dairy subsidies had the support of members of Congress from Maine, Pennsylvania and Vermont. Peanut subsidies had the support of members from Virginia, Alabama, and Georgia. Sugar subsidies had the support from the Florida delegation. The logrolling continued for cotton, wheat, wool, mohair, and other products. Unless Congressional leaders use party discipline to impose restraint, logrolling exacerbates the overspending problem in Congress".

Tax breaks justified to help the small farmer have been far more extensively used by agribusiness to the point that highly profitable companies pay little or no taxes. Drastic changes in farm policy are needed. Subsidies to large agribusinesses are unwarranted and should be avoided. Farming must be shifted from government subsidy to a market based and market driven economy.

Consider also that starting in the late 19th and first half of the 20th centuries, a great wave of expansion and development of agriculture was at its peak. The desire was to strengthen the agricultural sector of each national economy through expansion, research, mechanization, and improved farming techniques. And enormous advances were in fact made in farming technology: in planting and harvesting techniques, irrigation, land reclamation, mechanization, soil conservation, research, education, pesticides, insecticides, and fertilizers. Government assistance was highly popular and prevalent through crop loans, crop insurance, home ownership assistance and so on.

At the same time, another tide occurring around the world was urban migration, driven in part by the poverty of the countryside, and in part by the creation of new jobs in cities. But in countries like the United States and Japan, these two tides reinforced each other. Industrialization demanded a greater urban workforce and better farming released workers to the cities without reducing food production. Equally powerful was another tide— the conversion of the small family farming into larger corporate holdings, with a similar consolidation taking place among the processors resulting in what is now called "agribusiness." Despite huge public subsidies, the growing and harvesting of crops remains a marginal economic sector in most national economies, and there is the growing realization that the beneficiaries of government subsidies have increasingly been the large agribusiness corporations.

Even as early as the latter part of the 19th century, crops were purchased and processed by big businesses: millers of wheat, canning companies, meat and dairy processors, and distribution organizations. Thus, <u>farming</u> must be distinguished from the agriculture sector of the economy, which is a far broader concept that includes food processing, distribution, wholesaling and retailing. In the U. S. for example, the Department of Agriculture loves to point out that "agriculture accounts for 22% of the U. S. Gross Domestic Product." Yet less than 2% of this value is from the growing of crops, and the bulk of the value is in exporting, processing and sales. The largest segment of "agriculture" is in fact in retailing through big businesses like supermarket chains.

While government policy is focused on "the poor farmer", the reality is that the whole agriculture sector has been moving toward agribusiness because of the economics of the industry. This transformation is worldwide, and it has meant the decline of small farming. Even at the level of crop production, the movement has been to consolidate farms into larger production units for crops like wheat, corn, rice, soy beans, and even in fruits and vegetables and large plantation crops like coffee, bananas or pineapples. Livestock raising has gone through the same rationalization including beef cattle, dairy cattle, hogs, and sheep. This kind of intensive and specialized farming requires larger capital investment – millions of dollars – and such demands drive out small farming everywhere. Almost all of these production units have gone through various forms of specialization and intensification. For example, chicken raising has shifted from small hen houses on individual farms to huge barns full of chickens where egg production and breeding for chickens for sale have been industrialized. One company will do nothing but egg production. The next may run a hatching operation to produce pullets. The pullets are then sold to another company that matures the chickens for sale. Specialization produces real cost cutting from economies of scale and the reduction of labor intensity. Food processing such as grain milling, canning, and frozen foods preparation has gone through the same consolidation and integration for the same reasons. Small local canneries are being driven out in favor of very large production units because large operations are able to realize further economies in food transportation and distribution.

Agriculture markets are now very globalized. Faster transportation and the growth of economical refrigeration mean that fresh foods can be shipped all over the world. Foods like perishable fruits or vegetables now avoid seasonal declines. For example, bananas are available year-round; and fruits grown in South America are imported into the U. S. and Europe in winter, when local crops are not available. Large distribution companies (e.g. Archer-Daniels-Midland) specialize in food distribution on a world scale and large processing companies (e. g. General Mills) deal directly with large retailers (e.g. Safeway or Giant) to market products at prices that local suppliers can't match. National branding and advertising creates loyalties among retailers. Competition now occurs between these large companies, and not between large and small producers. But competition does function (mostly) and it does tend to drive down prices for the consumer.

The old fear that the growth in world or local populations would outrun the food supply and cause starvation has proved unreal, and there is no concern of that kind for the foreseeable future. Examples of starvation in the world are the products of wars or terrorism and not inadequate food production capability. Despite the fact that there are fewer farms and fewer farmers overall food production has soared. Much of the increase is attributable to research and technology: newer seeds, better farming techniques, concentration on highest productivity lands, better fertilizers, and better herbicides and insecticides. One of the tragedies of food production is that, in developing countries there are still food shortages. Local agriculture is inefficient and food must be imported. But some of these countries are so poor that even the cost of food can scarcely be afforded. It is outrageous to recognize that often corruption and mismanagement dissipates the money that might have gone for food. It is not just that enough food can't be produced, but that the related functions of food processing, transportation and distribution have failed, leaving valuable food rotting in the fields, storage facilities, or on the street.

The sum total of this shift to agribusiness has produced conditions under which farm employment, and even total agricultural employment has been vastly reduced, with extraordinary cuts in the total cost of labor. Less than 1% of the American workforce is now earning a living from farming. This has meant that many people working on the old style farms have been driven into the cities. It is not necessarily true that the cities are good places to be; but it does signal that they are better than the "nothing" that small marginal farming now represents. Also, as the farm base has changed and shrunk, it has produced a kind of second revolution in small towns, and small supporting businesses that were designed to serve large rural populations. These too have shrunk and gone through a different form of trauma.

So called "land reform" has been one of many techniques by which authoritarian governments sought to control the agricultural sector of the economy. Crop price supports have also been common, distorting both the domestic markets, and the prices of crops in international trade. Governments relied heavily on price controls for production, distribution and processing, and in many countries the government itself insisted on being the main purchaser and distributor of agricultural products. Import controls were used in an attempt to protect domestic production, but at high cost to consumers. Governments, including that of the U. S. have subsidized farmers in an amazing variety of ways, from price supports and crop insurance to special assistance programs for irrigation, soil conservation, subsidized fertilizers and pesticides, to education, research and development. Special lending organizations such as lending cooperatives, farm credit banks and rural development banks were widely used. Most of these programs were applied to varying degree by the American government.

But perhaps the most widely used approach was in the arena of agricultural financial aid. Take for example the USDA Market Access Program which provides to farmers money grants, low interest loans, (often forgiven), loan guarantees, subsidized insurance and "market access" grants to food producers to support food exporting, including money for foreign advertising and access help. What producers are helped?

Almonds	Grapes
Apples	Honey
Asparagus	Hops
Beans	Kiwis
Beer	Live stock
Blueberrys	Mohair
Confections	Oranges
Cotton	Papaya
Cranberrys	Paper products
Dairy products	Papaya

Peanuts	Seafood
Pears	Soybeans
Pet foods	Sunflowers
Pistacios	Tomatos
Popcorn	Walnuts
Poultry	Watermelons
Potatos	Wheat
Prunes	Wine
Raisins	

The point of this tedious list is deliberate: everybody can use special interest politics to get money or preferment from the federal government. Everybody – and if anybody gets funding, then everybody gets funding. Government funds are paid to trade associations, commissions, institutes, councils, boards, departments, international groups, coalitions, bureaus, federations or just plain companies. If cotton or tobacco gain preferment, can raisins and aspargus be far behind? In fact, the raisin guys are not behind at all. The raisin lobby has already taken $ 38 million out of the public purse to pay for its overseas marketing

Large special lending institutions lent money for farm investments, operations, and even home loans – often at borrowing rates below the normal lending market. Additional subsidies came in the form of cheap electrical power or fuels, rural telephone development, special subsidies in the tax structure, and finally in direct subsidies to farmers as a form of welfare or in the name of income maintenance. But despite several decades of such support, the numbers of farms has continued to decline and remains a hot political issue. The pathology is that governments have continued to subsidize agriculture despite the very obvious changes in the realities of agribusiness. Production units have become larger and more efficient, but also far more expensive to finance and maintain. The large farmers and the processors and distributors have been able to capture the bulk of the profits of the agribusiness, and more and more small farming has become marginal in nature. Thus, government efforts to help the small farmer often fly in the face of economic reality, and have succeeded in skewing the market, and keeping agriculture protected from true market tests.

Agriculture remains a political hot spot for two main reasons: a lingering and emotional concern for the small farmer; and the special interest politics of agribusiness. To quote James Bovard about the U. S. experience in the 1980's, "Prosperity is created through organized scarcity" and this has often been the goal of many United States Department of Agriculture (USDA) farm programs. The USDA rewarded farmers for not planting 78 million acres of farm land. Government shut down some of the best farm land in order to limit supply and drive up world corn and wheat prices. But each time Congress has driven up American crop prices above world prices, American farmers were driven out of the world market. Thanks to political mismanagement, one of America's leading industries is becoming a ball-and-chain on the American economy. Every year between 1983 and 1987, the total cost to consumers and taxpayers of welfare for farmers equaled or exceeded total farm income. Federal subsidies for wool, cotton, rice and honey are so lavish that they routinely exceed the value of the entire subsidized crop."

"Farm policy is the best American example of government controlled industrial policy in action, and it is a classic example of the debilitating effects of providing welfare for businessmen. The more welfare farmers have received, the less competitive they have become. Every farm handout program has reduced efficiency, raised costs of production, and increased federal control over farmers. Many farmers have gone bankrupt because they received too many subsidized government loans." "Federal agricultural policy has long been based on the supposed superiority of government central planning over private sector decision making, and it is as close as the federal government has ever come to adoption of a State Socialist economic sector. In California as in Poland or Hungary, government policy is designed almost solely for the benefit of the producers, with open contempt for consumers. In China and E. Europe, there are stockpiles of unused, often worthless manufactured goods; in the U. S. we have our mountains of surplus cheese, butter, wheat and corn." In Romania and on Capitol Hill, economic planners scorn the future and attempt to prohibit innovations that would disrupt government control."

Many of the policy positions of the Eighties as cataloged by Bovard, while often moderated, still occupy the hearts and minds of USDA and national politicians.

Agricultural prices have declined not because of the government, but because the cost of production has declined, thanks to new technology, new seed varieties, better fertilizers, and other innovations. Politicians perennially misunderstood this economic trend and cited the decline of crop prices as proof of market failure justifying the need for political intervention. But there is a striking farm revolution occurring around the world. Crop yields are soaring on every continent, costs of production are falling rapidly, and comparative advantages among nations are shifting. Politicians are being forced to admit their failures and reduce government controls over farmers.

RURAL DEVELOPMENT

If there is a new and more rational wave of government impact on the agriculture, it is that of rural development. Instead of "farming", government policy is now concentrating on rural development which is a "quality of life" concept. Many people still want to live in the rural/small town environment because they prefer the life style. The new emphasis for public programs therefore has begun to shift from "how can we help the poor farmer?" to "how can we revitalize the rural/small town economies?"

There are some more recent assessments from the U. S. Census Bureau that are relevant, since they show not only a disparity between rural and urban incomes, but a stagnation in income improvement in the country. "Non-metro" incomes have been essentially flat since 2014, while urban incomes have risen, and the disparity is now about 25%. But the moderating circumstance may be that, to a large extent, costs of living are markedly lower in rural/small town areas than in the "big city", especially for housing, by more than 20%, and for a lot of food and fuel costs.

There is a new emphasis on making sure that government programs are equitably available in rural communities: education, health care, social services, community services, and others. There is also a greatly enhanced interest in bringing non-farm employment to rural communities, along with an effort to pay attention to community revitalization. Rural/small town communities themselves are taking such steps, whether the national government participates or not. One manifestation of this new attitude for example is the increasing concern about how powerful retailers such as Safeway or Wal-Mart may be adversely affecting the health of existing rural town centers. Finally, there is a deliberate effort to assist in the development of rural cooperatives for everything from equipment sharing, to volume discounts on purchases of seeds, marketing cooperatives, and community development projects. This appears to be a real success and is a pattern that can be made to apply in any country.

PROGRAM MANAGEMENT AND OPERATIONS

The numbers of public programs are counted in the thousands. A single enabling law can create the capacity for some government agency to initiate many programs, and each of them then assumes a life of its own. The usual measure of success for each program is that it will be made bigger and broader and deeper – and thus more expensive. And no program ever seems to die. The Government Accoountability Office (GAO), an arm of Congress, has pointed out numerous instances where the laws enabling a program or set of programs has expired, but the programs remarkably continue and demand to be funded in the President's Budget, or by some other means.

Each of these thousands of programs have to be managed. Managers are appointed, staffs are hired, policies are puzzled out and promulgated. Processes are developed, procedures are implemented, evaluations are created, checks and balances are checked and balanced. And of course, the budget for each program is artistically created and forwarded for approval.

In olden days, government programs were managed by managers, but contemporary governance has become more sophisticated and more of the management is political as defined by politicians. But a tide that has been quietly running since about the time of the Nixon Administration is that gradually, the politicians have been deliberately taking control of policies, program management, and program operations that traditionally and properly had been controlled by professional managers. And it has proved true that **bad politics makes bad management.**

Program managers have increasingly been faced with having to manage programs that are useless, dysfunctional, misdirected, obsolete, excessively expensive, overlapping and duplicative and often the product of preferment and favoritism. For example, the Government Accountability Office (GAO) issued a report in 2013 including the following conclusions:

1. There are seventeen major areas in which agency programs substantially duplicate one another, overlap each other or are fragmented across several agencies.
2. There are fourteen areas where agencies have failed to create possible cost savings, or bring in additional revenue.
3. There is no form of accountability where multiple agencies are involved.
4. There are, for example, 209 programs dealing with science and technology, energy and mathematics, in thirteen agencies. There are 160 programs and tax expenditures dealing with housing. There are fourteen programs dealing with diesel emissions.

Such a mess is highly vulnerable to the even more distructive but highly profitable skills of bribery, collusion and good old fashioned theft. A very high proportion of the failures of governments reported here will show some degree of political manipulation. Would it not be common sense to return the the professional manager the decisions and actions that should be driven by the well known elements of efffective management? Is it not the real responsibility of the political leadership actually to support and encourage this return to managerial leadershiip, and to have the courage to resist the urges for political meddling and dysfunction?

Most agencies now employ contract organizations to carry out public programs, and these contractors emply sub-contractors, suppliers and providers of services, all of them learning the arts of political influence. In addition, government agencies may execute elements of their program through private non-profit organizations (NGOs) like Planned Parenthood, the League of Cities, the Sierra Club or the American Civil Liberties Union and the National Rifle Association. Government program relationships are also maintained with independent but government-like organizations such as universities, research laboratories, Underwriters Laboratory, training centers or conservation groups.

Thus, the essence of governance is probably now its politics. The essence of the government is probably **program management** – not just administrative skills like accounting or procurement administration or human resources, or budgeting, or security or communications technology. All of these skills are admirable, but what pays off is when factories actually produce things, stores sell things, hospitals treat patients, and teachers actually show up and teach. Drivers climb in and drive their trucks, police patrol, firefighters put out actual fires, and so on and on.

Said another way, all management, including government management is built around two centers. The first and most important is management of actual service delivery. The second is built around a series of administrative skills. The key concept behind the first center should be <u>accomplishment.</u> The key concept behind the second center should be <u>facilitation.</u>

Every government program has stated purposes and loosely stated objectives such as to provide elementary education, or deploy military operations, or run hospitals and treat patients. The basis of each program should be linked closely to the reality of the arena in which it is undertaken. It is not enough to have hospitals somewhere. Managers should make a positive determination of exactly where each hospital should best be located to do the most good. It is not enough for hospitals to open their doors and wait to see who shows up. Hospital managers should deliberately determine what care citizens will require and should make their hospital ready to meet these needs.

Management is one of the most taught subjects in the entire American academic world. Everything needs management, from huge manufacturing plants to space exploration to military operations, to housewives, to corner hot dog stands. Some of the most discerning persons in modern history have been management gurus, thoughtful economists and far seeing corporate executives. So if those in the world of government management want to know how to manage their programs well, they certainly can find out; and the U. S.public should be gratified that most government managers have done so. The governments of the United States, from top to bottom, are seen as among the best managed in the world.

But the thesis of this book is that our governance world has become excruciatingly complex and sophisticated and utterly confusing, and thus increasingly difficult to understand much less manage. Therefore, it is still useful to analyze where the management of government programs and their administrative support services have fallen short and warrant an agenda of reforms. It can also be admitted that our governments exhibit their own fair share of managers who are incompetent or lazy or obsolete or corrupt. Somehow, such failings seem far more damning within the public service; politicians and government managers have a deeper commitment because they are responsible to the people and not just to owners or shareholders.

Somewhere along the line, sombody invented the term "bureaucracy"; perhaps it referred to the palace staffs of the Egyptian Pharoahs, or the ink stained copiers of Roman documents. In any event, bureaucracy remains alive and well and it can be so negative that it is seen as the source of much that is wrong with management. It's origin stems from two peculiarities of government operation, dealt with in more detail elsewhere. The first is that the basis for creation of government programs, and for the definition of their purposes and objectives is in the form of a law – an enabling statute then buttressed and elaborated by case law, implementing regulations and political protection. There is nothing wrong with the demand for such a statutory base. The problem comes from the fact that such laws have, in the American system, become unbelievably complex and almost impossible to change. Thus, when the world changes, as it inevitably will, it may be impossible for the laws to keep up with that change. This in turn freezes the world of the operational program managers who are bound to carry out the mandates of their statutory base, even when it frustrates the kind of change that managers see as needed.

It is hard for the public to realize how pervasively the concept of governance has become, and how the programs of government have entered almost every facet of American life. And it is hard for people to believe that this universality of governance is anything but "good". Yet slowly and reluctantly the American public may be reconsidering this somewhat innocent attitude. Tides are now running that have begun to question the range and penetration and cost of public programs in their several dimensions:

1. That the ultimate cost of these programs in total and in many specific cases is excessive and potentially collectively unacceptable.
2. That many programs are beyond the perceived range of what is considered the legitimate role of governments.

3. That special interest politics have produced a perverted and improper allocation of public resources, where special interests are dominant rather than the general public interest.
4. That the expanded range of government has unfortunately weakened an important attribute which calls for citizens to provide for themselves.
5. That many programs are overblown and have improperly gone beyond their legitimate purposes.
6. That some programs may have become obsolete, pointless, unneeded, ineffective; and that the political leadership is too weak or too cowardly to close them down.
7. That management has come to mean merely paper shuffling. Bureaucracy and regulation can stifle human endeavor, and government management can cease to aim for achievement and seek merely to fill out the right forms. Thus, it is wrong in the long term to seek such universal and massive extensions of the government's tidal wave of regulation. According to Philiip K. Howard in his book "The Rule of Nobody" self responsibility requires people to think for themselves and that energizes human creativity and goodwill. It is this ownership of life's choices that empowers people to take risks, to innovate, and to stand for what they think is right."

Forty years ago, the government was generally well respected, as was the civil service. But this perception has radically changed, and has become ominously worse. In 1972, when public opinion polls posed questions like "do you trust the government to do the right things?" or "how well is the government managing programs?" the public response was favorable at the level of 70% or more. But a similar poll conducted by the Zogby Organization in 2007 showed positive views down to about 47%, and negative views at an all time high. A similar poll conducted in May of 2011 by Hart Research Associates, for the Center for American Progress was even worse. The "confidence in government" was' down to 35%, and the "no confidence" factor was at an all time high of 33%. Many polls now are not about politics; they are about management. Many newer polls are now asking questions that more clearly relate to the terrain of the government's executives and managers, and these ratings make difficult reading. There are increasing concerns about programs that are wasteful or ineffective, contractors overcharging the government, smelly tax breaks, concealed bribery, excessive military spending, government duplication and overlap, lack of technological advancement, and high cost/low value programs that are obsolete.

The great and remarkable American tradition has been that the lives of each citizen will be self defined and dependent on self reliance. Individuals also formed themselves into associations where broader activitiy beyond the capacity of the individual was warranted. Local governments initially were seen as extensions of defined local needs, with the national government strong in arenas such as national security, relations with foreign governments, multi-state roads and waterways, or a national banking system.

Gradually, the country began to "nationalize" – to become more integrated and complex. As this happened, the government too began to broaden its range and responsbilities, but on the continuing basis of citizen self reliance. Private businesses grew beyond their early local homes, becoming larger and more regional or national, or increasingly, "global". Huge tides like millions of immigrants, the expansion and development of new land, and especially the Civil War, further called for the presence of larger and more assertive governments at all levels. Slavery was abolished, unions were formed to counter industrial oppressors, elementary and secondary education became almost universal, the concepts of insurance emerged, travel became easier, and people and governments waxed and prospered.

During our nearly 250 years of history, government has, despite many lurches and staggers, been seen as a good thing and vital to the country. The checks and balances designed into the government system may have occasionally slowed the action, but they also seemed to have avoided dangerous excess. But the very growing range and importance of our political system has had a lot to do with the powerful emergence of the very special interest politics so heavily criticized today.

After WWII, governance around the world crossed a social and political watershed when a high percentage of governments in the world drew away from the concepts of citizen self reliance and bottom up representative government, and adopted instead some form of top down

State Socialism. America managed to draw back from the allure of State Socialism, but it has been deeply impacted by a growing reexamination of our national social and cultural environment. The consequence has been that both governance and governments have increasingly become deeply involved in a broad range of social concerns, and this has registered in the structure and programs of the federal and local governments. At the federal level for example we how have agencies for health and "human services", housing, urban development, labor, small business, primary education, local transportation, environment, civil rights, and many many more.

Add to this enormous expansion of social governance through several hundred "sub-agendas", established as public programs serving some specific special interest. This expansion is, of necessity, enabled by a national law, and they tend to be immortal, since it seems almost impossible for legislative bodies to abolish anything.

There are many ways in which the performance of public programs can be implemented. One is direct performance by government employees, such as the military or police or fire departments or schools. Also, programs may also be implemented through government contracts such as electric utilities, or military weapons development. Other programs may involve a designed partnership between governments and private enterprises, such as Planned Parenthood, which obtains more than 40% of its $1.3 billion annual income from the federal government. Or programs may simply flow money through the government budget line items: government grants, loans, guarantees of private borrowings, etc. In some cases as discussed elsewhere, funding may be entirely indirect through tax waivers or tax relief, tax expenditures or financial advantages realized through the application of some government regulation.

In a very great number of cases, government programs are families of more or less related activities. For example, what is called the government health care program involves complex patterns of activity involving states, counties, cities, hospitals, clinics, health insurance companies, medical technical providers, pharmaceutical manufacturers, scientific research centers, medical suppliers, and about 95% of the entire population of the country. Money enables and lubricates this enormous set of enterprises in ways that defy common understanding, and that in fact, often seems beyond control.

Similarly, governments at all levels vigorously support and fund the arena of education from kindergarten to post doctoral research. A range of programs deal with school systems, school buildings, teacher qualifications and their salaries and benefits, the substance of what is taught, and how it is taught. The costs of education are shared with these several levels of government, with the parents of children in primary/secondary classes. Later, much of the funding at the college/university level is borne by the students themselves, but with considerable help from governments. States provide a huge number of public universities. There are special programs for poor people, for the disadvantaged, for the handicapped, and for other educational needs. Millions of adults have benefitted over more than 70 years from the educational funding available through the GI Bill as a benefit stemming from military service.

The urge to do public program "packaging" is well illustrated in the formation of the federal Department of Transportation. Ever since colonial times, American governments have been vitally involved in the development of national transportation systems of roads, canals, waterways, and railroads, since all served the absolutely vital purpose of linking a growing and expanding country. Then, obviously the Wright brothers created another special interest, and airlines, airports and air traffic control systems became an increasingly important element of the transportation package. Finally, cities, faced with burgeoning populations and the universality of cars and trucks, and the demand for workable streets, roads and traffic control, formed new alliances to seek federal government money by getting the feds involved in highways and roads and in urban transit.

The range and complexity of public programs is absolutely staggering, and almost nobody really understands its totality, what it demands of the country and what it really costs. These costs are of two types: the cost of the programs themselves, and the cost of delivering and managing them, enforcing the federal interest, and federal regulation.

The extraordinary surge in government programs has increasingly been considered as a mixed blessing at two or three levels. First is the growing feeling that the government has created programs that are not necessary for it to undertake; that people who control parts of our lives have overreached their mandate, or succumbed to too many questionble pressures, or tried to buy too much political support. Perhaps the acid tests should more forcefully become whether any activity can be pursued outside of government; and whether a program serves the general public interest and not some specific private special interest.

The Government Accountability Office (GAO) has often entered this fray, speaking both to the Congress and to the agencies of government. GAO is an element of the Congress, and its charter permits it to work across the whole range of the U. S. government, and its connections with local governments, private companies and even voluntary organizations or individual citizens. GAO started out as more or less an audit agency, but over time, and by Congressional invitation, their work has shifted upward from audit to evaluation of both government management and underlying political policy setting. GAO routinely assesses individual programs and specific situation where there is a concern that something has gone wrong. But GAO too began to recognize that some of the most important problems of government went well beyond the follies and foibles of individual programs, and stemmed instead from broad political policies or general managerial malfunctions, usually cascading down into the government's enormous networks of interrelated agencies and activities.

It is to its credit that GAO itself is very aware of the ominous consequences of the incomprehensible magnitude and complexity of today's governments at all levels. Does anybody really understand it all? GAO tries. Does anybody really control the whole government? GAO knows the answer to that one. Nobody, not the President, not the agency heads, not the Congress, nobody. Does anybody even understand it all? No.

As stated by Senator James Lankford in his fascinating reports "Federal Fumbles: 100 Ways the Government Dropped the Ball" in two volumes, "Each year, GAO and agency IGs issue thousands of recommendations to federal agencies to improve their operations, eliminate waste and fraud, and save taxpayer money. In 2015, agencies successfully implemented 79% of these recommendations which saved the American taxpayers a record $74.4 billion. However, agencies still leave thousands of recommendations and their potential for billions more of savings on the table each year."

And to some greater degree, the institutions of governance are trying harder to get a broader and firmer grip on those thorny problems of mysterious complexity and interrelatedness. There is a law called The Government Performance and Results Act, and a more recent version called The Government Performance and Results Modernization Act which manates agencies to develop and actually use measures to assess the effectiveness of programs. All government programs are required to use performance measures. But there is a reality here: the real purpose of any evaluation system is to point the way to making improvements in the management of public programs. And even when the way has been pointed, does the agency actually act to improve program outcomes?

GAO issued another major report, dealing with the consequences of uncontrolled government in the form of its overlap, duplication, fragmentation, confusion of purpose and unrecognized failures and obsolesence. This report bears serious attention, and here are some of the major conclusions that it reported:

1. There has been a long and discouraging record of the failure or lack of support for many past efforts to promote better government performance and effectiveness. Much of this failure stems from a simple lack of will to enforce anything.

2. The government has an enormous holding of land, buildings, facilities and equipment, and stocks of inventory in its warehouses, but it has a poor and miserable record of proper management of such physical facilities and the control of government stocks.

3. DOD, across a broad range of its "weapons portfolios" needs serious efforts to upgrade these weapons systems acquisitions from design to deployment and maintenance. This is seen as a very broad and very expensive set of problems.

4. Part of the concern has been DOD's woeful record with respect to the identification and removal of obsolete, excessive or no longer needed supplies and equipment – ammunition for weapons no longer in use, or boots that are no longer worn.

5. The government has for too long missed opportunities to enhance its own revenue by greater leasing of public lands, or the charging of user fees for public services such as for parks or monuments, or the provision of public services such as Great Lakes ice breakers

or tolls on more public highways, or leasing of space in federal buildings.

6. All too often, GAO has found that the government does not adequately protect itself. There are literally hundreds of examples where the government has been overcharged for goods or services; that money has been paid for services never rendered; that bills have mistakenly been overpaid; that the government has paid contractors for phantom employees; that hundreds of thousands of people have been able to cheat on tax obligations; that well people are claiming health care benefits; that people without physical disabilities are collecting benefit payments — and on and on and on. GAO over decades, has pressed government officials to sharpen their control over their own programs.

7. In a similar vein, GAO has urged government agencies to "shop", when it purchases. All too often, the government buys at prices higher than it might have gotten if it had bothered to shop the market place.

8. The IRS has a disturbingly bad record about tax payers who skip out payment; of income lied about and hidden; of the basic capabilitiy to reach out and grab the tax dodgers. Also, IRS itself has paid out billions for fraudulent refund.

9. Surprisingly, the federal government has a lot of money just lying around. There are appropriated funds for specific programs that, at the end of the fiscal year, have not been spent. There are funds judged not needed after all – but not recovered. And there is the absurd tendency for federal officials, who fear the appearance of laxity over unspent funds, who shove the money out the door on questionable stuff.

10. In a somewhat murky way, it would be possible for the government to become a better comparison shopper. The GAO report cites the example of widely different rates for the purchase of medications and medical services. Obviously, doctors and hospitals share the blame for not being more effective shoppers.

The essence of this report is not about politics or policy, but about management, or specifically, the lack of it. GAO is fully serious about pressing government agencies to "wake up" and go beyond passive paper shuffling toward more positive high energy management effectiveness. And increasingly the American public has begun to reflect this same concern.

A simplification of the interrelationship between governmens would have gratifying advantages in trimming back the government thicket, or as President Trump would put it, to "drain the swamp in Washington." A single program may involve federal, state, regional, county and urban governments. At each level, expensive offices operate amid intergovernmental friction and maneuvering. Two major approaches are usually apparent. One is the prediliction of governments at the delivery level to hustle money. Cities would like to avoid city taxes by getting program money from counties or states. These governments in turn have lobbied, often successfully, to induce funding from the federal purse. In turn, the federal government engages in what has been tabbed the "unfunded mandate" where the implementation of a federal program is "delegated" to some level or local governments, but without federal money allocated to carry it out. This crafty maneuvering is exceedingly wide spread, and it totally baffles the public, and sometimes the very agencies that are doing the maneuvering. But this swamp is very expensive, and has begun to raise questions about whether the swamp reall does need more serious draining.

CORRUPTION FOR FUN AND PROFIT

=======★═★═★=======

L OTS OF PEOPLE HAVE invented lots of excuses to "justify" corruption, or explain it away. Some see corruption as a way of life, part of the culture, and therefore somehow acceptable. But in a deeper sense, it is clear that no society in history, and certainly not the U. S. society, has really endorsed corruption; all consider it wrong; every religion or secular philosophy condemns it; and our laws make it specifically illegal. So the "way of life" argument is merely a feeble rationalization when tested by these broader societal views.

Some say "everybody does it; how can you stop everybody?" But it is not true that everybody does it. Most people are remarkably honest, hate corruption, oppose it where possible, hate to be its victims, and will support anti-corruption efforts.

Others have argued that corruption is a lubricant, helping to get things done. But this is the kind of argument that is advanced by those organizations that see advantage in corruption. Corporations may argue (especially around tax time) that bribery is a necessary business tool to avoid bureaucratic process (e. g. the "speed bribe") and help to gain business. But the cost of corruption is properly perceived in the U. S. as far exceeding the cost of reduction many times over; a corrupt government is never a "cost-effective" government, nor is it serving any public interest. Hopefully, one of the adjuncts of a truly democratic government will be openness, transparency, lots of watchers, and managerial measures to fight corruption. But these means must be deliberately cultivated and will not happen spontaneously because a government has the democratic apparatus.

Given the will, there are many ways in which management corruption can be prevented or mitigated. Some involve broad government-wide management policies which can be mandated in law or implemented through individual agency adoption. Perhaps the most important is the use of maximum feasible competition in all government activities that allocate resources – systems such as awards of contracts, grants, loans, or the use of public lands or facilities. This may also include careful control of licenses for valuable assets such as broadcasting wavelengths or the allocation of access to airport gates.

It is also vitally important to require internal transparency of agency operations. The processes by which agencies carry out their programs should be clearly defined, made as simple and understandable as possible, and widely published for all employees who can then know what is acceptable and what is not. This transparency must also extend to the outside through published summaries of agency authority and operating procedures. This can and should be accompanied by some form of public review and comment <u>before</u> important divisions are made, or key processes changed. Special emphasis, often neglected, should be placed on making visible which official makes key decisions and why.

No public official, including political leadership should be authorized to have what are generally known as "slush funds"; that is, funds that are available without controls or justifications or audits.

As argued more fully elsewhere here, there are serious conflicts between good management and bad politics. It may become necessary to develop some forms of protection for career officials from the unwarranted intervention of political leadership into decisions that should rest on merit or competition. Obviously, political leadership is necessary but what should be restricted is the tendency o politicians to meddle in management decisions such as contract awards.

There are many measures to increase the likelihood of detection and prevention of corrupt practices. Inspectors General should be legislatively mandated, with strong independent powers of investigation and discovery. Either independently or as a part of an Office of Inspector General, a skilled corps of auditors should be authorized to insist on the examination of all agency records and actions. But even more importantly, it is first and foremost the responsibility of program managers to assure that their program is free of corruption or mismanagement even before the auditors arrive.

There is an old axiom for auditors and inspectors: "follow the money". Special attention should be given to the creation and enforcement of close controls over financial flows from initial collection of revenue to the authorization by legislatures of funds for expenditure by the agencies. Within each agency, authority to authorize the commitment of expenditures should be carefully limited to as few people as possible. A second internal control should be maintained through the use of separate officials who can approve the actual disbursement of funds. Then, there should be management reviews and post-audits of whether the funds were actually used properly and for the purposes for which they were authorized. This sort of managerial discipline is simply good program management, but sometimes politicians are unable or unwilling to contemplate the possible constipation of the happy flow of government funds to their voting constituencies, even for good reason.

Experience shows that perhaps the best "auditors" of agency actions are not necessarily official auditors, but the general public and sometimes employees of an agency with inside knowledge. Good confidential methods should be available for the public to lodge complaints or report corruption. The best intelligence about government corruption often comes from its victims. Those agencies that operate hotlines are often amazed and gratified by the numbers and sharpness of public responses. Internal agency whistleblowers may also be remarkably valuable but they are often punished by agency officials who have something to conceal, even if it is only their own mismanagement.

Finally, in truly scandalous governments, corruption is not just ignored, it is organized and encouraged. Corruption shows up at each and every level of government institutions, and this is especially true when it starts and flourishes at the top. There are distinct patterns where illegal funds, generated at the working level of government operations are shared up and down the chain of command in secret by carefully negotiated percentages. Corruption at the top may involve a certain degree of pass-down to secure loyalty, but these shares usually magically dwindle on the way down, and seldom reach the bottom. The cardinal principle for reform: be sure to "get" the top guys!

One of the great mysteries of modern American governance is the response of our government to this world of corruption in the international arena. How is it possible that we have donated year after year to recognized oppressive and corrupt governments, only to see the money diverted to improper and illegal purposes, or simply to disappear?

Even where the apparatus for controlling corruption exists, they may be ignored or underpowered. What the public deserves and wants to see is that the corruptors are caught and removed, and that corrupt acts receive serious punishment. For situations of entrenched corruption in agencies, it may be impossible for the organization to purge itself from the inside and the only alternative may be the creation of external anti-corruption campaigns mounted and enforced from outside of the agency. Thus, it is vital that there exist a forceful government-wide posture against corruption and a set of instruments by which this posture can be carried out. U. S. governments employ inspectors general, government-wide auditing and evaluation agencies, a government-wide budget review organization, and often, a contract review and oversight boards. There is a growing tendency too to create a special anti-corruption agency with strong independent powers.

But of critical importance is the participation of the national legislative body. The rule of law can become perverse if the laws themselves are pathological. Part of this responsibility involves the oversight of the executive agencies of the government, and these agencies can be aided and abetted in preventing corruption if the laws themselves make it clear exactly what practices are defined as illegal or improper. Further, anti-corruption controls can be deliberately incorporated into laws and mandated in more detailed government regulations. Legislatures can and should maintain their own forms of transparency and openness to public comment, review, complaint and education. Every public official at senior levels should be required to disclose the state of their personal finances; however, a mistake often made is not to extend this requirement to politicians.

GOVERNMENT GRANT/
CONTRACT PATHOLOGIES

=====★=★=★=====

ALL GOVERNMENTS CONTRACT FOR goods and services in many cases as a preferred alternative to having work performed by staffs of regular civil servants. The ability to contract out work is perfectly reasonable and it is a vital policy and management tool. Each contract is a binding agreement between the government and commercial suppliers of goods or services, and is enforceable in law. In addition, governments may use the instrument of "grants-in-aid" which are usually made to other levels of government such as states or municipalities. Grants are essentially an award of funds to a recipient for the performance of some defined activity which may range from the conduct of scientific research to information processing or the provision of some public service such as health care centers or municipal transit services. Grants are usually of two forms: one is a categorical grant paid for the performance of a defined "category" of work such as assistance to the handicapped or the provision of low income housing; the other is a formula grant where the amount of the payment is calculated under a defined formula such as population, population density, average income or age ranges.

Contracting is justified where the government lacks some specific skills or institutional capacity, or where the work needs are temporary and would not justify hiring permanent civil servants, or where contractor performance would produce cost savings or superior performance. Contracting may be used for a tremendous range of activities from scientific research to the purchase of paper and pens. It is important to understand that, when a government agency contracts for work it never relinquishes its ultimate responsibility for that work. Some public official must remain responsible for defining what will be contracted out and for the supervision of the resulting contract. The public official must draft specifications for a contract that defines what the government needs, and defines standards and controls to be imposed on the contractor to assure that the government needs are met. The public official must oversee the performance of the contractor to assure that the work is performed in accordance with defined specifications or statements of contract objectives. The official must make sure that all contracted work is in fact performed – no performance should mean no payment. There must be evaluation of costs under the contract to make sure that they are justified and realistic. Goods and services must be inspected or evaluated to make sure that they meet the terms of the contract.

It is exceedingly difficult to find out how many contractors the federal government employs. Even the Congressional Budget Office (CBO) says that they do not know for sure. The best estimates are that there are about 7.5 milllion people working for federal contractors, (about 770 million for DOD), under contracts worth about $500 billion per year. Add to this approximately 18 million contractors working for state and local governments. The obvious and most basic means to control the costs of contracts is to use as few contractors as possible in the first place.

If there is a single most important policy to be followed in government contracting, it is to seek competition from interested companies for each contract. Competition is vital in assuring that the government has really sought out the best combination of cost and performance from the private sector. Often, the unwillingness to seek competition is an ominous signal about what the government is doing. "Sole sourcing" is justified only in limited instances where only one company can perform the work.

Contracts usually state that the government commits to paying all legitimate costs plus a reasonable fee, fixed in advance. A somewhat more sophisticated approach may be used where the government pays all legitimate costs, plus an award fee which may go up if performance is better than expected. When the government is buying routine things such as office supplies or equipment it may just purchase from the most convenient source, but even here, if the government is purchasing large volumes of material or services, a price competition is easily possible.

While the use of contracting is vital in the work of most governments, it is also perhaps the single most important source of corruption and perverse policies and operations. Contracting is a contact sport, full of rough and tumble in both the public and private sectors. Companies seeking contracts routinely test the capability of those letting the contract. A price may be quoted for work that is heavily overstated, to see if the buyer is smart enough to reject it. If the buyer is too dumb, the bidder will happily enter into a perverse contract to its own advantage.

Every element of contracting from the initial decision to contract down to detailed operations is highly vulnerable despite government protective mechanisms. Many governments have corruptly contracted for things that they do not really need as a perverse way to pay off certain companies or as the source of bribe seeking by government officials. A good example is the purchase of expensive military hardware even though there is little military threat. Even where the need for a contract is justified, there may be perverse rules applied for determining who is eligible to bid. For example, eligibility may be limited to domestic companies, even where it is clear that foreign companies might offer better capabilities. Eligibility criteria may be skewed to give unfair advantage to a single company, owned by somebody's brother-in-law, or located in some politicians voting district, or by a company that is willing to pay for the privilege. A "sole source" decision may be driven by the prospects of later payoffs.

The whole process of soliciting bids and evaluating them to determine which company will receive the contract is highly vulnerable. Legitimate bids may be rejected for many technical reasons so that "friends" of selecting officials may win the bid. One of the major sources of fraud is called "bid rigging" where bidders and public officials collude to fix the outcome of the competition in advance. Often, such bid rigging arrangements are organized by industry associations to share the wealth among its members. Public officials can and do provide insider information (at a price) to their favored companies to make sure that they win. Another form of corruption is called "bidding in" – a deliberate understatement by a bidder of the expected cost of the contract in order to win the bid. The contractor relies on the high likelihood that they will be able to pump up costs once they have the contract. Many so-called contract cost overruns are the inevitable and plotted outcome of low bidding in the first place. The whole bidding process may have been a false front to mask the fact that the winner has already been selected by the public officials involved. A bidder may simply offer a bribe to the selecting official.

Once a contractor begins work under the contract, whole new forms of corruption become possible. The work itself can be pathological: shoddy work, substandard materials, failure to perform required work, unwarranted expenses, overstated costs, deliberate cost overruns, and many more failures. Cost may be overstated. The government may be billed "phantom charges" for work or supplies not actually provided. The workforce may be overstated and phantom wages and benefits for "ghost" employees billed to the government. Work delays may be deliberately created to pump up costs. Management salaries or overhead costs may be excessive. Unfortunately the contractor may feel that the quality of government oversight is so poor that such illegalities will never be caught. In other cases kickbacks are simply made to public officials to turn a blind eye to such cheating. Government managers and inspectors may not be competent, or may be too few to adequately cover all contracts. Performance is not evaluated, costs are not verified, goods are "lost" or stolen, and accounts are not audited. Where a contractor is caught in an illegal or improper act, the overseeing government official may be bribed or coerced to ignore the fact. Even the protections of auditors or inspectors may be frustrated through bribes or political pressure.

Each year, a government may have hundreds or even thousands of contracts in force, with additional contracts or contract renewals being let. Most governments suffer from inadequate resources to oversee these contracts, and in some cases, this shortage of oversight capability is deliberate, where corrupt politicians and officials want to keep oversight as ineffective as possible. The single most effective curb against contract corruption continues to be the mandated use of competitive bidding. A carefully drafted law mandating competition can be used as the basis for defending agency contracting practices, and giving leverage to reformers and those officials in agencies who genuinely want fair and legal contracting to prevail.

But a legislative mandate for competition even if it is achieved, is far from enough. Much depends on the willingness and ability of public officials to implement such laws fairly and free of corruption, and this is not easy. Each agency of government should be required to supplement the law with a carefully defined and published set of procedures for bid competition. All bidders should be made aware of these procedures, and bidders can and should police each other to make sure that the procedures are followed. The reputation of each bidding company can be tested by checking their performance on previous contracts and their financial and management ability to carry out the contract must be evaluated. The initial contractor selection process is critical because it is here that the likelihood of corruption will first manifest itself. If bad public officials and companies capture the contract at this point, it is likely that subsequent operations under the contract will be a constant problem. All contract bids should be subjected to an opaque evaluation process aimed at getting a realistic assessment of bidder capabilities. This evaluation should be open to review, at least for auditors and other bidders to examine. That way, if a selecting official makes a decision that runs counter to the technical evaluation; such an arbitrary selection can be more effectively challenged.

Another significant protection is created when the government has the authority to debar bidders from future contract opportunities if there is evidence of collusion, factual misrepresentation or intent to conceal relevant information. Debarment is an administrative action, and it puts the burden on the alleged offender to upset the decision either by law suit or by appealing for help from political allies who, however, may regard it as dangerous to interfere. Even informally, any rumors or partial evidence of improper bidder practices can be made known to other contracting organizations in both government and the private sector.

Another important way for public officials to protect their position is for the government agency itself to prepare its own estimates of the expected costs for all significant elements of the intended contract. Such estimates should be available at the time of the contract competition so that the government officials have a basis for judging the costs proposed by bidders. This is especially valuable if there is the likelihood that few bids will be received, or that there may be bid rigging collusion among bidders. Substantial variances from the government estimate should be suspect. If the bids are too low, it may signal that the bidder is trying to "buy in" to the contract. If the bids are too high, it may signal that bidders think they can soak the government. The need for government officials to have their own independent capability to evaluate costs is even more critical during the life of the contract because the potential to cheat is so high. Every single activity under the contract can be manipulated.

Since corruption involves both sellers and buyers, every government agency must start with the premise that some improper approaches will take place. This means that the measures to protect against improper actions by the government's own staff are just as important as protections against outsiders. Special oversight of bidding processes can be provided by auditors, inspectors, or even outside investigators, and it should be made clear to the staff that such assessments are to be expected. Each agency should have formal procedures which clearly state that any form of bribery, collusion or improper information disclosure will be sought out and punished. The evaluation of bids should be conducted by multi-person teams, and their evaluation and recommendations should be in writing and signed.

The most difficult problem comes where the decision rests with a political official who is not controlled by the mechanisms applied to the career staff. Many agency heads have broad and unchecked authority under agency enabling statutes. They may make arbitrary decisions based entirely on their own judgment, and on political factors not considered in the staff technical evaluation. Factors such as the geographical location of bidding companies, or contributions to political campaigns, or the desire to reward the allies of the regime are not uncommon. Few career officials will have either the authority or the courage to challenge such political distortions. In some countries, provision is made for a "Tender Board" or Contract Review Board that has independent authority to review the outcomes of bid processes and challenge any instance of serious impropriety. But again, these boards may be ineffective unless they have the courage to press their objections. At the very least, their challenge of a contract selection can serve to fix public attention on the suspect decision.

During the performance of each contract, there should be multiple responsibilities. First, the official in charge of the contract must be made clearly responsible for its effective management. This is the first and most important line of defense against impropriety, and no amount of post audit can substitute for it. This responsibility includes real time determination that the demands of the contract are being met, that only authorized work is performed and billed, that all costs are realistic and appropriate, and that costly overruns are avoided. In support of these procontract managers may be allies in the agency who will audit, inspect or investigate contractor performance if necessary. Auditing and inspection should be performed constantly and not left to post audits months after the fact. These government oversight systems should extend down to subcontractors or suppliers of the prime contractor. Some form of appeals process is also valuable so that factual disputes can be reconciled, or contractors may appeal what they believe to be improper or incorrect actions by contracting officials.

INTERGOVERNMENTAL RELATIONSHIPS

═══════════════★═★═★═══════════════

ONE OF THE MOST compelling approaches to the restraint of centrist authoritarian governments is to press for the devolution or delegation of authority over many government programs to regional (e. g. state, county, city) governments. There is a continuing debate about the kinds and levels of decentralization and devolution in governments; the main basis for this debate is the overwhelming concerns about the nature of centrist power. The central government is in charge of this debate, and will certainly guarantee its own power. Cities are de facto sources of power, and they will be the main sources of leverage for local government authority. The most uncertain element in this debate is about what power should be given to regions. Typically, the strongest views against devolution come from the centrist power holders, and from macroeconomists who believe that economic development is best when driven from the top. There is also a strong element of simple inertia, in part because many do not want to change the current allocation of power because they fear or do not understand what to replace it with, and they do not want to face up to the need to do some heavy lifting in the face of substantial opposition.

Consider the following list of the great range of public programs which are shared between governments:

EDUCATION

Strengthening educational administation
Facilities, equipment, renovation
Teacher training
Library resources

Vocational/adult education
Special programs for handicapped, disadvantaged children, migrants
Grants to associated non-profit organizations

HEALTH

Medicaid
Medicare
Social Security
Aid for the disadvantaged
Unemployment compensation
Aid for the handicapped

WELFARE

Supplemental Nutritional Assistance Program (SNAP, formerly Food
    Stamp Program
Aid to Families with Dependent Children (AFDC)
Housing assistance
Tax exemption and subsidy
Handicapped programs
Social Security and retirement assistance

WORKFORCE

Workforce training assistance
Labor protection laws
Employment services
Youth Corps and youth employment assistance

RURAL LIFE

Agricultural crop assistance and subsidies
Subsidies for fertilizers, pesticides, insecticides
Subsidies for land development and protection
Loans and loan guarantees at subsidy rates
Rural school assistance

Programs to spread communications systems and cpmputers

State administrative expenses

Rural community development; Extension services, community facilities, family assistance, farm income supplements, marketing assistance, foreign sales assistance, forestry and land conservation.

LAW ENFORCEMENT

Law Enforcement Assistance Administration

Grants for law enforcement equipment and facilities

Grants to improve law enforcement skills

Open discretionary grants.

TRANSPORTATION

Aviation: planning grants, general aviation assistance, Airports and Airways Trust Fund

Highways: the Highway Trust Fund, funds for primary highways, fund for secondary roads, urban extensions, rural routes, bridges, tranportation safety, beautification.

PUBLIC FACILITIES

Power plants

Power distribution systems

Water system development

River/lake development and water conservation

Water distribution systems

Airports

Water ports

Public land development

Communications

THE LEGAL ESTABLISHSMENT

Definition of what is legal and illegal

Civil rights, race, gender equity issues

Definition of taxing authority
Definition of the authority to regulate – many issues
Definition of the range of legal discretion
Regulation of private sector practices

ENERGY

Mining and minerals extraction
Oil extraction, fracking
Gas, oil transmission
Power generation
Power transmission and distribution
Solar/wind power
Water power
Energy regulation, taxation and safety protection

What are the best arguments for devolution or decentralization?

1. Sharing power promotes democracy because it is easier for citizens and organizations to reach and influence local governments. Especially with social services programs, most national governments are seen as remote and preoccupied with broader issues. Decentralization also enhances the total cadre of public leadership.

2. Local governments offer the potential of achieving higher public service effectiveness and responsiveness, and of creating a better and more capable public service. In general, local administration of public programs is seen as more practical and less theoretical or doctrinaire. Program success is more likely to be evaluated in terms of how well the public is served.

3. Devolution will take power out of the hands of centrist elites, reduce elitist collusion and the power of centrist government organizations, and reduce the range of public activities that are vulnerable to corrupt control. It also importantly shifts the attention of special interest lobbying groups from a single target

to a variety of governments, more attuned to the general public interest.

4. As more power and authority is decentralized, it makes the relationship between the central government and local governments more balanced since these relationships will be more often negotiated rather than dictated. Regional governments have roles to play which are genuinely regional in nature – for example, regional road nets, the allocation of land uses, the provision of public utilities or the priorities between conflicting demands on government. But to achieve these advances, regional and municipal governments must be independent and not just administrative units of the central government.

5. There is even a valid line of argument that says that regional governments are also good economic development tools. At the very least, it can be argued that a wiser allocation of scarce government resources is an economic advantage, and that local governments will be smarter about how to improve the value and performance of local economies. But the stronger argument centers on the capacity of regional governments to pursue regional economic development. The 50 American states all feel free to pursue economic development programs with international outreach. In some of the smarter countries in E. Europe, privatization and the revitalization of a private sector economy has often been delegated to regional governments freed from the straight jacket of central economic command and control. These governments are then free to initiate their own economic development strategies, plans and development objectives, and to control the allocation of whatever funds are available to carry out their own objectives rather than those of the central government. As local governments assume more control of their own economic fate, this enhances the likelihood that eventually, they will be able to free themselves from the power of central government funding. This means that decentralization or devolution must be accompanied by a shift from national funding sources to local taxation powers.

6. Part of the rethinking of the roles of local governments will involve the relationship between regional and municipal governments. In some cases, states may share some of the burden of financing key urban based social programs. In other cases, states may assume primary responsibility for some programs such as highway construction and maintenance, universities, some parts of the health care system or parts of welfare program financing.

One of the new challenges to the role of governments has come in the form of the emergence of the private provision of elementary/secondary education by private organizations. There are few things that have been more certainly the responsibility of government than the education of children, which is generally seen as a necessity but also a "right" that parents can demand from their governments. This responsibility is firmly imbedded in the role of local govenments from the bottom up, and it has long been strongly supported and supplemented by the volunteer efforts of parents and community groups. Parent-teacher associations are diversified and active, and parents support sport teams, and dance classes and a wide range of extracurricular activies.

But in recent times, there has been a growing feeling that all is not well. Local politicians have increasingly proven unable or unwilling to collect the taxes needed to finance the construction and maintenance of school system physical plant. The national population increase has put a rapidly increasing nmber of children into school systems, and this flood has been supplemented in many communities by a second flood of immigrant children, both legal and illegal. Some school systems have lacked the capacity or the will to keep up. There is a growing concern that there are too few really capable teachers, and that the demands of the class room containing larger numbers of students are driving too many teachers into administration and out of the class room.

As these political and managerial concerns have been impinging more on public school systems, local politicians have increasingly begun to pressure state governmenrts and the federal government for more money and support, and teacher leadership has turned vastly more political. The National Education Association (NEA) and other teacher organizations have turned themselves into powerful lobbyiing organizations, less interested in improving teaching than in supporting the Democratic Party, and lobbying for more and more government funding.

There has been a gradual sense that the provision of primary and secondary education by government school systems is declining in quality and relevance, especially in minority communities where the need is perhaps the greatest. As this belief has grown, new providers in the private sector have begun to emerge. As the numbers of private schools have increased, so has the political tension. Teachers unions are implacably opposed to this competition, and have used their considerable political power to resist them. But the teachers themselves have proved to be more practical. If teaching in private schools is freer and better paid, why not move over? If private schools are less conflict ridden, why not move? If private schools allow more latitude in classroom content and technique, isn' t this a good thing for a really skilled teacher?

At the heart of this growing debate then is the concept of competition, and it seems that more and more parents – and even some politicians – are beginning to respond. One popular theme that has emerged is the concept that public funds can be paid not only to school systems but to parents themselves in the form of vouchers which they could then use to pay for their children's education in the best school available, whether public or private. Even those who continue to see the provision of primary education as an obligation of government may be willing to accept the competition as a good thing, hoping that it will push up public school quality of instruction, and perhaps pare back some of the excess ministerial overhead. Financially, it seems still unclear whether private schools are more cost effective than public counterparts. Right now, comparisons can be made only on a school-by-school basis.

THE DEMANDS OF INTERNATIONAL
RELATIONSHIPS

THE PUBLIC DEBATE ABOUT the international responsibilities and obligations has become more seriously threatening because it seems to want to insist that the U. S. is obliged to "solve" a whole series of international crises. The nature of U. S. obligations seemed to have been fixed by a surge of the creation of international institutions following WW II. The United Nations, the World Bank, the North Atlantic Treaty Organization, the Association of South East Asian Nations and other regional organizations in Africa, South and Latin America and the Middle East represent the formulation of a wide-ranging series of commitments for the U. S. Each demands action, often risky and expensive, and the United States, because of its wealth, usually ends up being the principal financier for everything.

These international organizations have evolved around a broad range of initiatives. First, they are a forum and principal enunciator of what might be termed a set of common principles and objectives, to assure world-wide peace and prosperity for all, and more than 65 years have now been spent pursuing these ambitions with varying degrees of success. One of the principal parts of this agenda is economic, where it is reasoned that international economic aid must be extended at very high levels by richer and more developed nations to developing countries, because economic growth and development are preceived to be keys to the generation of enough wealth in each country to afford the provision of needed public social services and public infrastructure.

Further, these international organizations have also gotten heavily involved in many efforts to prevent destructive conflict within and between countries. UN and NATO forces have spent years and lives and funds in intervening in crises in many countries. Current operations are being maintained in The Central African Republic, Mali, Haiti, the Democratic Republic of Congo, S. Sudan, Cyprus, Kosovo and even in conflicts between India and Pakistan. In the past, major peace keeping operations were conducted in Angola, Rwanda/Burundi, Ethiopia/Eritrea, and Sierra Leone. More than 100,000 uniformed troops and 10,000 police officers are available for active duty, provided by more than 120 countries.

The United States has, from the beginning, been fully engaged in all of these efforts, and usually, the American government, and U. S. private interests have been the largest and most effective contributors. But this then has encouraged an ominous view of this commitment. Whenever a new crisis breaks out, many voices around the world cry out one of two things: "What is America going to do about this?"; or "This is the fault of the Americans!" The fear then is that the Americans are being forced into the role of "the policeman of the world", and that somehow, dozens of horrible conflicts around the world are our responsibilities.

Further, the same kind of attitude is reaching beyond issues of security and economics and broadening into the social fabric of countries. In the world's 196 countries, almost all including the U. S. suffer from a lack of the adequate provision of vital social services such as primary education, health care, support for the elderly, and help for the disadvantaged. In addition, there is a lack of infrastructure such as transportation, electrical power, water and sanitation. And there is a growing fear of the negative tides running in the environment and the consequences of global warming.

These problems are posed against the U. S.: what is the United States going to do about these problems? You are rich; how can you let childen starve?" Thus, in addition to being asked to become the "policeman of the world", many are asking the U. S. to become the "social service provider for the world".

The sum of these demands for U. S. responsibility are utterly overwhelming. They demand a compelling U. S. obligation with respect to the following countries: Afghanistan, Pakistan, Iraq, Yemen, Philippines, Puerto Rico, S. Arabia, S. Sudan, Sudan, Syria, Libya, Ethiopia, Eritrea, Nigeria, Cuba, Haiti, the Gaza Strip, Honduras, Venezulea, and perhaps others. In addition, the U. S. is expected to maintain a whole series of highly important and often prickly relationships with world powers: China, Russia, India, Japan, Mexico, Canada, Vietnam, S. Korea, Egypt and Turkey and Israel. And then of course, there is Iran and North Korea—!

It should be obvious that the U. S. cannot allow itself to be burdened with the responsibility for the success or failure of the fate of some 36 countries. Half of them are in hopeless condition – bottomless pits of failure and endless conflict. Many cannot provide a competent government or society. Many are in the clutches of centrist elites that are dictatorial, oppressive and corrupt. They cannot and should not be addressed by military force from the U. S. or anybody else, and they are largely immune to rational diplomacy.

As an example of these dilemmas, one of the most soul searching problems now challenging U. S. international policy is tht of the growing breadth and depth of human hunger. No sane person wants to see any person starve or suffer from inadequate food availabiliity. This problem is in fact endlessly complex; it exists at several levels, each of which requires its own special set of policy positions and operational responses. In the last 100 years or so, several great tides of expansion and development of the agricultural sector of the economy emerged. The first was reality that the whole sector could be substantially upgraded through the expansion of education, research, mechanisation, better seeds, animal stocks, fertilizers, insecticides, and indeed in the improvement of farming techniques themselves. Advances were made in planting and harvesting techniques, irrigation, land reclamation, mechanization, and soil conservation. Government assistance was substantial and highly popular and prevalent through crop loans, crop insurance, farm home ownership assistance and more.

At the first level of hunger is simply the need for foods to have proper levels of nutritional value for all, especially for mothers and young children. There are well known and readily available foods and nutritional supplements like vitamins or energy products to deal with this nutritional level, and it is generally expected that people will take of these needs themselves, and that the government has little responsibility beyond assurance of food safety and purity.

And despite the fact that there are fewer farms and fewer farmers, overalll food production has soared.

The second level of human hunger occurs when, to some considerable extent the normal food supply system fails to deliver adequately. This might occur as a consequence of reduced food production or food import brought about from technical, economic, or managerial shortcomings. In the United States, it would seem apparent that there is surely enough national wealth to avoid hunger through lack of money – and yet, it remains true that there are arenas where indefensible hunger continues to exist. Hunger may be unstoppable elsewhere in the world, but its presence in America is simply inexcusable. Hunger at this level invokes greater governmental responsibility, but really only to the extent in which the government aids and supplements a national system that runs itself, and rises from the bottom up.

The third level of the hunger issue is far more serious, where it rises to the level of long term, serious, protracted and punishing shortage. It is astonishing to realize that many of such situations are directly related back to the failures of government. This has been extensively seen in many foreign countries, and all too often it is linked to the massive disruptions caused by civil and intercountry wars, revolutions, insurrections, convulsive civil unrest, and the collapse of necessary public services such as the water supply systems, roads, electrical power generation and distribution and the production and distribution if seeds, animal stocks, fertilizers, and pesticides.

Finally, and at an unbelievably disasterous level have been the horrors of total, abject starvation where literally millions and millions of people have starved to death. Perhaps the worst example is that of the old Soviet Union under the oppressive rule of the dictator Joseph Stalin. The government took over the ownership of all land, and reallocated most of it for use by the peasants themselves. But what followed was disaster, and it was a disaster deliberately insisted upon by Comrade Stalin, the Great Leader himself. He decided, somehow, that the peasants were guilty of instigating and sustaining all of the ills facing the new Soviet Union. He insisted that all land had to be owned and managed by the State, and he thought that the notion that land held privately by peasants was intolerable and deeply suspicious. He therefore decreed country-wide collectivization of all agricultural land. This meant that rural people were to be forced into organizations called collectives where all property was owned by "the people" but controlled and managed by supposedly skilled managers on behalf of all of the people in the community, now members of these collectives. The collective would not only own the land itself, but all homes, farm animals and farm equipment. The collective would decide what would be planted, how and when crops would be harvested, to whom they would be sold and at what prices. It is not surprising that the peasants strongly resisted this tyranny, and in some cases there were armed clashes and violent resistance.

Stalin was outraged and he pushed the collectivization program even harder. This was of course highly disruptive of every element of rural life and the agricultural economy. The peasants were subjected to terrorist tactics, including killings, imprisonments, beatings, threats against family members, and of course the seizure of all property by the new collectives. Crops did not get planted, or were not tended or harvested. The ranks of people to produce food were decimated. An estimated 15 million people were removed through murder, starvation, consignment to labor camps, deaths in labor camps and deportations. In the peak years of 1932-1933, an estimated 10 million people died. Robert Conquest, the great chronicler of the Stalin era estimates that, during the extended period of Stalin's rule up to 1952, an estimated 20 million people died, many of them from abject starvation. The total numbers of those "repressed" exceeded 40 million, half of them during the reign of terror from 1929 to 1933.

Or consider another of the most horrible examples of government induced starvation – that of Chairman Mao in Communist China. One of the worst terrorist governments in world history has been that of the Chinese. For thirty years, from the rise of the Communist Party (CCP) in in 1949 to just beyond the death of Mao Zedong in 1976, the CCP created the worst government in the world. It should be remembered that this included the oppressions invented during "The Great Leap Forward" and the "Cultural Revolution" which were among the most distructive acts of government in modern history. The notorious Red Guards arrested and tortured millions of people with the approval of Mao and the CCP. And because Mao had forced farmers to forego planting, and made them shift to some rudimentary form of industrial production, crops all over the country never got planted, and huge food shortages occurred, with the result that 20 to 30 million people simply starved to death.

Or consider the actions of The Great Leader, the Light of Human Genius, Kim Jong Un, the dictator of North Korea. Under his disasterous economic policies and political oppressions, the government pursued a deeply damaging policy of rigid price controls under which farmers were paid less for their crops than their actual costs, and thus very many were simply driven out of business. Since foreign importation was generally forbidden, the inevitable consequence of these huge blunders was the drying up of the food supply – and almost everything else. The result was a total collapse of the government controlled food distribution system with the utterly unbelievable consequences that people began starving to death because there was no food. Even farm animals starved. People wer eating rats and boiling grass. Much of the available food was grabbed up by the Korean military, or simply stolen by smugglers, black marketeers, and senior government officials.

Similar starvation horror scenes have been played out in many other countries: Vietnam, Cambodia, Myanmar, Yemen, Syria and others. The consequences of these disasters are still reverberating decades later, and they illlustrate a sinister reality: often, the government is totallly unable – ever – to deal with these horrible kinds of problems; and that all too often and even worse, the government, far from being the solution, is really the problem. It is unrealistic to suggest that somehow, the American government should have prevented these disasters, or that it can now somehow make them all right.

The issues of hunger cover a range of seriousness. At the lowest level is simply the need to produce foods that have adequate nutritional value, and that these are the foods that reach to public. At the next level is genuine hunger, but specific and possibly managable situations, and the issues here are to get the government and private sources to do this kind of management. Beyond that are situations in which there is long term and protracted hunger, perhaps leading to periods of starvation. These problems may be a function of an inadequate economy, a lack of public funding, a weak and congenital lack of food production, or some failings of government capability. Normally food can and will be imported to fill gaps, but this may prove to be economically infeasible.

At the ultimate level are the horrible examples of mammoth starvation, where whole populations die. These have increasingly been the result of the disruptions of wars, insurrections, revolutions, or the depradations of terrorist organizations such as ISIS, al-Queda, or Boko Haram. These conflicts not only kill people but they destroy infrastructure and public services, and they almost disrupt agricultural production and the food distribution system. In the longer term, children become widely undernorished and physically debilitated, revenues from food production decline, food prices for consumers rise sharply, and the whole system founders. More than half of those impacted by such massive starvation live in the areas of such violent conflict, including perhaps 20% of Africans and 10% of those in the Far East.

It is marvelous to recognize however that this problem will be taken care of. Of course.

In its "2030 Agenda for Sustainable Development", the United Nations and most national leaders have promised to end hunger and malnutrition by the year 2030, detailed in a report jointly prepared by the UN International Fund for Agrricultural Development, the World Food Program, and the World Health Organization, along with the UN Children's Fund. Right.

Certainly, there many valuable things that can be done. International organizations will continue dozens of involvements to strengthen economies, resolve conflicts, provide emergency relief, and vital social services, and the U. S. is fully able and willing to play a major part in these valuable interventions. And now, there are literally thousands of private organizations – non government organizations or NGOs – that play a vital humanitarian role in dozens of countries. These NGOs are voluntary organizations, and much of the funding available for support of government related activities has been provided privately, and then supplemented by government support. As they have emerged, they have rapidly strengthened their capabilities and broadened the range of their involvment so that now there is almost no kind of human endeavor that does not benefit from their presence. Their international organization, the World Alliance of Non Government Organizations (WANGO) has published truly astonishing information about the numbers and kinds of activities that NGOs represent:

Aging
Agricutlture and food production
Animal health and rights

Economic/business development
Children and youth
Communications and media
Conflict resolution
Education
Environment
Heath and nutrition
Human relations
Law and legal affairs
Population and human settlement
Refugees
Relief services
Religion, ethics
Science and technology
Trade
Transport
Women's status and rights

Their international organization, the World Association of Non Government Organizations (WANGO) has published truly astonishing information about the numbers and kinds of activitiesk that NGOs represent. WANGO lists more than 54,000 NGOs currently active, including the following:

EUROPE

Southern Europe: 1088
Eastern Europe: 8361
Northern Europe: 4676
Western Europe: 378
AFRICA

Northern Africa: 222
West Africa: 2279
East Africa: 1209
Mid Africa: 550

ASIA

Eastern Asia: 405
Southeast Asia: 973
South Central Asia: 4287

N. AMERICA: 23071
S. AMERICA: 653
CARRIBEAN: 480
OCEANA: 651

It should be noted that, while most of the NGOs in Africa, Latin America, and the Far East are foreign to the countries in which they operate, a growing number are emerging as native enterprises.

A new Muslim world is now emerging. Fifteen or twenty Muslim governments and countries are in deep trouble, and their citizens are slowly trying to gain the ascendency against both oppressive governments and vicious Islamic terrorist organizations. Women especially, all over the world, and remarkably, in the Muslim world are emerging as a strong stabilizing force. Slowly, the economies of countries like China, India, much of Africa and the Far East are being expanded and upgraded, providing the wealth to meet social needs more adequately.

The budget of the American government can be better balanced by far more careful investments in the international arena. The true posture for the United States should be to buttress the constructive forces in the world however possible, <u>from the bottom up;</u> to try and reach the people directly and not just indirectly from the top down through oppressive, incompetent and corrupt governments. There can never be any final declaration of "victory" on 100 fronts, but their can be a vital and honorable assertion of the best efforts possible to protect humanity from itself.

One of the most vexing U. S. governmental tangles centers around the role of the State Department in dealing with this question of how much effort and wealth is spent on foreign aid. Over many decades, the institutional role for the direction of U. S. government foreign aid around the world has been the State Department. Then, after WW II, and with the creation of the United Nations, the World Bank, NATO and dozens of other international organizations, the U. S. apparatus for providing foreign assistance has been vastly expanded. The Agency for International Development (AID) was created for the specific purpose of expanding and broadening aid in a rapidly increasing number of recipient governments and organizations. Then, the Defense Department got into the act in a big way, furnishing allies with billions of dollars worth of weapons systems each year, plus a confusing array of programs to buttress the governments that use the weapons.

The funding of foreign assistance has now become the enthusiastic role of half of the agencies of the federal government. According to a report prepared at the request of the Congress, under the auspices of the Atlantic Council, there are more than 25 federal agencies that are engaged in foreign assistance, with no single point of integration, no mechanism to hold them accountable, no evidence of improved performance. The authors of the report were ten former senior officials who served under both Democrat and Republican administrations, and who not only addressed the muddle surrounding the apparatus of foreign assistance, but the muddle of the State Department itself, and that of the DOD as well. The essence of the report is this: get the State Department out of the operational services for the provision of foreign assistance and concentrate these operations in USAID as a beefed up independent agency. Let the State Department concentrate on the policy and diplomatic functions, which surely need all of the attention they can get. The role of USAID would be deliberately cast as the coordinator of the federal government activities, including those of DOD, which are clearly outside of the central responsibilities of direct combat operations.

The State Department was characterized in the Atlantic Council report as seriously over-structured. There are dozens of big organizational units, 24 regional centers, dozens of "issues" bureaus, and a vast and confusing array of overseas units, beyond the major ambassadorial headquarters. Thus, a reorganization of the department would seek to rationalize this collection of units, many of which overlap or duplicate each others roles. President Trump has proposed to cut the State Department's budget by as much as one third, but he has also called for a program of reforms and management improvements. It would be unfortunate for budget cuts to reduce the department's diplomatic effectiveness, but serious agency restructuring and reform could absorb much of such a budget cut, along with a new emphasis on strange and magical concepts such as "efficiency" or "cost effectiveness" and "higher productivity" and the reduction of bureaucratic paper pushing.

THE MILITARY ESTABLISHMENT

=====★=★=★=====

ALL OVER THE WORLD, conflict is an enormous curse. Since WWII there have been ten or more major wars, and perhaps 300 insurrections, major liberation movements and countless lesser conflicts. Millions of people have been killed, wounded or injured. Many more millions have been displaced from their homes, either forced to shift to safer places in their own country, or to flee the country as refugees. In every case, the issue has been raised: why did America permit these outrages? Why didn't we prevent them? What will the U. S. do now to prevent future wars and revolutions?

But such criticism is preposterously wrong, both in substance and perception. The United States cannot and should not try to be "the policeman of the world", and should not be urged to try. There are now more than 105 substantial governments (out of a total of 196) that are in deep trouble, most with conflicts involving some level of armed conflict. Many conflicts are the consequence of desperate struggles by people against their own horrible rulers. Most are conflicts between two groups of serious oppressors about who gets to be the next dictator. No form of American intervention, either military or diplomatic, could have prevented these disasters. Sometimes, external intervention can mitigate the horror or pick up the pieces. But a good heart and good intentions are not enough. The American role was not enough in Korea, or Vietnam, or Afghanistan, or Iraq, or Syria, or Sudan, or S. Sudan, or Egypt, or Yemen, Venezuela, or Somalia, etc. etc. etc.

Much good has been done, and some international victories have been won, but the point is this: such crises will continue to occur of their own creation, and it is neither reasonable nor rational to blame the U. S.

as a false hope for salvation, or cynically to shift the blame for their own failings onto somebody else. The U. S. has a duty to help, within the range of moderation, but it cannot possibly be everybody's salvation.

The same sort of argument emerges over the idea that the U. S. should be "the banker of the world". This argument is not about whether the U. S. should help other nations financially; or whether it should continue to support international organizations supporting international stability and financil progress. Of course it should. But reality is that the majority of governments and populations of people are in serious financial difficulty and there is no way that the U. S. could somehow bail them all out.

Within the legitimate range of U. S. security needs, the Department of Defense (DOD) is facing the need to rethink its strategies for the future. Gone of course is the day of the battleship, and perhaps the day of the aircraft carrier, increasingly vulnerable to long range guided nuclear missiles. Probably, gone are the days of the 70 ton tanks that can't cross most bridges or maneuver in narrow urban streets; or perhaps the day of the high capability fighter-bombers with few targets they can attack. The threat around the world in about 50 countries is now strike forces of terrorist groups that conceal themselves among innocent civilians populations. The modern U. S. infantry soldiers must now act more like the police in order to ferret them out. Nuclear weapons are now irrelevant since no sane leader can order them to be used to obliterate cities and slaughter milllions of innocent civilians.

Meanwhile, many of the expensive aspects of the defense establishment need now to be rethought, and the military leadership knows it and seems to hate the prospect. Does the U. S. and its allies really need 2400 F-35 fighter-bombers at a unit cost of $100 million each? Do they really need 10,000 Abrams tanks, or the eleven massive aircraft carriers?

Is the "war" we are facing really between the military leadership locked in with the special interests of huge weapons devlopment contractors and their political allies, versus the interests and the wallets and purses of the general American public?. How many bases around the world are still needed? How many warehouses must there be, filled with bullets and boots? President Trump wants to reduce the number of government employees. Will this desire ever be extended to the more than one million civil servants and contractor employees in the huge defense establishment?

In short, the challenges the military is facing are changing faster than the military establishment appears able to react. It is falling behind on three important fronts:

1. Size and complexity: There was a time when the Pentagon argued that it must prepare to fight two major wars on two fronts simultaneously. Those days are gone forever, rendered obsolete by the widened possession of great nuclear arsenals. No nation – not Iran, or Russia, or even mad North Korea – could launch a war without inducing utterly distructive nuclear counter attacks. Neither the UN or NATO nor the United States could bear to deliver such an attack, which would kill millions of innocent civilians; so barring some individual lunacy, nuclear war seems to have been eliminated. Large masses of infantry and armor are now vulnerable to smaller tactical atomic weapons of high kill power. Aircraft carriers are vulnerable to nuclear weapons dropped with high precision from hundreds of miles away. This change seems to suggest that the conflicts of the future will be smaller and more concealed and more tactical than strategic.

2. It appears then that the conflicts of the future will be produced more by locally based insurgencies, and by limited invasions of less heavily armed forces, and by small secretive terrorist groups. These conflicts are not to be faced by aircraft carriers or 70 ton tanks. They are first and foremost likely to be created by stupid, dictatorial regimes, or opposing groups using relatively small ill trained and ill armed troops. Small groups will prove adept at hiding in the hills and jungles, and embedding themselves among the masses of innocent native populations. U. S. military strategy and tactics must uncreasingly be directed to combatting these types of threats.

3. Another consequence of these strategic and tactical changes is that the military of the future probably should become smaller and less complex, and hopefully much cheaper. There will have to be a long and searching reassessment of all of DOD's physical plant and facilities, human resources, contract structuring, logistics and

supply chains, and command structures from top to bottom. In fact, the whole grand design of the military – with separate and stubbornly independent Army, Navy, Air Force and Marine Corps – seems now to be overly complex and duplicative. The logistics of supporting the current enormous structure are truly amazing and hideously expensive, and it simply has to be true that serious efforts to revise and reform and simplify the structure could yield billions of dollars of cost reductions, without reducing overall military capability. If the future of warfare is more likely to be small wars and small unit street fighting, then the constant evolution of weapons systems technology seems less crucial. Remember, that's why we no longer build battleships. At the very least, DOD might continue the cost of weapons system technology research, so that it continues to dominate that technology, but to refrain from entering every new system in its more expensive production unless proven to be urgently needed.

In other words, this line of reasoning is a way to beg the eternal question: when is enough enough?

Two other arenas of concern are developing. There is a subterranean discontent within the U. S. government that spending on essentially military matters in the international world may have yielded many benefits but it has also increasingly led to two serious problems. The first is increasing concern that, in the past, we have found outselves foolishly or deliberately financing the affairs of dictatorial regimes, helping them to oppress their people and deny civil rights, using U. S. military money. American political and civic debate is proving less willing to accept the standard justification that our governmen must deal with whover is in power, good or bad. And unfortunately, two thirds of the world's major governments are bad, to some degree and in some confusing ways. It would be highly desirable to shift U. S. international commitments from top down support of centrist regimes to bottom up direct support of social services and citizen enablement.

But here again, confusion reigns. U. S. funds, well intended, often unfortunately end up in the hands of theives and corrupt officials. And foreign governments frequently "sucker" the U. S. and other international donors by deliberately using foreign funds to reduce their own investments, especially in social services. In Israel for example, their government has long used U. S. funds both from the government and from private donors to shift much of their own money into wepons purchases and support of their military establishment.

It is a tribute to the American public that they highly honor our military personnel and leadership. We have never stinted in providing what these military leaders say they need. But the Gates assessments, and those of many others, strongly point out that DOD owes that American public a higher level of disciplined planning, management, and realistic financial control than they have been getting. This is especially true with the election of Donald Trump as President. He has made it clear that he will be a strong proponent of the strengthening of our military establishment, and he has already proposed a 2018 Budget for defense at $639 billion – one of the largest defense budget increases in history, and more than $50 billion higher than that of the previous year. The debate over this budget is already reflecting the growing necessity to rethink future military needs, strategies and on-the-ground operations. Surely DOD leaders owe President Trump and the American people a higher order of attention to these changes.

Serious allegations were made, for example, in an internal DOD report prepared by the consulting firm of McKinsey and Co. (reported in the Washington Post of Dec. 6, 2017) that asserted that there was " a clear path for the Defense Department to save $ 125 billion over five years". The report did not advocate any specific reduction of DOD employment, but it did urge the streamlining of the bureaucracy through early retirements and curtailment of the role of high priced contractors, plus faster and more effective use of new information technology. Adding contractors in the past has proved to be too quick and easy and too vulnerable to political interference and favoritism – a bad substitute for internal enhancement of productivity, efficiency and cost effectiveness within the existing workforce.

The McKinsey study for example pointed out that the Army employs about 200,000 full time contractor employees – which exceeds the employment of the whole federal government departments of State, Commerce, Education, Agriculture and HUD combined. In addition, the report lists 200,000 contractor employees of the Navy Department and another 122,000 employed by the Air Force. And nobody – nobody

– seems to plan this tide, much less really manage it. A Washington Post front page article (Dec. 6, 2016) reported that the Pentagon had "buried (another) internal study produced by DOD itself, condeming the agency's "enormous back-office bureaucracy" which wastes more than $250 billion that could be better spent on actual military capability."

More than 25% of the defense budget goes for human resources, current and retired, and for financial management, budgeting, logistics, property management, and other administrative chores. So Trump should be beginning to perceive what should be the true nature of the defense agenda; to enhance its fighting effectiveness, but also to cut the costs of its bloated bureaucracy. It would appear that the White House does recognize that the Civil Service is not directly at fault. All of these 1.1 million DOD and contractor employees are there because of the enormous structural overburden of hundreds of programs, projects, facilities, and services. First, reform the system and structure; reform of the staff could then follow.

A perfect example of the obsolete psychology of the defense establishment can be seen in the current emergence of the Navy's new carrier, the Gerald R. Ford. Even such a defense stalwart as Sen. John McCain called its procurement "one of the most spectacular acquisition debacles in modern memory – and that is saying something!"

The design and authorization of funding of the Ford carrier began more than 10 years ago. It's current cost is now estimated to be just under $13 billion. And two other Ford class carriers are planned! And yet, the Navy already has **ELEVEN** fully operational carriers, in a world where nobody, not even the Navy itself, can explain why 11 carriers are really needed, much less 14 carriers in the future. And it must be remembered that it is also true that in the era of the long range guided nuclear missile world, carriers are newly vulnerable, and must be accompanied by a fleet of other ships to protect it (the Carrier Group).

In its broadest context, the entire national security establishment of the United States has shifted to some substantial degree away from the primacy of "military effectiveness" to a disturbing emergence of a highly complex and incestuous web of power politics. Every major defense contractor has become a powerful political force, and they are motivated almost entirely by their own self interest and not that of the general American public. It is a toss-up these days to figure out who the leaders of the Pentagon truly represent.

PART TWO

TWO HUNDRED WAYS TO GALVANIZE PROGRAM PERFORMANCE AND BUDGETS OF AMERICAN GOVERNMENTS

★ ═ ★ ═ ★

I T IS NOT MISSION impossible for American citizens and their governments to bring their huge and complex public public programs to higher levels of performance, and their budgets into desirable balance. There is no lack of means and methods for doing so. What is lacking are the attitudes needed to make this a serious objective, and the will and the courage to make it happen. America's political leadership has said loudly and endlessly that it intends to do so. For more than 60 years President after President, and Congress after Congress have announced that the public budget will soon be under control, but instead, the reality is that it has gotten worse. Unremittingly, the federal governments and the governments of states and counties and cities and school systems and police and fire departments and transportation facilities have gotten bigger and fancier and far, far more expensive. The Federal government has extended the range and depth and cost of its programs under pressure from a widely expanded range of special interest political supplicants. The political leadership has the will to collect more revenue, but not the courage to cut back its commitments. The richest country in the world is creating the capacity to spend itself into bankruptcy.

Based on the discussions of ways and means explored earilier, the following summary is the author's intent to try and put into one listing two hundred of the potentials for achieving sound and tolerable government budgets. These items deal both with revenues and expenditures. They start with some deep philosophical concepts about the true role of governments and the moral and responsible elements that any government should maintain, and then further defined along the following outline:

I. The Philosophy and Morality of Governance

II. The Nature of Current and Future Public Policy

III. The Remarkable Role of Special Interest Politics

IV. Economic Development

V. The Effectiveness of Government Operations

VI. Reform of Tax Systems

VII. The Power of Government Regulation

VIII. Human Resources

IX. Intergovernmental Relationships

X. National Security

Many of the potential things listed here will by judged to be impossible. Others may seem to be infeasible, or wrong headed or just plain wrong. Others are perfectly valid as potentials, but are beyond the range of current levels of political courage. This is understood. But from this listing might come the means, over time, to bring American governmence under financial and managerial control and at higher levels of effectiveness and success. What is lacking now is the recognition of the need to move to the middle; "moderation in all things"; the need to move more to the realm of common sense; and the need, somehow, to find the courage to do what we keep telling ourselves is really necessary.

I. THE PHILOSOPHY AND
MORALITY OF GOVERNANCE

1. Perhaps the most fundamental issue facing the evolution of governments is the almost universal choice being considered between the old tradition of people's <u>self reliance in all things, versus the growing sense that human wellbeing must be provided and guaranteed by the State</u>. The American government has evolved into a compromise between these poles, but the tide for the last four decades has been in the direction of greater government assistance and a growing sense that such assistance is a "right" and not just a help or supplement. As discussed elsewhere, the post WWII tide of governance moved massively toward state socialism and the concepts of government "from the cradle to the grave". The U. S. largely avoided such a massive shift, but it did augment the role of governments more widely into the cultural and social issues facing the country. Still, it is fortunate that the country stayed out of the tide toward state socialism, because it is now widely seen as a failure or at least as substantial disappointment. Obviously then, the greater the growth of government involvement in a wider range of affairs, the greater the cost of government will become.

2. **The morality of governance**. It is widely argued that the government has a positive moral responsibility to enter the arenas of human problems and failings, and that such a government role is boundless, endless and forever. It is argued that, if the government does not act, people will live in poverty and misery,

and that people will not be kept healthy or live in good homes or have decently paying jobs. Limits on government involvement are argued as inherently immoral. The counter argument has been, and continues to be, that there are many aspects of people's lives that should be self controlled and not controlled by government. In addition, it is argued that fiscal prudence is also a serious government obligation, and perhaps even a moral obligation. In this conflict today, the spenders seem to be solidly in the ascendance; and it is no longer possible to have a balanced government budget. But if it is necessary for enhancing the sense of moral responsibility of governments, is it not also vital to enhance the sense of moral responsibility of the people themselves? By themselves?

3. **The triumph of centrism.** All over the world, including the United States, the form of governance is persistently centrist and elitist. Almost every government since the dawn of time has been centrist in nature which means that what is defined as right is defined by the holders of power. Rightness means anything that retains or expands their grip on the levers of power. Anybody that disagrees or opposes is wrong. Such governments remain political beasts and are not immune to cultural doctrine or even rational decision making, but public needs or rational choices can be denied if they challenge centrist power. Public officials are appointed not mainly for their competence, but for their loyalty to the power leadership. Such governments are not wholly incompetent, but they do redefine the basis on which "success" is judged. Every government has the right to seek its own continuation, but these authoritarian governments beg the question of how much of such power they should be able to exercise, and how such centrist power clashes with doing what is really right for citizens.

4. **The concept of "least feasible government".** Whatever the outcomes are in the debate of the nature of American governance, it is still an obligation to avoid expending resources that are not really necessary, or to impose controls that are not even wanted, or

even to supply goods and services that are not even needed from the government.

5. **The "rule of law" dilemma.** Even where there is a substantial framework for the rule of law, those mechanisms can be perverted because they rest on the often invalid assumption that the laws themselves are good and proper. This has been largely true in the United States and in most other developed countries, but it is increasingly apparent that keeping the laws good and proper is an enormously complex and sophisticated process. In many countries, rules of law and the institutional mechanisms to protect them do not exist or are not strong enough. Thus, laws themselves can become perverted and made to work against the very people they are supposed to protect. Anything – any pathological, corrupt, perverse, outrageous and dysfunctional thing – can and has been made legal and the law of the land. Pathological politics has proved time and time again that it can frustrate the intent of the rule of law and turn it upside down. Thus, part of the drafting of any law governing the workings of government should deliberately limit the authority that can be exercised under that law.

6. **Special interest politics vs. the general public wellbeing.** In the American political system, special interest politics is almost universal, and highly successful, almost to the point that it could be argued that it has substituted itself for the more traditional Constitutional philosophy of representative democracy.

   All of the actors in the political world must commit themselves to the posture that their obligation is mainly to their current bosses or to their organization, or to their party or two their special interest supporters. It is to the American public and the country. There are far too many ominous cases in which the influence of special interests is secret and carefully concealed, and deliberately intended as the absolute antithesis of "representative democracy". The history of countries is filled with the perversities of special interest politics as being immutabley self serving and insatiable. It should be perfectly possible to mount and maintain a public state of mind that instructs their political leaders to return to legislation and oversight that is designed to serve citizens and not high powered organizations.

7. **Promises not kept.** It is a deeply discouraging process to watch a government that knowingly makes promises in political utterances where it is really known that such promises cannot and will not be honored. There ought to be greater honesty and frankness in the commitments made, especially by politicians, who know full well that such commitments will never be realized. Often, the consequence of such misrepresentation becomes a habit of dissembly, misrepresention, falseness, and craven lying.

8. The role of American governments can be defined as **promoter of cooperation**, tolerance and assistance as opposed to the concept of government as controlle, enforcer and punisher.

9. **Government vs. the private sector.** The great wave of movement after WWII toward State Socialist governance was heavily justified by the concern that private companies were suspect; that they acted against the interests of the average citizen, were in conflict with the government, and sucked too much wealth out of the national economy. This conflict has been one of the most powerful forces justifying larger, more powerful and more ubiquitous governments. In recent years, this movement is largely being reversed, and many governments, even those such as Russia, China, India, and Vietnam have had to retreat from this philisophical terrain toward a greater degree of national reliance on the private sector for vital economic concerns. It is highly desirable to press for a renewed attitude of demanding that each existing or proposed public program be subject to some legal requirement to make a serious determination: "Is this really a government responsibility?"

10. **Government rigidity vs. government flexibility.** Increasingly, in the U. S. and in countries around the world, concern has been building over the impact of public regulation. In the U. S.,

regulation has become one of the most valuable means by which the government deploys its power, ostensibly to protect the public and to advance the common good. Almost every country benefits now from proper regulation of health protection, public safety, environmental protection, and modulation of the functioning of the economy. But regulation knows few limits; there almost no ground rules to define where regulations exceed reasonable limits and become instruments of oppression and petty tyranny. There is virtually no serious intellectual reasoning that helps to define the limits of regulation. Almost nothing in society and life is unregulated, and nobody can say when it should stop and at what level. The basic questions are the hardest to answer: how safe is safe? How safe is safe enough? What, in society should be left essentially unregulated? When and why does regulation become excessive and pathological? For the regulatory mind, the answer seems to be Never!

11. **Managing complexity.** For most of its life, the U. S. has simply assumed that whatever government is created, it can and will be effectively managed and controlled. This basic philosophy is now under serious question. As American society and economy have evolved, they have become vastly more complex and sophisticated, and the government seems increasingly unable to keep up with the demands of this new complexity. Change can be extraordinarily swift, but the ability to change the government is excruciatingly slow and often simply impossible. Governments increasingly are seen as far too rigid: laws are forever, rgulations never die, costs now always overpower income, the political system seems permanently locked in stalemate and inadequacy. The question is now being asked: it it time for the U. S. to develop a new form of governance, and a new set of political principles? A key principle: simplicity!

12. **Black is a Country.** In 2005, Nikhil Pal Singh, a professor of history at the University of Washington, published an insightful book entitled "Black is a Country". While it deals extensively with

the unfinished struggle for racial fairness, part of his message is also that African Americans in the U. S. do not necessarily want to become just like the white middle class. Instead, blacks are seeking to evolve their own society, equal to, but parallel to, the white society. Blacks have their own moral standards, ambitions, goals, even language, and art and music and other elements of a substantial black culture. Thus, failure to become "just like whites" is not a sin, and the proper goals of the citizens of the black country are to become better blacks. And it is very possible now that part of the growing complexity of American society will become a new philosophy of understanding why black is a country, and why we might see hispanics as a country, and Muslims as a country, and governments may need to learn how to deal properly with a set of different but strongly held social elements.

13. **Urban vs. rural interests.** Until about the 1930s, the compelling political balance of power lay with the predominant population of rural and small town America. But the nature of the economy began to change. The national economy rested less and less on primary economic activities such as agriculture, fishing and mining, and more and more on city based manufacturing, retailing and office occupations. In addition, agricultural technology had advanced to the point that greater levels of crops could be produced with less and less manpower. Nor were cities always successful for all residents, and the needs for assisting and supporting urban dwellers became more demanding. Reality has swept more than 85% of U. S. population into cities; politicians however, continue to cling to habits of agricultural subsidy and assistance.

14. **Government honesty.** It has always been government policy that neither people or organizations were allowed to lie to the government or to withhold information demanded by the government. In the United States, it has generally been believed that the government in turn should not lie to the people. The fact is that every government, every place, all of the time has lied when it was necessary or desirable to do so, but these lies were seen

as unfortunate deviations from a general policy of relative truth telling. This pattern of relative honesty has undergone a serious change, probably starting with the Nazi regime in Germany in WW II. Today in many countries it is **official government policy** to lie. Countries like N. Korea, China, Russia and Iran have whole large and very active agencies which produce government, misinformation, misrepresentation, exaggerations, distortions, "spin", and just flat out lies. The official policy now is that there is no such thing as absolute truth; what is true of false is what the government says it is. The United States government is less inclined to lie because there are so many sources of independent observation, but we sure have learned to love the skills of "spin."

15. **Lack of political/bureaucratic courage.** There are characteristics of every government that make it very hard for the political system to really deal with the hard problems of governance. Most politicians and government officials see themselves as providing highly desirable things to citizens, thinking "we are the good guys". Therefore, it seems somehow improper to even think about limiting the flow. In a more cynical vein, politicians are very aware of the fact that the dispensation of public goods and services is a popular way to "buy' votes and to keep themselves in office. Whole governments around the world have absolutely lived on this principle. But the strongest resistance to finding the courage to change has been the vast influence of political special interests which freeze the political system in favor of their interests, and intimidate their political allies. Finally, there is simply just cowardice; the politicians lack the courage to act against any kind of resistance, and confine themselves to the skills of pompous utterance, full of sound and fury, but merely a means to obscure their lack of real action.

16. **Greater and more forceful citizen involvement.** Elections of course, but far more is needed, and it is perfectly feasible and often actual for it to be forthcoming. Increasingly, dissatisfaction with the performance of governments has led to growing citizen

self involvement. There is more awareness of the problems posed by government inaction. There is more self-awareness – of how individual lives may be negatively impacted by inaction or failure. There is much more willingness – much more – to exercise an activist role; to communicate, to protest, to march, or to finance bottom up organizations that challenge governments. It can be argued that the last two presidential elections, and the election of numerous Congressional members or governors have been all about the perceived need for "change". Hopefully, this tide will continue to surge, and it will pump up political courage to act, beyond pompous utterance.

II. PUBLIC POLICY

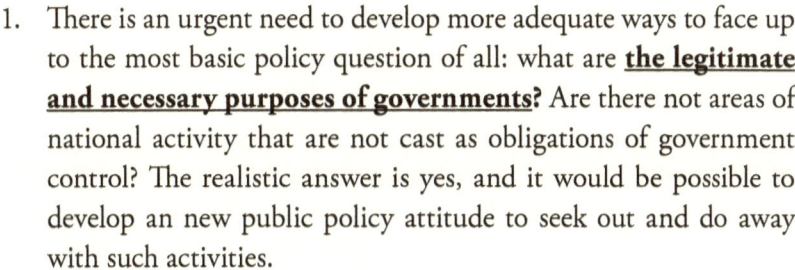

1. There is an urgent need to develop more adequate ways to face up to the most basic policy question of all: what are **the legitimate and necessary purposes of governments?** Are there not areas of national activity that are not cast as obligations of government control? The realistic answer is yes, and it would be possible to develop an new public policy attitude to seek out and do away with such activities.

2. The philosophical conflict discussed above is fully articulated in debates over the public policies that drive government. One conflict is that centering around **the government vs. the private sector.** At one extreme is the socialist philosophy to constrain the private sector and deploy a controlling government instead, but this extreme has been rejected in the U. S. At the next level is the real U. S. model with the private sector dominant in economic terms, but with the government locked in a vastly complex and sophisticated set of interrelationships with it, both good and bad. The other extreme would be a society and economy with minimum governmental primacy, but this has long been abandoned in the U. S. Governments in the United States have played out literally hundeds of these debates, almost to the point where, in major arenas of national activity, it is extrrordinarily difficult to tell where the private sector ends and the government begins.

The is the same dilemma facing governments in the arenas of social services and public infrastructure. It is really very human to ask for "more". It is sort of natural for politicians to want to say "yes", but they are pressed by conflicting motives: a desire to be posiitive and helpful; a somewhat cynical urge to say "yes" as a populist measure to promote political backing; and the need as a public official to be efficient and prudent in the dispersement of public money.

The interpretation now is growing: the demands for "more" have not been adequately resisted. Special interest politics are now excessive and ominous. The political system has failed adequately to protect the public purse. Without allowing this argument to be addressed simply along political party lines, it is increasingly necessary for all of the political leadership to find the courage to be more constraining and judgemental against any excessive and unwarranted demands against the sources of public money. A more stringent acid test is needed: to resist funding programs in which there is no legitimate federal interest or responsibility, and/or which are clearly designed to favor some special interest and not the general public. A policy must be defined that seeks to reduce, rather than increase, demands on the public budget. Each line item in every government budget should be subjected to assessment as to whether it can be pared down or eliminated, or have its marginal beneficiaries removed. There can be great value in concentrating available funds on those with greatest needs.

3. It is possible that what has emerged over time is a government **so complex that it cannot be governed**, and such complexity is the enemy of democratic understanding. There is no such thing as "the government". What exists is a great, huge, extraordinarilly complex, complicated and utterly incomprehensible mass of organizations and relationships. And experience has proved that what the people really want is often very different than what politicians think is good for them. It it even possible to simplify this mess? Probably not much, within the limits of today's weak political courage. But it is important therefore to argue that government laws should be kept as simple as possible, and within the range of what people can understand if they try. A target should be to define the "least"

government that is consistent with national need and intent. As collateral to this reasoning, the more complex and confusing a body of laws become, the more possibilities are created for misuse and corruption. Therefore, laws should be written to meet the general public good and this standard should always be held up against legislation proposed merely for the advantage of some special elite or specific special interest. It is astonishing to learn that a number of public programs are operating under enabling statutes which have expired, but nobody seems to have the guts to call for their termination.

4. The **Constitution and supporting legislation should clearly authorize the conduct of political parties**, and preferably they should lay down the rules for honest elections in some detail if possible. Constitutional definition of proper elections would highlight the nature of such pathology and provide a stronger basis for opposition to a system that is increasingly not only smelly but ineffective.

5. Also if possible, Constitutions or basic laws should provide mechanisms to prevent the **abuse of presidential appointment powers, or the "reinterpretation" of laws.** Since time immemorial, perhaps the greatest problem of govenments has been the overwelming application of executive power. Sometimes, such power is just siezed, and is beyond control, but where there is some formal framework for the definition of power, its limits should be established and carefully asserted.

6. Politicians have always known the popular appeal of providing public goods and services, and many have cynically used this fact **to curry the support of people as voters.** The intent of this approach is deliberately perverse. It spends public funds not necessarilly to deal with legitimate public needs, but simply to direct funds to the things that would produce votes. This misdirection of public expenditure may have serious consequences in those areas that are neglected. A classic example is the case where the government

wants to provide very cheap bread for urban dwellers, and in order to do so, the government will distort the pricing structure from beginning to end. It will deliberately set prices paid to the farmers who grow the grain – often so low that they make no profit, or even get forced into a loss. Then, millers of the grain are underpaid; the bakers of bread are underpaid; and the urban population happily votes for their government benefactors. Populism in this political sense is a deliberate policy choice and can be applied across an extraordinary range of activities - gas and fuel oil, food, clothing, housing, electricity and water, communications, and of course who gets to pay taxes. But it seems clear that U. S. wellbeing would be advanced if this perversity is stoutly resisted.

7. **Politics vs. management.** Bad politics makes bad management. The American public is largely unaware of one of the great hidden policy conflicts that is taking place in the hundreds of government programs and projects. Each program is created and financed by basic enabling statutes, and the formal political leadershiip has a quite proper right and obligation to oversee the proper conduct of these programs and the validity of funding deployment. And yet, each year, there are <u>hundreds</u> of situations where perverse political decisions overpower common sense and managerial decision making. The political system has created governments that suffer from programs and projects that, by any rational evaluation, are unnecessary, ineffective, low payoff, duplicative, obsolete or of low value. Some of these political demands are simply illegal, such as those that represent bribes, deliberate overpayments, improper contracting or nepotism and political preferment. In most cases, political distortions are not illegal but they are certainly inappropriate, blatantly irrational or arrogantly outrageous.

The classic game that is perhaps most recognized by the American public is the game played by members in legislative bodies from top to bottom, called "the earmark" or the "set aside". Congressional members are constantly on the hunt to identify ways to seek money for their legislative district out of some government agency. It does not matter whether the cost is justified; for them, the only criterion for justification is "give it here – or else!" For example, the Pentagon has long maintained a sophisticated information system which shows how much money flows to every Congressional district in the country, and there is a deliberate policy to make sure that somehow every district gets something out of the money pump. Another feasible move would be to outlaw any undefined "contingency funds" or open ended "trust funds" in which there is no trust at all.

The public should understand that many of the political earmarks payoffs run against the realities of managerial evaluations, or even of common sense, real need, or cost effectiveness. Bad politics has made bad management time and time again. There have been two or three efforts in Congress, or by the President or some governor to prohibit or impede the tide of perverse earmarks. Some have succeeded for a while, but all seem eventually to fade, and this hidden policy seems to be immortal. What is the ultimate solution to the dilemma of weak incompetent politics? It is for the American voting public to stop electing cowards, fools and incompetents.

8. **"Semi-Socialist" policies.** The U. S. government wisely and thankfully avoided the great surge of State Socialism that swept through the rest of the world after WWII. We can congratulate ourselves now, as Socialist governments all over the map have been forced by economic and social failures and incompetence to move reluctantly back to a broader private sector, and more bottom-up democracy. In the end, State Owned Enterprises (SOEs) proved not to be so much efficient instruments of economic delopment, but highly inefficient economic vehicles, most of them running at congenital deficits, to the great embarassment of the socialist politicians that were forced to defend them.

There are numerous vital lessons that the U. S. can learn from the Socialist experience.

All too often, economic operations proved to be heavily impacted by ceaseless elements of political intervention into their supposedly superior economic capability, and thus, SOEs are now being disposed of in many countries, and this tide should be continued. Capital for creation and development of SOEs has been provided by governments at little or no cost, while private companies have generated such funds themselves or borrowed for the purpose. But still, in the end, the total cost within the national economy is far better through private asset creation than for heavy taxes to finance incompetent SOEs.

Socialist governments can, by law or regulation, effectively blocked out private companies from certain markets and reserve them for SOEs. In some cases, SOEs were given absolute monopoly control of a market, against both domestic and international alternatives. But again, the failure of SOEs has meant that this practice damaged the economy. It must be a determined policy of the U. S. government to avoid such monopolies like the plague.

Governments can control national prices so that SOEs could obtain goods and services at subsidy discounts. In some cases, government price controls forced on some suppliers to sell to SOEs at prices lower than their actual costs. In turn, the government can set prices for SOE goods and services at the highest possible level to maximize SOE income, but at great cost to the buying pucblic. The U. S. should understand the perversity and negative consequences of such a policy and resist it.

In a similar vein, when an SOE produces low quality and unreliable products as a means to hold down their costs, or because of poor management, the public has to live with inferior goods.

The lesson to be learned in the U. S. out of this almost universal negative experience is not only that state enterprises are dangerous, but more importantly that it is at the very great advantage of our government to become commtted to the support and stimulation of private enterprise. This however has been a constant dilemma in the U. S. for almost 200 years. Tax, yes; but not "too much". Regulate, yes; but not beyond reason. Encourage, yes; but not subsidy and preferment.

But the U. S. has still had to struggle with advocacy groups who espouse some of the more important elements of State Socialist policy. For example, during the 2017 presidential election campaign, Senator Bernie Sanders declared himself to be a "democratic Socialist", and he enthusiastically advocated such popular socialist policies as free public college education, universal government funded health care, and fuller "tax the rich" policies. Remarkably, President Trump has toyed with the imposition of new taxes on foreign imports into the

U. S., apparently unaware that this is an old socialist policy, known widely in socialist governments as ISI: "Import Substitutions Initiatives". This policy theory was that taxing potential imports would prevent their entry, thus protecting domestic producers and service providers. The almost universal reality was that ISI left the natives with domestic goods that were more expensive and of lower quality, and local businesses were prevented from getting vital imports that they needed to develop.

A very similar policy argument centers around people. Some policy advocates seek to prevent the entry of foreign immigrants and refugees because they are seen as "taking jobs away" from domestic workers. Closed borders were a hallmark of great Socialist regimes such as the USSR and China. But here, the consequence seems the same. Many immigrants in fact possess widely needed and wanted skills and abilities, and their record over several decades of U. S. experience has that they have made valuable contributions to national wellbeing. In other cases, low skilled workers are still eagerly sought for certain kinds of jobs such as crop collection where the domestic workforce is not adequate. In sum, under an open borders policy, the U. S. has allowed immigration of more than 40 million people both legal and illegal – far more than any other country in the world.

In essence, policies seeming to stem from the Socialist base are justified in the U. S.as being more humanist than "greedy capitalism", and that democratic socalism would be offered by a noble and caring government. The counter policy position is that, in reality, socialist governance in almost all of its manifestations represented more control and domination than it did assistance and service. Almost all socialist governments have been economic disasters and serious cultural disappointments.

9. **Rural vs. urban.** Over several decades, government policies have been based on the premise that rural America is under-developed both economically and socially, and that it was necessary to maintain a comprehensive set of government polcies and programs to bring rural/small town areas forward. At the same time, reality has been that the American future is already urban, that cities and suburbs are burgeoning, that 81% of the population is now

in cities. Rural America meanwhile is well able to take care of itself. It might be reasonably argued that current rural wellbeing is largely the result of all of those decade-long government support programs. In any event, it is time to face up fully to the new opportunity: deliberately and drastically cut back on no longer needed government largess, and reinvest the money in programs for the urban poor.

10. **An aging population.** It is widely recognized that a very large generation of citizens is now moving inevitably into the age of retirement, and this surge is demanding some "retooling" of public policies. Is the health care system sturdy enough to support the needs of this aging population? Will the economy stand up to a great decline in the numbers and the earning power of these retirees? Are retirees financially albe to support themselves in retirement? If there are large numbers of people who are physically or financially unable to care for themselves, who will care for them – their sons and daughters or the government? If the burden assumed by the government is greatly more expensive, where will the money come from?

Much of the answer to these questions is already apparent. People may be able to draw upon the Social Security retirement system, and they will become eligible for Medicare or perhaps Medicaid. Their taxes will be radically reduced. There are special programs for the elderly who suffer from many forms of disability. Most will probably be covered by some form of retirement earned by work in a company. Many will be covered by retirement programs provided for civil service retirement programs or those provided by the military.

In fact, studies show a reassuring pattern: of people over the age of 65, more than 80% say that there are financially "safe", and at least 80% say that their financial resources make them "secure". This creates the prospect for a new and more rational debate about retirement policy; it is possible to more broadly apply a "means" determination to retirement qualification, where the relatively well off receive less, and the money flows instead to the most needy. It might also make sense to recognize the increasing physical well being of the middle aged, and simply raise the age of eligibility for most social services designed to serve the elderly. Could the lobbyists that constantly demand "more" be induced to argue for "more rational"?

11. **Rate of inflation.** Another possibility, as an option to the battles over "most needy" or "means testing" is for the government simply to force a limitation on any changes to the funding made available for social programs to the rate of inflation, then dispersed to the states as a fixed amount block grant, thus making the states decide on how these limited funds are deployed.

12. **Separate but equal.** Beginning with the Constitution and continuing through almost 250 years of thousands of laws, regulations, policies, programs, actions, interpretations and pleas, the United States has sought to maintain a policy where people may be separate and distinct in their lives and culture while remaining equal under the law. Here surely is a policy that has never fully succeeded. Women, minorities, the social variant, and the economically disadvantaged all feel that their world remains unequal and often unfair.

As argued elsewhere here, the African American community in America appears to be saying that "equal" does not have to mean "same"; that blacks have evolved their own society in all of its manifistations that is separate, equal in legal stature, but parallel to the long traditional culture of white European origin. Is this a good thing for the country? Almost certainly, the answer is yes. And so it may be necessary to start rethinking all kinds of public policy in terms of whether they not only permit, but perhaps enhance the best elements of this equal/parallel world. And it is possible that American society will become even more complex, with a parallel Hispanic culture, and perhaps - an American Muslim culture?

13. **Priority setting.** The current political policy culture is that all demands on the public purse and the public policy base are equal, and that all should be "honored". This is a critical base for the success of special interest politics. If the government says yes to

one client demand, it must then say yes to all similar demands. If the government provides subsidies for tobacco, or cotton, or corn, or cows, it must then – as a necessity of populist politics – say yes to subsidies for wheat or hogs or apples or asparagus.

What if the government was able to shift this policy into one calling for priority setting? Priority setting would mean a more useful and powerful assesssment of public programs based on value or payoff or outcome. Whatever money is available, it would thus be spent on the top priority activities as defined by need and actual results. As Lord Acton, the illustrious British scientist put it "Gentlemen: we have run out of money – so it is time to start thinking."

Priority setting does not necessarily mean the total elimination of some low value programs, but may include changes at the margin to buttrress high payoff patterns and cut useless or low value program elements. One of the limitations being discussed centers around the proposal that the government's role in social services should be defined by the concept of "the truly needy". Those that are truly needy in either humanitarian or financial terms should be helped by the government, but government programs would not extend to those who can care for themselves, including institutions such as health clinics and universities. One of the main targets for such a limitation would be federal payments for local "community development" — a money pit of limitless depth.

14. **Special interest politics.** Can anything stem the tide of the triumph of special interest politics? Yes – the rise of bottom up public demand to stop the pump and insist on the application of the primacy of the general public interest. That plus encouragement of the political courage in deciding when to say no.

A number of policy changes have been advanced to curb special interest politics. One is a policy of passing more laws that have a fixed termination date. This would force the political special interest advocates to have to make their case again, hopefully more in public than previous back room deals, and more in the face of a general public resistance to their private preferment. A more drastic approach may be to sponsor and support a new public policy which simply says "no more new subsidies". There is nothing wrong with a hightened public debate over what constitutes a proper and needed public program versus what has been typically a series of political back room deals for narrow interests.

15. **An effective election system.** It is expected, and vitally important, that the American government maintain an effective election system at all levels of government, and that such a system be as invulnerable as possibe from the perverse possibilities that money can buy elections. There is a growing concern that the current election system is far less independent than it used to be. We are now seeing elections in which literally billions of dollars are being spent to control outcomes – even to the extent that there is the fear that money from foreign sources can enter the system and influence the results. It is frankly widely known that political contributions, made by special interest organizations have a decisive influence on elections and on the minds of those whom the funds support. And once such a candidate is elected, he/she feels compelled to favor their funding backers with decisions impacting their reach into the largess of public programs.

16. **Political effectiveness.** It would seem to follow that if sound elections are held, the right people will get elected, and they will do the right things in office. Unfortunately, this is not inevitable. There is a growing perception that those in office are far too passive, and the political system is failing to produce results. Problems that are clearly understood and opposed are simply not dealt with. The system has become ominously inhibited by a preoccupation with divisiveness and sterile infighting between key political leaders. People plead for action, but they get stalemate. They plead for action, but they get passiveness. What is needed is the courage to tackle problems, but instead what is seen is timidity and cowardice. Our political system is built around the need for bottom up cooperation and negotiation, but what we are seeing is opposition and enmity and the triumph of useless and pompous rhetoric.

17. **Immigrants vs. refugees.** Immigration into the United States has had a long and valued and honored 200 year history. In the modern era, the U. S. has allowed more than 42 million persons – 31 million legal and 11 million illegal –into our country. We, along with Canada, are by far the most welcoming home for immigrants in the world, and the most sought after. Legal immigrants are required to possess some capacity to sustain themselves. Current laws require that they have some degree of education, some form of skill, a job, or some other support here in the country. They are asked to profess a desire to obey our laws and to seek citizenship if they wish to stay. Illegal immigrants are in a more precarious situation, but even for them, there are paths to ultimate legal residence. Immigration here has never ceased. In fact, threats in other countries are driving more and more people to seek refuge in the U. S. along with the more than one million legal immigrants who enter each year.

The special case of "refugees" is what has seriously muddied U. S. policies. Refuges are those people who claim that they are in great peril in their home countries, and that they fear for their lives and/or the loss of their wellbeing. U. S. laws permit the entry of refugees, but require some validation of the legitimacy of the threats. There are many vastly overburdened courts trying to undertake these proofs. But this is a classic example of the difference between law and justice. To deny entry to a person through the proper application of the law might nevertheless send persons back to a corrupt and oppressive government where they will be killed or brutalized. Sanctuary cities in the U. S. are part of this policy dilemma because these cities argue that their policy may be illegal but it is just and humane.

There are two other critical dimensions to this argument. One is cost. Refugees or illegals gain access to public services and financial aid, to medical care, to assisted housing, and to the education of their children, and somebody has to pay for these things. Is it "fair" to make American citizens pay higher taxes to meet these outsider demands? Isn't this money that might have been spent on our existing urban needy? The ultimate dimension of this debate is the horrible fact that more than 60 million people are refugees somewhere in the world, and it is threatening to think of what it might cost if too many of these unfortunates attempt to throw themselves as a burden onto the U. S. economy and society.

The second issue has to do with the reality that some immigrants and refugees are bad people, or even terrorists infiltrating under the cover of the flow of immigrants and refugees. Some are thieves and crooks. Some are members of vicious gangs like MS-13 who terrorize our urban neighborhoods. Some may be agents of terrorist organizations such as ISIS or al Queda who want to attack U. S. interests. This fear is what caused President Trump to deny access to people from certain countries widely seen as sponsoring or harboring such terrorist organizations. Unfortunately, this fear tends to poison relationships at a broader level. There are, for example, people who now hate or fear all Muslims despite the obvious fact that 99% of Muslims are perfectly fine and decent people who suffer most from the viciousness of their own 1%.

18. **Intergovernmental relationships.** One of the crucial elements that emerged in the formulation of the country and in public policy intent of the Constitution was the creation of a government structure where individual states would exist formally and legally separate from an overarching federal government. States were intended to stand by themselves with their own laws, revenues and separate policies. Over time however, the laws of separation have not changed but the nature of intergovernmental relations have – in remarkable and utterly confusing ways. There is now almost no facet of American life and culture that is not imbedded in some complex ways with these relationshi;s, and it is now estimated that more than one third of state revenues flow from some federal source. The most compelling of these relationships are those that center around social programs: Medicaid, Social Security, Medicare, unemployment compensation, food stamps, housing and education. But there are hundreds of other programs where the three levels of government are welded together –roads, and bridges, and urban transit and rural development and labor relations and the environment, and citizen equality – and on and on.

Increasing the range and complexity of these relationships has been vigerously pursued in both directions. National policies are often mandated to be carried out at the state level, or by state subsidiaries like counties and cities. State governments benefit from these relationships; but they do not appreciate the Washington tendency toward top down meddling and control. The worst case has become known as the "unfunded mandate" problem where the federal government delegates performance by states but declines to provide the money to carry them out. On the other hand, states and especially cities are masters of easing into Washington to solicit federal funding or federal force in mandating some preferred policy position. It is simply true that many of these demands are a reflection that local politicians have often lacked the courage to generate the tax base to finance their programs, and they turn to the feds to get bailed out. The author personally experienced this in the federal mass transit program where cities and counties caused the creation of a program of support for local urban transportation that really could not be justified as a true federal responsibility. In addition, the transit agency had to design and enforce a policy called "maintenance of effort" which sought to prevent efforts by local governments to use federal funds to reduce their own funding so that no real total money increase occurred.

So reality is that public policy has, for decades, been aimed at the expansion and intensification of these policy and financial relationships. Is this a good thing or a bad thing? As usual, they will be seen as good of they are pursued with common sense, moderation and courage. They are bad if they are stupid, excessive, of low value and as mere exercises of special interest politics. Let local governments finance their own local services and activities including public transit, law enforcement, schools and facilities construction and management.

What are the best arguments for devolution or decentraliization?

a. It promote democracy because it is easier for citizens to reach and influence local governments, and strengthens the capacities of local governments.
b. Local governments in turn achieve the potential of achieving higher public service effectiveness and responsiveness. In general,

local administration os public programs is seen as gaining the ability to be practical, simpler, less theoretical and less constrained by doctrine.

c. It is also argued that, to take some power out of the hands of centrist governments is a good thing. It reduces overburdening control, reduces structural complexity, limits some opportunities for corruption, and diffuses some degree of special interest centrist influence.

d. It is also argued that devolution leads to more balanced negotiations between levels of government. Local governments have many vital roles such as road nets, land use control, public utilities, urban services, etc. Regional governments must be independent and not just administrative subsidiaries of the central government.

e. It is argued that a wiser allocation of scarce government resources is also an economic advantage and that local governments will be smarter about how to improve the value and performance of local economies.

f. These lines of reasoning extend to the complex relationships between state governments and their subordinate country and city jurisdictions.

19. **Balancing the government budget by force.** It has been argued that it is useless to expect the current political leadership ever to balance the budget by addressing hundreds of specific budget line items, so some draconian measure must be forced upon them. One feasible approach might be to apply some universal across-the-board budget cut when program-by-program cutting has failed. Another feasible approach would be to enact a law requiring a balanced budget, with a cap applied on any proposed budget increase unless matched by a cut in other budget line items. This has been tried in the past, and it has failed, because the political courage ran out, and the Congress or state legislators, under pressure, simply raise the ceiling. Such an attempt would have to be accompanied by a provision that the law cannot be canceled or modified for some fixed period like five years. Another approach

has been simply to freeze all descretionay spending for one or more fiscal years.

20. A more drastic version of this approach has been advocated in the sense that the budget limitation would be set by an **amendment to the Constitution**. Such a Constitutional amendment may be to require that the federal government would be forced to operate under a balanced budget, or it might be to limit the federal government debt to a fixed percentage of the gross domestic product (GDP).

21. One of the most powerful and valuable tools that the President possesses for controlling the federal government budget was created by the passage, in 1996, of what is called "The **Line Item Veto Act**". The motivation for this act was the recognition in the Congress – yes, even in the Congress! –that there was a nasty tendency to load up crucial proposed legislation with extraneous and often bad and wasteful budget item, deliberately counting on getting this junk enacted because the President could not veto the critical legislation in which these items were deliberately buried. The Line Item Veto Act allowed the President to veto any specific provision in proposed legislation without having to veto the overall bill.

There were two other factors. The wisdom of any veto would have to be debated, and the President had to summon up the courage to act. Again, the enemy of such a rational authority will be the special interest politicians who got their payoffs embedded in the legislation in the first place. There will be hundreds of such interests fighting rejection. How many of them can a president take on? How many will he win?

22. **Hard unpopular choices.** It is at least theoritically possible for public policy to turn more flinty to the extent that some effort would be made to retrench popular and valuable social programs. Very expensive targets: Social Security, Medicaid, the Supplemental Nutritional Assistance Program (SNAP, formally the Food Stamp

Program), the agricultural subsidy program. Retrenchment might be considered at a variety of levels. A basic public policy option might be to limit assistance only to the "truly needy". Another option might be simply to legislate cuts in the funding of these and or other programs. Another relatively feasible option would be to legislate that spending increases would cease to be automatic and pension and welfare spending increases would not be allowed to exceed the national rate of inflation.

Another alternative would be to apply much more stringent limits on eligibility, as for example to raise the retirement age for access to Social Security. Another might be to apply a "means" test which would mean that people with slightly higher incomes or assets would be denied access to a given program. For the federal government, there might be an option to shift more of the costs to state and local governments. One such appoach that has been proposed would be to convert the present Medicaid Program from an open ended "no limit" system to one of fixed annual block grants to states. Another proposition has been the idea of shifting a number of public programs from payments to governments or organizations to one of vouchers paid instead directly to citizens, who then have the personal option of where to spend their money. Such ideas have been advanced for Medicare, Medicaid, primary/secondary education, public housing, etc.

23. **Physical plant.** Eliminate federal subsidies to local governments for many physical facilitiess programs where there is no clear federal interest: AMTRAK, city streets, state roads, urban transportation, public buildings, public school physical plant modernization, vehicle purchases, etc. In a somewhat different vein, the government itself has thousands of physical facilities, and it is almost certain that many of them could be disposed of, shared, or run more cheaply. One tempting target must be the more than 1000 military facilities around the world.

24. **Social service subsidies.** Similarly, eliminate federal subsidies for many social programs that are clearly local responsibilities: law enforcement, school operating costs, community development,

family planning, low income child school enrollment, child support, family assistance, home purchase tax credits, immunization projects, neighborhood assistance, fire stations, etc. The current political debate in America over health care is heavily engaged with this debate.

25. **R & D.** Eliminate federal spending for R & D that can/should be done by the private sector. There is a case for the federal government to continue to support new basic science research where there is no sufficient private ability to do so. Also, major federal programs such as those of NASA or DOD will produce legitimate fallouts of valuable technology.

26. Cut **Labor Department programs** to subsidize labor unions: worker training, worker education, job creation, literacy encouragement, vocational education, welfare-to-work programs, youth job training. It is not that these programs are not desirable; it is that they are not federal.

27. Eliminate the program to **extend broad band services to rural areas.**

28. Decline to finance federal programs to create **electric car connection** infrastructure, fund local government purchase of fuel efficient vehicles, or to purchase equipment for law enforcement agencies.

29. **Overseas investment.** There was a time when the federal government felt compelled to subsidize American companies to invest in operations in other countries. That tide has turned, and private companies are fully able to make these investments on their own. In fact, the new policy attitude is to worry about how to stimulate the growth of our domestic economy, even including efforts to resist sending business overseas.

30. Refuse to fund the DOT program for the development of **high speed rail systems.**

III. ECONOMIC DEVELOPMENT

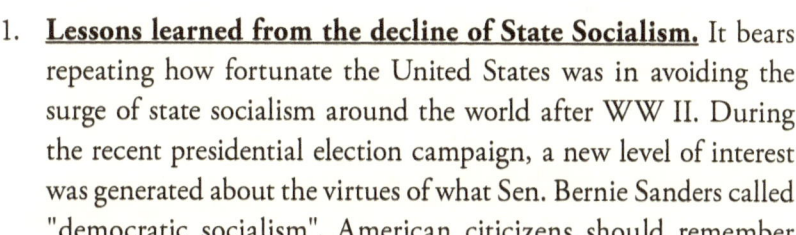

1. **<u>Lessons learned from the decline of State Socialism.</u>** It bears repeating how fortunate the United States was in avoiding the surge of state socialism around the world after WW II. During the recent presidential election campaign, a new level of interest was generated about the virtues of what Sen. Bernie Sanders called "democratic socialism". American citicizens should remember that state socialism was almost never democratic, and was almost always a failure.

2. **<u>Government/private sector relationships.</u>** Government relationships vis-à-vis private enterprise are both positive and negative Past history has emphasized the development of hundreds of ways in which the government, through policy control, a tangle of laws and tons of regulations has constrained private sector activity under the premise that it is protecting the interests of the public. Where there are government actions that appear to reward or protect huge corporations and the very rich, there are growing public resentments and resistance, but at the same time, the government has indeed become excessively regulatory, and there is a good case for some very seriou efforts to weed out the dysfunctional.

3. **<u>Economic payoff.</u>** One important line of thinking centers around the capacity of the U. S. economy to move itself up the scale of economic sophistication from low value output (farming,

fishing, forestry, etc.) to higher value output. This can be aided by government policies that encourage investment and technology development and adoption, and tax policies that pose the least restraint on such upgradings. A counter argument has always beeen that automation and technology adoption causes unemployment, so special attention should be paid to ways to educate and train people for the more sophisticated types of jobs that an upgraded economy demands. The U. S. has a fairly active informal economy, but it is far less important than in some other countries where it is almost the part of the economy that works best.

4. **"Value for Dollar"**. Every government program, whether influencing the private sector or not, should be placed on a basis of maximum effort to pursue a program of "value for dollar" of pubic expenditure, along the lines of a program recently successful in Canada. This is a good argument to use in considering the machinations of special interest politics. If federal programs actually produced more value for dollar, who would capture the added value?

5. **Structural reforms.** Similarly, the effectiveness of the U. S. government structure is heavily negative and excessively costly because of its almost incompehensible complexity – thousands of units, organizational overlap, internal conflict and confusion, duplication, top-to-bottom layering, an excess of petty unproductive detail, long delays, needless repetition, and every other bureaucratic sin. Simplify! Flatten! Reduce! Cut! Courage!

6. **The sins of preferment.** More vigorous attention should be paid to the distinction between government connections with the private sector that are truly productive, and those that are payoffs, and preferment to special interest political relationships. Could the federal government manage to establish a policy of **"no more special interest subsidies"?**

7. **World trade.** This is the subject of disagreement, and it centers around two conflicting perceptions: one is that, by facilitating trade more openly in the world, the pace of development of economic capability will grow and be more equitably distributed and more profitable. The counter view is the fear that trade openness simply shifts jobs away from developed countries where wages and benefits have become more satisfactory, to less developed countries where workers are paid less and will settle for fewer benefits. The realistic answer seems to be all on the side of optimizing world trade. The most compelling case in support of this assessment is the extraordinary experience in China and India, starting around 1980, after each had been forced to abandon state control. The switch to far more open economic competitive enterprise literally raised hundeds of millions of people out of their abject poverty.

8. **Import substitution.** Over the course of almost 50 years, there were several theories about economic development which proved to disastrously wrong. First, one of the prime justifications for major public ownership and management of state enterprises was that it would facilitate the highly desirable Federation of State/CountyMunicipal Employees, contibuting policy of import substituting industrialization (ISI), often called import substitution. This policy sought to encourage as many domestic enterprises as possible to produce things that were being imported from outside of the country. This was seen as having two valuable consequences: it captured domestic consumption and forced it to purchase goods and services from domestic enterprises; and it reduced the outward flow of scarce money. This kind of program is inherently government based since it requires the selection and massive support of certain industries, often in the face of negative market realities. At the same time, it required the government to exercise an increasing degree of control over the banking system so that it could direct the preferential or subsidy flow of lending to the elements of the economy that it had chosen to develop.

In his book "Exposed to Innumerable Delusions" – a study of state enterprises and their import substitution policies over more than forty years in Egypt, India, Mexico and Turkey – John Waterbury put it this way: "The need to protect and subsidize the ISI public enterprises led to multiyear planning, heavy regulation of all economic activity, administered prices, control or modulation of normal market forces, subsidization, cross subsidization, partial or even total control of banking/lending, heavy government oversight of enterprise performance and the politics of state control." He goes on further to condemn SOEs in general: "The track record of one of disappointment in the performance of the SOEs – chronic losses, inability to avoid import reliance, the high cost of sheltering both industries and labor, and a growing realization of the failure to capitalize in real export development potentials"[1]

There are two similar but more moderate versions of the failed ISI policy – a "domestic content" policy and a "mandated exporting" policy. The domestic content policy loosened up control of an economy to the extent that it permitted FDI, but the goods and services produced could not exceed some arbitrary percentage of the total, usually 50%. The purpose of such a policy is to force foreign investors to partner with domestic enterprises and use locally produced raw materials, fabricated parts or subassemblies, and domestic labor. This policy is almost purely political and is widely used; it is even popular in the U. S. Mandated exporting policies are also based on the political urge to assist domestic industry, and the usual approach is to use government mechanisms such as tax waivers for export earnings, fast depreciation of assets used in exporting, preferences in the granting of export licenses, waiver or reduction of export fees, and even government help in exploring overseas markets.

Import substitution had the effect of depriving national consumers of superior foreign products in favor of what all too often proved to be inferior local products, and the U. S. should congratulate itself in staying away from these curses. Domestic content regulations and "Buy American" policies were almost always quickly abandoned simply because they seriously inhibited the willingness of investors to invest in a country where the government officially forced them to combine with obsolete or inefficient local enterprises. It also appears true that when such a domestic content involvement is mandated, the venture begins perversely to act more like a "protected industry" and less like a dynamic private enterprise. Most will lobby to retain and enhance their subsidies, and there is a high risk that, unless the government is very skilled, they will subsidize enterprises that are never capable of making it on their own and will survive only as long as the government props them up. Export encouragement has often failed because the government's policy makers proved to have an almost pathetic lack of grasp of the markets their subsidized enterprises were trying to enter.

An interesting example of the complexity of trade is that of coal. In the United States, the growing use of natural gas has occurred because the cost for gas is now lower than for coal. Coal mine companies have, however, greatly increased exports to countries around the world. In Europe, Germany is phasing out its large nuclear power capability, but the odd result is that it is burning more imported coal, or local brown coal which has high emissions patterns. The U. S. also exports to the Netherlands, Great Britain, S. Korea, Italy, Brazil, India, and Turkey. Germany's ultimate goal is to produce 80% of its energy from renewable resources by 2050, with coal filling the gap for the next 35 to 40 years – or maybe forever.

The United Kingdom almost killed off its own coal sources in the 80's, but the consequence is now that imports of U. S. coal are up more than 70% since 2011 (Washington Post, Feb. 3, 2017). European countries are betting on huge surges of renewable energy sources, but this is expensive, and takes a lot of effort and courage. The private sector will share in these costs, but would be happy to shift as much of the cost as possible to some government.

9. **Technology ownership.** Many private companies have found that, gradually, it has become easier and safer to enter dangerous or unprofitable markets such as China and India, Russia or Vietnam and a few other national economies in the Far East and Africa. In a surprising number of economic markets, the key advantage has been in the ownership of some technological advantage, and the ability to apply it at a high level. Here again, the Chinese policy is revealing. The Chinese Communist Party (CCP) and the Chinese government have always maintained policies that are aimed at

gaining access to key technologies. Many foreign companies are allowed access to the Chinese economy only when they do so as partners with some domestic Chinese company or state owned public enterprise, and these partners require that the technologies of their foreign partners must be shared with them. Then, the government sees to it that such technologies are made available beyond the original partnership.

The hope is that while a technology is "lost" as a condition of market penetration, the home company back in the U. S. or Europe or Japan will be staying out ahead of the power curve by developing the next wave of technological innovation for the next future. A collateral concern is the parallel evolution of the skill base, where schools and universities and laboratories and tech savvy employers keep developing the higher order of skills demanded.

10. **Still: the need for competition.** In its broadest sense, what a world economy leads to is probably a rise in more countries of economic entities capable of new competitiveness with those in the developed world. If you are the top dog, you may fear the threat of new dogs closing up behind you. If you are a customer or client however, competition may end up being a good thing. But in another sense, the competition may be more about capable providers everywhere.

11. **The dangers of promoting deliberate divisiveness.** There is a whole range of natural divisions between human beings: young vs. old, rich vs. poor, men vs. women, blacks vs. whites vs. hispanics, the high skilled vs. the low skilled, labor vs. management, managers vs. workers, police vs. crooks, Mets vs. the Yankees, and kids vs. the third grade.

12. **Structural Adjustment.** Structural adjustment is not just a dilemma for less developed countries. In fact it is happening all the time in most countries, including the most developed countries. The difference is that, in most countries it occurs

through voluntary and slow paced evolution of the economy and not through authoritarian impositions of the government or the requirements of lending institutions as conditions for the granting of loans. In addition to the earlier adjustments such as the shift from a rural to an urban economy, and government assumption of a broader agenda of social services recent trends in the United States typify the major adjustments that have been happening in its economy and in most developed countries around the world.

The United States, more than any other country, is a "consumer economy"; that is, the greatest leverage in the economy is consumer preference and demand and not industrial development or public sector strategies. In most developing countries the opposite is true. Economic development is usually driven from the top down, emphasizes industrial development, and is almost indifferent to consumer interests.

In the U. S. there has been a shift from manufacturing and industry to a service sector economy. More than 70% of U. S. employment is in the service sector, which also provides most of the growth in jobs. The U. S. leads the world in this shift, which has many important consequences. Despite perceptions to the contrary, the service economy is very profitable and "value added". It requires large numbers of well educated people because it includes education, banking, government, insurance, communications, media and others – all high value sectors. It is certainly not confined to lower value jobs such as janitorial or food service. The service sector has a history of not being as productive as manufacturing activities but computers and better communications are changing that, and there is a new trend in economic development pointed to enhancing the productivity of the service sector. Here again, the U. S. leads the world. In addition, world competition, especially from Japan which caused deterioration in the U. S. manufacturing sector has now sparked a recent trend to reexamine and revitalize manufacturing.

The shift from manufacturing to services has been accomplished by several critical human resources based shifts. College training is now almost mandatory. Those with less education or comparable upgraded technical skills are falling into a "second tier" level in the economy. Unions are declining; organized labor now constitutes less than 15% of the workforce. Individuals with professional skills are now negotiating directly one-on-one with employers, and unions have seemed unable to connect with newer industries or to attract the growing numbers of minorities and immigrants in the country. The service sector is very "bi-level" – a top level of professionals, and a second level in low skilled low paying jobs. These low level jobs have helped absorb the influx of more than 20 million immigrants, but there is a lack of adequate "bridges" from the low level jobs to the more valuable positions. The obvious answer is education, at least for the next generation. Finally, workers are now more mobile and less tied to fixed manufacturing sites. This enhances the likelihood of finding a better job somewhere and increases worker bargaining power.

13. **Working Women.** To an extraordinary degree, the recent trends in the increase of the percentage of workers of "prime age – 25 to 54 " have been driven largely by the entry of more women into the workforce. The greater openness to the top ranges of the labor market, and the shift from manufacturing to services have favored the access of women. Women now represent the majority of entering college students, including in the historic male arenas of law, medicine and engineering. At the same time, women are also entering the ranks of unskilled job holders in increasing numbers, especially in what have been seen as more-or-less female sectors such as primary education, health care and retailing.

14. **Organized labor.** Part of this shift in the patterns in the workforce has been the decline of organized labor. Part of the reason lies in the fact that corporations recognize that the cost of wages and fringe benefits is usually the largest single category of business expense and they are constantly looking for ways to reduce those costs. This is especially true for small and middle sized businesses where labor costs are crucial, and it is these smaller businesses that are the primary source of new job creation. In some cases, the introduction of automation and other new technologies has reduced the need for human labor.

But is it also true that organized labor has almost aways been implacably opposed to a lot of technology innovation because it is seen as destroying jobs, or holding down wages and benefits. And organized labor leadership, if not membership, has been heavily political, and always in support of the Democratic Party. According to the Federal Election Commission, of the top ten largest contributors to Democratic Party political campaigns, 13 have been labor unions – and 25 of the top 100. In the last election campaign, the largest single contributor to any campaign was the Service Employees International Union, having conributed $222 million. The next was ActBlue, a west coast Political Action Committee (PAC). The next was another union: The American Federation of State/CountyMunicipal Employees, contibuting $93 million. The National Education Association is next with $92 million and the American Federation of Teachers is #6 with $69 million. Unions contribute almost exclusively to the Democratic Party, and teacher organization representatives have made up a majority of the delegates to the DRC national convention. As a consequence of this influence, there is a broad national pattern of state and local governments that have raised pension benefits to such a high level that they are having extreme difficulty funding them. Some states are seen as on the brink of financial failure, driven hugely by these retirement costs and employee benefit costs, and often caught in legal binds which prohibit any reduction in these benefits. Political leadership in these states have been part of the problem, and it seems unlikely that they are able to become part of the solution.

15. In other cases, the **import/export stance** of a corporation will have crucial workforce impact. U. S. corporations that have fairly people-intensive activities will be drawn to overseas locations where labor is relatively cheap. U. S. firms that are more technologically advanced tend to stay at home but tend to rely on their technological advantages. But U. S. firms will not export their activities just because of cheap labor since there are other critical factors to be considered. One of most important is the attitudes of the foreign governments. Also, any company considering investment overseas will look for a workforce that is educated and industrious.

In summary, structural adjustment in the U. S. is voluntary, steady but more gradual, and is tied to market forces rather than central planning or government mandates. The U. S. is the largest and most lucrative economic market in the world and is the target of entrepreneurs in every other country. It is also one of the most open national markets in the world despite certain highly visible exceptions like tobacco or cotton. This gives consumers greater advantage as the economy evolves. In this environment, governments, and especially the federal government are largely irrelevant to the realities of economic development. There is no "National Economic Plan". In fact, the government trails along behind the power curve of economic development and is largely confined to efforts to stabilize the economy and mitigate unwarranted excesses. The main relationship between the government and the private sector is regulatory.

Life in the U. S. is inevitably a world of friction between economic interests in ways that range from the benign and cooperative up to serious and violent conflict. In comparison the the rest of the world however, the U. S. experience has been relatively moderate and well maintained, and the great bulk of our mutual lives is friendly and secure. In other countries, these conflicts have become so distructive that they have all but destroyed the country, or caused unblievable pain and horror. Think of the fate of Afghanistan, Bosnia, Cambodia, the Central African Republic, Chechnya, Colombia, the Democratic Republic of Congo, Cote D. Ivoire, Cyprus, E. Timor, Gaza City, Guatamala, Haiti, Honduras, Iran, Iraq, Laos, Lebanon, Liberia, Libya, Mali, Mauritania, Myanmar, Nepal, Nicaragua, Niger, N. Korea, Pakistan, Philippines, Rwanda, Sierra Leone, S. Africa, Somalia,Sri Lanka, Sudan, South Sudan, Syria,Thailand, Tunisia, Uganda, Yemen, Yugoslavia and now the emerging oppressive dictatorship in Venevuela.

In other words, depending on the nature of national conflicts, more than 45 countries, or almost 1/3 of all of the substantial countries of the world have suffered from poisonous and distructive internal conflicts, and in the majority of cases, the government itself has played a powerful role in creating and supporting, for perverse political reasons, the very divisiveness that ends up destroying the country. It is important for the American public to realize that conflicts within our economic system are relatively tolerable compared to the horrors found in other countries. Economic development in the U. S. can be comfortably and productively shared between the public and private sectors in encouraging major improvements in the national economy:

16. It would be particularly productive to find ways to move the economy increasingly up the power curve from low value <u>to **high value economic sectors.**</u>

17. To deliberately do more to use the influence of governments to force the pace of economic development in all arenas of economic activity. One of the most urgent of these targets should be **cities** – the population of the country is now heavily urban, and many cities (Detroit? Chicago?) are experiencing great difficulty keeping up.

18. It is usuallly wise economic policy to diversify the nature of the economy, often **away from agriculture** to elsewhere in the economy such as consumer services and information technology, and to invest more effort in the revitalization of the manufacturing sectors, and the evolution of cities.

19. One of the most effective means for change is for the government to help in the development of **small/middle sized companies**, and to deliberately promote greater competition. A very serious collateral issue is the acceptability of the growth of enormous organizations and persons of very great wealth. Ever since the concerns over the concentration of money and power in the 1870's and beyond in the hands of Standard Oil, or John D. Rockefeller, governments in the U. S. have acted to curb such power, primarily by what became known as anti-trust law enforcement. But there is a feeling that the adequacy of current laws and the apparent reluctance to enforce have allowed the emergence of companies of threatening size and power, and the inability of the government to prevent abuses. What then is needed as a new and more courageous approach to the prevention of dangerous abuse.

20. There is a growing feeling that there will be a rethinking of the so-called **"military-industrial complex"**, to move it away from

large weapons systems and more to (less costly) intelligence and joint on-the-ground operations.

21. It is likely that more and more can and will be done to facilitate the economic participation and success of **women, minorities**, and new immigrants in the national economic system.

22. It is increasingly recognized that major elements of the physical structure of the country are in the forms of **public infrastructure** such as dams, rail lines, power generating stations, power distribution networks and urban transportation systems. It is therefore an important need for governments to support the development, maintenance and repair of such systems. The economic implications are very powerful; while infrastructure development and maintenance is very expensive, the economic impact is huge and benefits are far, far greater and simply cannot be ignored.

23. And it is always both economically and politically astute to do whatever is possible to promote national employment, **wages, benefits and labor protections.**

24. The World Bank has attempted to define what it considers to be the basic essential elements of any national program for **structural adjustment** and is now promoting this policy instead of opposing it.

25. It is critical to **control of inflation**, to maintain a strong central bank, and to keep a tight money supply.

26. Concentration of our econmic strategy for economic development **on export development** and promotion and not import substitution.

27. Federal **government borrowing** should be primarily for economic development purposes, not financing of day-to-day government operations. A key mandate is that international debts must be honored and gradually paid off, but loans can be refinanced or

even forgiven if "adequate" structural adjustment progress is being made.

28. **Prices** should be brought into line with market reality – wages, consumer goods, industrial transfers, financing of state enterprises.

29. Reduce **trade barriers** to a minimum.

30. Eliminate **redundancy in the labor force**, particularly in government agencies.

31. **Privatization**: It is probably wise in the last analysis to sell off most state enterprises (AMTRAK, Alaska RR), unless economically justified.

32. Promote **environmental sustainability.**

33. **Local governments** and not the federal government must accept the responsibility for making major improvements in education and training.

34. And finally, there is an increasing concern, both economic and moral, about the huge d**isparities between the wealth and income** of the average citizen and the "top %". It does not seem that most Americans object to personal wealth, but they do object to the moral acceptance of people of enormous wealth, beyond reason and justification. Shifts are possible though the tax system, special interest politics and greater competition in market places. But it may also be necessary now to revitalize the concept of "anti-trust", where the government does more to prevent the oppressive concentration of power in economic institutions.

IV. REFORM OF THE TAX SYSTEM

1. **System reform**. First and foremost, the tax system began its existence in colonial times primarily as a means of raising revenue for governments, but even that early, it also became a means of control and then of reward. The tax system as revenue source is driven by government demands for money. The tax system as control and reward is driven by politics. Because of this, the whole system is viewed by the public and some of the political leadership with dark suspicion, and recent federal administrations have regularly announced their intentions to undertake "tax reform".

But why has so little actually been done? The unsettling answer is that the beneficiaries of tax system preferment are more powerful than the political and public forces seeking reform. And it is true that the whole system is so blindingly complex and complicated that the public may hate taxes, but they don't really understand what would "fix" the system. Once again, the newly elected Trump Administration has announced this reform intent, with some substantial allies in the Congress, so once again this test of courage will be undertaken.

2. First and foremost, the ultimate reform would be to enact laws that **tighten controls on borrowing, and set upper limits on indebtedness.** But this is a death wish, since such limits would destroy the federal budget because spending could not be limited to live within such an artifical limit.

3. **Tax subsidies.** As part of this argument, a trade-off often discussed is to eliminate some substantial number of preferential subsidies now carefully embedded in the system in exchange for a general reduction in the level of taxation of corporate income. This kind of agreement may eliminate some of these objectionable subsidies, but it would reduce government revenues, in the face of mounting expenditure demands. The worst case then would be for the government to be compelled to raise other taxes instead – probably on the middle class tax payer. Big business argues that corporate tax cuts would "stimulate the economy", and thus, in the long run, provide a greater base for government taxation.

4. **Spending reduction.** Of course, the ultimate influence on the tax system is to the reduce the demand for taxation by reducing government expenditures. While strictly not tax reform almost every tax reform study has emphasized this point.

5. **Tax evasion.** Tax evasion has risen to the level of a valued skill; a game that anybody can play. Reform would have three components. First, the system itself can be improved in ways that eliminate gaps and loopholes that are openings for tax evasion, including the establishment of a minimum tax requirement to be paid by all corporations. Second, the system could be made to provide more serious penalties for tax evasion. Third, pursuit of tax evaders can be made more vigorous and successful. For example – laws should be strengthened to force politicians to reveal their personal and official finances. Sometimes, the tax evader is the government itself, when it grants special "tax waivers" or pays "tax subsidies".

6. **Fraudulent refunds.** The Government Accountability Office (GAO), an agency supporting the Congress has urged the federal government to "prevent paying $480 million in fraudulent refunds in fiscal years 2015 and 2016."

7. **Special interest purge.** Many have urged a major assault on special interest advantages: a purging of the whole tax code of special interest breaks and tax loopholes, especially for profit making organizations. This would purge breaks not only for companies but also for social organizations like labor unions, environmental groups, lobbying groups, and many, many more. One element of this thinking is the possibility of raising the present cap on payroll taxes. There are many possibilities involved in our system of tax expenditures. We might rethink all tax expenditures including employer health care benefits and the provision for mortgage interest deduction. How about "no tax subsidies for profit making organizations?" One valued provision is that which requires at least an alternative minimum tax on organizations that may otherwise maneuver their way out of taxation.

8. **SALT!** Perhaps the single most compelling argument for tax avoidance is the ability of taxpayers to take as a deduction taxes paid to state and local governments from income tax paid to the federal government. Under President Trump, the proposal to eliminate this deduction has again been advanced. Again, it will retreat., but —.

9. **Tax collection:** Many people who owe taxes feel that they can simply not pay, or can delay payment as long as possible – to see what happens. In too many cases in the past what happened was nothing Obviously, the government needs to be much more serious about collecting all taxes due – on time. Strengthen the ability to collect taxes. One of the most questionable tax impositions is that which was newly imposed by the Obama health care legislation, where any person who does not have some form of health care insurance would by punished by the imposition of a tax. Many of the people effected have made reasonable and conscious decisions not to buy health care insurance because they are young and healthy and resent being forced to buy something that they do not need and would not use.

10. Enact legislation to reform overly suppressive **tort laws.**

11. **Reduce tax expenditures**. One of the most politically popular forms of tax evasion is the deliberate public policy of deciding not to collect certain taxes that might have been collected. An example is a tax on payment of home mortages which are forgone for most home owners. Maybe this tax expenditure is iron clad, but other similar measures might be eliminated. Potential candidates might include employer-provided health insurance costs, charitable giving, retirement savings, and provision for payers to take a fixed standard deduction instead of the tricky business of itemizing deductions. In some cases, income can be declared to be "capital gains" and thus taxed at a level lower than income taxes.

12. **Eliminate estate "death" taxes.** One of the most powerful of such tax expenditure targets is any tax on the estates of people when then die. It is argued that assets of an estate have already been tax when they were earned, and that it is unfair to tax them again.

13. **Greater public knowledge**. Legislative bodies or offices of a President should be required to publish a list of all tax advantages contained in the tax code, and their costs. Tax laws are also prime targets for limited time authorizations.

14. **Expand the tax base** to all but the very poor. More than 40% of American earners pay no federal taxes, but many often very profitable companies also pay little or no taxes through legal and regulatory maneuvering. There should be no policy to subsidize profit making businesses, and every business should be made to pay its "fair share".

15. **But – corporate size.** While all businesses should pay their fair share, there is of course the argument of what is fair. A good case can be made for more carefully designing the tax structure so that, in a common sense way, it puts a greater burden on large and wealthy businesses, and is kinder and lighter on small business

owners who can ill afford heavy taxes, along with the heavy burden of paperwork for tax preparation.

16. **The special case of health care.** There is increasing concern about the soaring costs of health care, and it is felt that significant savings could be realized if these costs can be controlled. This might involve reform of Medicare payments to doctors and health workers, and by placing firm limits on potential future cost increases. Perhaps the most serious kind of proposal for both Midicare and Medicaid is to retrench the range of program eligibility, by a means test or an age test. It might also be said that the level of overpayment and downright cheating within the system is another major target.

17. **Other spending reforms.** Similar arguments are advanced for other federal programs such as Social Security; the Supplemental Nutritional Assistance Program (SNAP, earlier called the Food Stamp Program), farm subsidies, local school aid, and more.

18. **A gas tax.** One of the most successful taxes of all time has been the taxes levied on gasoline, imposed by both the national and local governments, primarily to finance the construction and maintenance of highways, roads and bridges. While it has been opposed by trucking companies and others for whom it is a considerable expense, it still is a fair tax which descends largely on the people who benefit most directly from its investment. The tax has not kept up with inflation, and it is more than time to upgrade it. Deterioration of streets and highways is becoming a more serious problem, and the possibilities of other forms of funding for this infrastructure range from slim to none.

19. One highly regarded option, widely used in Europe and elsewhere is what is known as a **value added tax**. This is a tax not on income but on consumption, and it is levied on producers of goods and services at each stage of their production and sale. The producer can attempt to recoup the cost of the tax in the price paid by the purchaser, but whether they succeed is a function of the state of

the market. The argument here is that the VAT is probably not regressive, and it is a better and simpler and less expensive form of tax collection. Local governments fear that such a consumer based tax will clash with their own efforts to impose local government sales taxes.

V. GOVERNMENT OPERATIONS

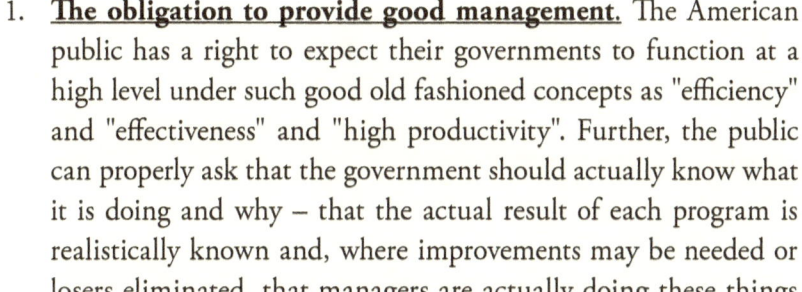

1. **The obligation to provide good management.** The American public has a right to expect their governments to function at a high level under such good old fashioned concepts as "efficiency" and "effectiveness" and "high productivity". Further, the public can properly ask that the government should actually know what it is doing and why – that the actual result of each program is realistically known and, where improvements may be needed or losers eliminated, that managers are actually doing these things – in essence, superior management of government programs. The public may also have the reasonable expectation that government will tell the truth, prevent corruption and theft, and work always to serve the public and not just its friends and clientele.

In other words, the great tradition of honest and effective management is a proper and vital necessity. What is good management? The answer is widely understood. It is taught in universities. It is learned on the job. It is absorbed and understood by millions of people at all levels as their profession and obligation.

Does the federal government of the United States provide such good and professional management? The answer seem to be "yes, but ------". Do state and county and city governments such good and professional management? The answer is also "yes, but -----".

To begin with, the totality of the national government system is unbelievably huge and complex, sophisticated, complicated, muddled and notoriously fragmented and yet interrelated. It is probably unwise to think of it as "the government" since it is literally hundreds of governments, program by program and place by place. In short it has never been a coherent entity designed to be "managed" as that term is understood in other contexts. The best way to evaluate government is first from the top down, and second from the middle down. From the top down, governments are created and designed not for management effectiveness but for political interpretations, and as discussed earlier, the political view of the world is often markedly different from the professional management view. Thus, public managers are faced with conditions far different than those face by the executives and managers in the private sector, and they are usually far more complicated.

The President is, by order of the Constitution, the Chief Executive of the government, and yet not even the President can really manage the totality the way a chief executive of corporations can manage. Much of the operational power and authority for specific government programs is vested by law not in the President but in the head of the government agency that delivers the program. Cabinet secretaries and agency heads may "work for" the President and be appointed by him, but each also "works for" the Congress which defines his or her programs, dictates agency structure, defines many of its processes, and ultimately controls its finances. The President cannot order his leaders to violate the law, and should be careful not to try.

So we go back to the interpretation of the civil servant's managerial obligation. Clearly, it is not just to be the sacred principles of classic professional management as taught in universities and corporate board rooms. It is a deeper and more compelling and more confusing form of management – but carrying both legal and moral obligations nevertheless. But is also clear that, bluntly, it should not be mere paper shuffling either. There is nothing – absolutely nothing – that really prevents every person in a position of authority in governments from making a maximum commitment to producing valuable and cost effective management for the American public, and the ultimate objective must be to develop and maintain a powerful motivation for both politicians and managers to accept the obligation to do just that.

2. **The obligation for government effectiveness.** Over a long period of U. S. governance, the reputation of public managers has been reassuringly high. But increasingly in recent years, there has been a growing public concern that the public administration community is failing to step up to the demands imposed upon it to provide effective management of the programs and activities of governments. These demands are very serious and complex. The provision of effective government is perhaps the must difficult thing that nations are called upon to do. Often, political leadership has proven to be disturbingly bad, pursuing policies and relationships that create conflict and reduce the capacity for the government's managers to function effectively. It is vital that every U. S. government recognize and try to live up to their obligation to be effective – both in political and managerial terms. All of the tools for achieving effectiveness exist; what seems to be lacking is the will and the courage to use them up to their real potential.

3. The central dilemma of American governments at all levels has become a system in which **special interests** have come to dominate the provision of funds and influence for political campaigns, which in turn translates into the creation of hundreds of government programs designed to favor these special interests organizations, often at some cost to the general public interest. Each of these special interest programs becomes locked into law, and they are then stoutly defended against any elimination, retrenchment or even reform. The legislation is, by design, so detailed that it blocks any capacity for managerial improvement. Then, the special interest groups will invariably continue to press for new increments of preferment and subsidy.

4. Among the upper levels of the civil service, this special interest ascendency is particularly disturbing. **The real world is constantly evolving.** Programs become marginal, less valuable, overly expensive or simply obsolete. But career managers are increasingly unwilling to press for management reforms in the

face of implacable, and often threatening and dangerous political resistance.

In this special interest world, there seems to be virtually no political capacity to say "no" to anybody, nor do they know how to set priorities based on public need or value. A look at the published lists of Washington lobbyists reveals the extraordinary number and range of the beneficiaries of this system. A look at the budgets of Federal, state and local governments shows thousands of budget line items financing these business and social advocacy interests. State and local governments in turn have become huge special interest in themselves, drawing funds from Federal programs ranging from health, education and environmental protection, to law enforcement, fire protection, road construction and maintenance and many forms of tax advantages.

5. The public manager is finding it increasingly difficult and perilous to function in this intense political environment. There is virtually no substantial **political** support for, or interest in, the values of effective management. Many senior professional executives and managers simply hang back from proposing change or reform. Despite these pressures and frustrations, the public administration community continues to have responsibilities to the American public that, if ignored, may mean great peril for the profession. The public needs to understand not only when and why politics may be bad, but also why bad politics produces bad management.

6. What is the effective course of action against this perversion? It lies in a deliberate effort, from largely public sources, to **educate the general public** about the dilemma of special interest politics. And indeed, the public does seem to be increasingly reacting to what it perceives as the decline in government effectiveness and thus the performance and reputation of the government's corps of professional executives and managers Yet, if one looks at the performance of governments around the world, U. S. governments remain among the best in the world, and American citizens really have much to be proud of in the performance of their governments.

The public administration community is seriously lacking in its ability to explain to the public all of the things that governments do well and effectively. In truth, the government's managers probably do better at their jobs than many politicians do in theirs.

7. It is **important for the public administration community to speak out** against the kind of bad politics that forces bad management. Governments should be able to rid themselves of programs and activities that are useless, of low value, or simply obsolete. Managers need more latitude to eliminate overlap and duplications in public programs, or to do away with mandated regulations that are overly complicated, too intrusive, time-wasting, costly and often simply pointless. Managers often know when some program is costing a lot and achieving little, or other programs that produce more harm than good. Often, they can point out to the political decision-makers where the government has involved itself in affairs that are not the legitimate roles of government, and are better left to private institutions.

8. **The size of the Civil Service.** Part of this growing dissatisfaction is the complaint that the government is "too large", and in fact, the federal government has grown enormously in the last 40 years in terms of size, range of authority, cost and numbers of programs. The government now involves around 1,000 identifiable programs of increased complexity. In 1970, the federal budget was just around $200 million. It reached $1 trillion in 1987, and it has now topped $3.6 trillion. That means that it is more than 17 times larger, and even allowing for inflation, it is a powerful statement of the magnitude and sophistication of the government that our federal executives and managers are expected to manage.

But meanwhile, the population of the federal civil service, which peaked at 6.6 million in 1968, is now down to about 4.2 million – an absolute decline of 37% since 1968. These figures provide a telling story of how the government has changed, and if they were better understood, they would be a powerful statement about the real effectiveness of the government and its leaders.

In summary, Federal, state and local government have become huge, complex and highly sophisticated groups of institutions that create demands for effective management far beyond the political layer at the top. The American public is right to expect these governments to employ the very best of professional management and leadership, and it is the responsibility of the career leadership to fight for an environment that supports and facilitates excellence in management instead of ignoring or even frustrating it.

It is easy – and necessary – to say that this pattern must be reversed, but it is far from clear how. Essentially, the whole professional ethic of thousands of civil servants needs to be galvanized and the importance of managerial competence and effectiveness pushed with greater seriousness across the whole range of government activities. Bland utterances of political and agency leadership are not and never have been enough. A subset of this argument is the need to somehow blunt the political tendency to give political appointments to friends, relatives, allies, supporters and others of doublful competence. More support for quality management leadership must come from the bottom up as well as better from the top down. What is needed is a longer term program to reform the organization and management of government agencies: to simplify, eliminate, speed up and create a greater attention to cost effectiveness.

9. **The war against corruption.** In truly scandalous governments, corruption is not just ignored, it is organized and encouraged. Even where the apparatus for controlling corruption exists, it may be ignored or kept deliberately weak. What the public deserves and wants is that corrupters are prevented – and caught and removed. For situations in entrenched corruption of government agencies, it may be impossible for the organization to purge itself, and the only alternative may be in the form of external organizations and external anti-corruption campaigns mounted from the outside.

10. In an extreme environment of agency corruption, the government has turned to a promising new approach: **the Watch Dog**

agency. These agencies are not designed for routine auditing but for mounting government-wide anti-corruption attacks. In designing such agencies or in assessing their track records, certain characteristics have been seen as critical:

a.   Such agencies may be established at the government-wide level or placed in individual agencies of government but in either case, they must be independent and must report to the highest possible level. Most are created by special legislation that establishes the needed independence. Many such laws provide that the reports of the watch dog organization must be submitted either to an agency head or to the legislature. The staffs should be politically neutral and not beholden to any organization or persons other than those who appoint them.

b.   The agency should be deliberately weighted to provide the maximum capacity to do operational field investigation – on-the-ground rooting out of corruption.

c.   The authority of the agency should be powerful. It must be given the authority to investigate any situation, have open access to all government records including the legal authority to subpoena such records. It should also have the right to interrogate any individual or to investigate the private records of persons where corruption is suspected.

d.   Authority should extend beyond the government itself into the institutions that are engaged in government financed activities such as state owned enterprises, contractors, grantees, local governments to which government authorities have been delegated, or to those holding government licenses or charters.

e.   In addition to the power to investigate, many watch dog agencies have also been granted "intelligence gathering" authority which opens up such tools as wire taps, surveillance, and clandestine ways to penetrate suspect groups or organizations.

f.   There should also be the means by which secret access is provided to whistleblowers or the general public who want to report suspected corrupt practices without fear of retribution. This access should include reports against politicians, since one of the greatest inhibitors of ant-corruption criticism is the fear of political retaliation.

g. The independent capability to prepare cases for prosecution is vital, since one of the "choke points" that a regime can most effectively control is that of the actions of public prosecutors who are public employees, subject to direction from their political superiors.

11. **<u>The art of bad budgeting.</u>** To a very serious extent, the nature of governance and its reputation rests on what emerges in the formal budgets of each department and agency. The content of an agency budget is defined by two categories: first is the programs and projects that the agency administers; and second is the "overhead" costs of agency personnel, its buildings and facilities, and its operational services such as power and transportation. Of these two, the far more complex budget development deals with the program base.

The development of program costs is not easy, and often it is perverse. If the public sees this as a simple process carried out on an adding machine, it is much deluded. The preparation of an agency budget is an art form of exquisite complexity, played from agency back rooms all the way up to the White House and the halls of Congress. Let us start with budgeting from the bottom up. The mid level program manager will start the process, and his/her motives may be quite complicated. The manager will assume that one of the prime motives for his superiors will be to appear fiscally prudent, and thus, each will "cut" some funding to appear to demonstrate such prudence. Thus, the middle manager will almost certainly inflate his/her initial estimates to neutralize the anticipated cuts. Some may not actually <u>know</u> what the program will cost because of inflation and the crafty managers of program recipient organizations. It may be the desire of managers to portray the program as a "success" by portraying the need for more money to support success. These earnest budget offerings are then passed upward through two channels; first, the line of command from boss to boss; and then through a "Budget Office" and other staff reviewers, whose roles are to be suspicious and negative.

In general, two criteria are important. One hopefully seeks to put the available money into the program elements that will have real impact and value. Second is to put the money where it will create the most political satisfaction. Agency budgets are advanced to the President through the Office of Managemnt and Budget (OMB) which plays several roles. First, it collects and consolidates the budgets from all of the agencies and forges them into something called "The President's Budget". In this process, OMB will conduct a content evaluation of each agency budget, hoping to squeeze out the trash, threaten the gamers, sustain the important and vital budget needs, and strike the "right" balance between the managerially desirable and the politically feasible. OMB issues budget guidance at the start of each budget cycle that defines presidential goals, objectives, targets, and inhibitions. OMB works for the presidency, not for the agencies or for Congress. In recent years, its role has been extended to give more attention to achieving government-wide encouragement of high quality management as a means for maximizing budget effectivenes. At the same time, it has been made more of a political instrument, pushing and often defining political control of budget allocation.

The President and OMB prepare the President's Budget which is submitted to the appropriations committees of the Congress, and here another reality sinks in. By Constitutional mandate, the federal government budget is ultimately the instrument of the Congress and not just of the President. There is always a titanic clash between the two over the ultimate budget that will emerge. In some years, this conflict has been so great that the presidential budget is said to be "dead on arrival". Conflicts are over policy, interpretations of program effectiveness, special interest political preferment, local government political influence, and the amounts of money (or debt) available for spending. Nobody—absolutely nobody – can predict the final outcome at the end of this dance.

What then would constitute "good" budgeting? One marvelous goal would be a whole major simplification and rationalization of the whole budget structure itself, with hundreds of fewer bits and pieces, more multi-year budgets for known, stable programs, and a deliberate effort to throw out the trash, including repugnant special interest payoffs, notorious earmarking, and the elimination of programs and projects whose legal authorization has expired. What is argued here is the high budget value of effective program management vs. the low value of political bargaining, cunning and payoff.

It seems also clear that it is very important to maintain and even strengthen two critical institutions: the Office of Management and Budget, in the Executive Office of the President; ; and the Government Accountability Office, which is an instrumentality of the Congress. Both represent a critical back pressure within the budget/policy world. Somebody has to say "Not so fast!", or "Prove it!". OMB works for the President, but in the larger and more statesmanlike sense, it really works for the institutional presidency. GAO clearly works for the Congress, but in that more statesmanlike sense, it really works for the legislative branch of government.

12. Another form of financial gaming in government agencies has been the quiet creation of a range of **secret and semi-secret funds** controlled only by some key official. These include slush funds, contingency funds, discretionary funds and emergency funds. But these funds are notorious for their vulnerability to corruption, and special efforts are needed to prevent their creation.

13. **Limits on program benefits.** Populist politics gains its traction not by advocating fiscal prudence, but on being the advocates of "more", and more rewarding public services, and for the expansion and deeping of all programs. Should poor people get more financial subsidy? Of course. Should the elderly receive larger social security payments? Naturally. Should the unemployed be paid larger benefits for longer periods of time? Good deal. Should Medicaid recipients get more care with no co-payments? Sounds good. Should large banks be bailed out? Well -------.

The noted economist Robert Samuelson said in an article in the Washington Post (Aug 9, 2017) that "There is not enough money to finance all of the things we want. Not enough money in the economy and in the country." This is a constant and eternal conflict not just in America but in all countries and societies around the world. The basic struggle has two parts: the expansion of wealth, and the provision of necessary human services.

If one trys to figure out the score, the U. S. has sort of a tie, and much of he rest of the world is in deep trouble. Perhaps the greatest triumph in these perpetual conflict has been occurring in Asia – in China and to a more limited extent in India where hundreds of milllions of people have been able rise up out of abject poverty, even if only to "poverty".

14. **Program priority setting.** One interesting theory is that of the fixed total budget. That is, the budget for the upcoming fiscal year would have a mandated ceiling total fixed by law. Thus, the budget in total could not add up to more than this fixed total, and it is assumed that this would force one of two courses of action. One would be a uniform cut across the board on all programs to keep the total below the ceiling (dumb approach). The other would be a deliberate program to determine priorities between and among programs with the lowest priority activities either eliminated or drastically reduced (smart approach). When this kind of approach has been attempted in the past, unfortunately they have failed politically. Either governments have chosen the dumb approach or when a budget cap has been enacted, it simply got raised when it began to bite. In short, the limitation idea has been on the dollar amount and not on the program base that causes the dollars to be demanded in the first place.

It is also necessary to realize that, even if the political leadership wanted to institute some significant program of program priority setting, there is absolutely no conceptual framework for doing so. Nobody knows what the groundrules would be for determining priority, and thus, what is needed is a politically valid intellectual framework to be developed for this fascinating possibility.

15. **Government contracts and grants.** Every agency of federal, state, county and city governments is a user of contracts, staring with the most mundane such as the collection of trash, or security

guard services, up to extraordinarily complex contracts for space exploration and weapons system development.

<u>The management of government grants and contracts is probably the single most important arena for the exercise of better government management.</u>

For many governments, the use of contracts may be a matter of choice or a matter of necessity. There has been a long term controversy over those who argue the careful reliance on the utilization of full civil service employees, both as legal protection of the rights and interests of governments and as a skilled and relatively inexpensive source of talent. The counter argument is based on the undoubted fact that there are many goods and services that governments can best obtain from contractor organizations.

In any event, the use of government contracting is so extensive that governments have, of necessity, evolved a whole complete and elaborate set of laws, regulations and managerial systems for selection and management of government contracts. The role of the manager is to contract for the right things, at the right price, and a satisfactory level of performance. Yet there is a vastly disturbing record of the mismanagement of such contracts and the failure to contract with the best bidding company. Then, once under contract, the government can be billed for things not really delivered; for goods and services that are overpriced; for "ghost" workers and activities; for services never delivered; and for plain old fashioned lying and cheating. Both politicians and managers are guilty of these sins.

16. **Contractor supervision.** Once a contractor begins work under the contract, whole new forms of corruption become possible. The work itself can be pathological: shoddy work, substandard materials, failure to perform required work, unwarranted expenses, overstated costs, deliberate cost overruns, and many more failures. Cost may be overstated. The government may be billed "phantom charges" for work or supplies not actually provided. The workforce may be overstated and phantom wages and benefits billed to the government. Work delays may be deliberately created to pump up costs. Management salaries or overhead costs may be

excessive. Unfortunately the contractor may feel that the quality of government oversight is so poor that such illegalities will never be caught. In other cases kickbacks are simply made to public officials to turn a blind eye to such cheating. Government managers and inspectors may not be competent, or may be too few to cover all contracts. Performance is not evaluated, costs are not verified, goods are "lost" or stolen, and accounts are not audited. Where a contractor is caught in an illegal or improper act, the overseeing government official may be bribed or coerced to ignore the fact. Even the protections of auditors or inspectors may be frustrated through bribes or political pressure. Just because some activities are performed under contract does not reduce the responsibility of government contract managers for the activities themselves.

17. **Advanced contract forms.** Contracts usually state that the government commits to paying all legitimate costs plus a reasonable fee, fixed in advance. A somewhat more sophisticated approach may be used where the government pays all legitimate costs, plus an award fee which may go up if performance is better than expected. When the government is buying routine things such as office supplies or equipment it may just purchase from the most convenient source, but even here, if the government is purchasing large volumes of material or services, a contract competition is far better. In any event, the government is responsible for spelling out a specific set of rules and regulations that define its relationships with contractors. These rules are different from the rules that govern the government civil service. For example, contracts are not governed by the government's system for determination of employee pay and benefits, but by their own corporate pay system.

18. **Competitive bidding.** The single most effective curb against contract corruption continues to be the mandated use of competitive bidding. A carefully drafted law mandating competition can be used as the basis for defending agency contracting practices, and giving leverage to reformers and those officials in agencies who genuinely want fair and legal contracting to prevail.

But a legislative mandate for competition even if it is achieved, is far from enough. Much depends on the willingness and ability of public officials to implement such laws fairly and free of corruption, and this is not easy. Each agency of government should be required to supplement the law with a carefully defined and published set of procedures for bid competition. All bidders should be made aware of these procedures, and bidders can and should police each other to make sure that the procedures are followed. The reputation of each bidding company can be tested by checking their performance on previous contracts and their financial and management ability to carry out the contract must be evaluated. The initial contractor selection process is critical because it is here that the likelihood of corruption will first manifest itself. If bad public officials and companies seize the contract at this point, it is likely that subsequent operations under the contract will be a constant problem. All contract bids should be subjected to an opaque evaluation process aimed at getting a realistic assessment of bidder capabilities. This evaluation should be open to review, at least for auditors and other bidders to examine. That way, if a selecting official makes a decision that runs counter to the technical evaluation; such an arbitrary selection can be more effectively challenged.

Another significant protection is created when the government has the authority to debar bidders from future contract opportunities if there is evidence of collusion, factual misrepresentation or intent to conceal relevant information. Debarment is an administrative action, and it puts the burden on the alleged offender to upset the decision either by law suit or by appealing for help from political allies who may regard it as dangerous to interfere. Even informally, any rumors or partial evidence of improper bidder practices can be made known to other contracting organizations in both government and the private sector.

Another important way for public officials to protect their position is for the government agency itself to prepare its own estimates of the expected costs for all significant elements of the intended contract. Such estimates should be available at the time of the contract competition so that the government officials have a basis for judging the costs proposed by bidders. This is especially valuable if there is the likelihood that few bids will be received, or that there may be bid rigging collusion among bidders. Substantial variances from the government estimate should be suspect. If the bids are too low, it may signal that the bidder is trying to "buy in" to the contract. If the bids are too high, it may signal that bidders think they can soak the government.

During the performance of each contract, there should be multiple responsibilities. First, the official in charge of the contract must be made clearly responsible for its effective management. This is the first and most important line of defense against impropriety, and no amount of post audit can substitute for it. This responsibility includes real time determination that the demands of the contract are being met, that only authorized work is performed and billed, that all costs are realistic and appropriate, and that costly overruns are avoided. In support of these contract managers may be allies in the agency who will audit, inspect or investigate contractor performance if necessary. Auditing and inspection should be performed constantly and not left to post audits months after the fact. These government oversight systems should extend down to subcontractors or suppliers of the prime contractor. Some form of appeals process is also valuable so that factual disputes can be reconciled, or contractors may appeal what they believe to be improper or incorrect actions by contracting officials.

To its credit, the U. S. government in its official roles has always taken this series of contract problems seriously, and it maintains a generally effective range of official mechanisms to press for effective contract supervision. Compared to about 120 other governments, ours is a model of rectitude. If there is an arena where better performance is needed, it is in the ability of the government to ferret out full understanding of contractor costs to permit a more forceful detection of excessive costs beyond reality, or the billing of improper costs, the inventions of "ghost" charges, or simple thievery. The government seems to need to consult some housewives to learn how to shop – meaning to purchase the goods or services that are the most value for money, and not those that are merely lazy or convenient.

19. **Less is better.** Governments have several means for providing funds for its programs, and there are some striking financial differences between them. The most expensive tends to be the grant-in-aid which is simply a gift of money. Hundreds of such grants are made, and they may be what is called categorical

grants which are paid for specific purposes or they may be block or formula grants which are paid, usually to local governments based on some statistical factors such as population, or population density or citizen income.

The next most expensive financing approach is for the government to lay out money through a budget line item. The advantage here is that the government can exert greater control over how the money is used, beyond the grant where there is usually no recourse. When the government pays out money through its budget, it may set some terms and conditions for how the money is used. It also has a greater ability to stop the flow of funds if it perceives that the flow of funds is being misused.

Next up the scale is the government loan. Here, the government fully expects that these loans will be repaid so that a valid public purpose has been achieved, but the government can recover at least some of its funding.

The least expensive funding alternative is for the government to provide not a loan but the guarantee of a loan between a government supported borrower and its own lending institution. Such loan guarantees have been used extensively for farmers and agribusiness, and for million of student university loans.

It is absolutely possible for governments to push its program financing up this scale of frugality. Grants can be converted into budget funded contracts. Budget line items can be shifted to loans. Loans can be restructured to guarantees. Some of this has been done, but as usual, any really substantial shift would depend on the ability of the politicl leadership to bite some bullets.

20. **Limits on program benefits.** Populist politics gains its traction not by advocating fiscal prudence, but by being advocates of more and more rewarding public services and funding. Should poor people get more financial subsidy? Of course. Should the elderly receive larger social security payments? Naturally. Should the unemployed be paid larger benefits for longer periods of time? Good deal. Should Medicaid recipients get more care with no co-payments? Sounds good!

The noted economist Robert Samuelson said in an article in the Washington Post (August 9, 2017) that "There is not enough money anywhere to finance all of the things we want". Not enough money in the economy and in the country. This is a constant and eternal conflict, not just in America but in countries and societies all over the world. The basic struggle has two points: the extension of wealth, and the satisfaction of human needs and wants.

If one tries to figure out the score in this contest, the U. S. has sort of a tie, and much of th rest of the world is in deep trouble. Perhaps the greatest triumph in this perpetual conflict has been occurring in Asia – in China and to a more limited extent in India. In China, the proportion of the population in absolute poverty has fallen from more than 50% in 1978 to about 25% in the early 80s and 8% in 1997 (official government figures). Those under the next higher poverty level definition are about 25% compared to 65% in the 80s. The Chinese maintain that they have raised more than 200 million people out of "abject" poverty since 1978. It is true that removal from such abject poverty is a modern day miracle, supposedly leaving China with just 28 million in this lowest poverty condition. However, it has to be noted that the definition of "abject poverty" as defined by the UN is less than $1 per day, and that the Chinese standard is just $.66 per day. If the UN standard is used, China would still have 200 million in abject poverty. Nor is it true that those out of abject poverty have escaped poverty itself. Yet – the Chinese miracle is real and important.

This pattern of the success of economic development began in Europe in the Industrial Revolution and it continues today. There are perhaps 100 countries that, right now, are in such debilitating economic condition that their governments cannot (or will not) provide adequate levels of vital social services and public infrastructure. After WW II, the nations of the world were heavily involved in two arenas; the emergence, world-wide, of State Socialist governance which was promised to make miraculous economic advances; and a new structure of internationalized multi-nation political and economic institutions that would spread the wealth in the form of aid and loans to under developed countries. Supposedly, a third wave existed in the form of the Soviet political bloc which also sought to galvanize socialist governments in the bloc; but flawed policies produced more economic constriction and deterioration than expansion and enlargement.

In any event, both the miracles of State Socialism and Internationalism proved illusory. Good has been done. Some successes have been registered. But the total weight of achievement was never close to meeting even basic levels of development. State Socialism has been a sobering recognition of wrongness and incompetence, and most socialist countries have had to shift, however, reluctantly, to more of a private sector, competition based economy. Thus, the Socialist world of government subsidy and largess has increasingly been in retreat. But the general enthusiasm for government provided goods and services remains unabated.

21. **The failure of fail safe systems.** Goverments are tempting targets for every kind of malfeasance and misfeasance ever conceived, and it seems that the more extensive and complex the government is, the more vulnerable it becomes. Every government acknowledges theswe problems and says that they have taken stern measures to protect themselves. But even in the relatively efficient government of the U. S., it seems true that the government's "fail-safe" protections routinely fail. The government takes the following measures:

    a. It empowers managers with real authority to guard the proper execution of their programs, and to take strong measures to stop improper actions.

    b. Up the chain of command, agency heads have further broader powers to detect and stop improper practices.

    c. Most agencies have substantial offices full of auditors with the power to examine every action within the agency.

    d. Agencies also have inspectors – even Inspectors General – who are more like detectives and have authority beyond that of auditors to investigate suspicious activity.

    e. Laws are written and contracts are utilize which give the government adequate leverage to scrutinize any activity of government contractors and grantees that they suspect to be acting improperly or illegally.

f. In many cases, where program performance is intergovernmental, there are layers of federal auditors, state auditors, county auditors, city auditors, and auditors of their own schools or hospitals or bus operators.

g. Both the President and the Congress have special powers of oversight, investigation and prosecution.

And yet ------ these fail-safe systems repeatedly fail. Why?

There are a number of serious ethical dilemmas that contribute to this failure. To begin with, both managers and their political leaders may not want any failure to be known because it may be <u>their</u> failure revealed. In some countries, this motive is so strong that audit and inspection staffs are mostly weak, under funded and under staffed. In some cases political pressures are brought to bear to prevent the investigation of organizations under political protection. Many contractors become so powerful that they become formidible political forces themselves, and can intimidate and fend off government oversight managers and auditors.

It is also true that the definition of improper action is a little slippery. In the relationship between a government agency and its contractors, some contractors will see if they can beat the system and get away with it. The government may for example be over charged or billed for work not actually performed. If the government manager is too dumb to catch the action, it is enthusiastically repeated. Contractors may literally not see this sort of practices as "corrupt", but instead as good sharp business. Nor are state or city agencies reluctant to see whether they can beat the feds.

It seem increasingly apparent that the principal protection of government activities – it huge and expensive cadres of auditors – is not stopping improper attacks. Auditing is almost always "after-the-fact". It audits activities many months after the action where the money and the malefactors are both long gone. The reality seems to be that there is little political or managerial interest in beating dead horses. This perception once again highlights the role of the program manager who has both the responsibility and the power to prevent improper practices in real time, or even if they are about to happen. This kind of real time control extends all the way from petty theft to major policy problems.

There are many brazen beneficiaries who are willing to beat the system: heath care recipients who are not ill; recipients of unemployment compensation who could be working; people on food stamps who hold jobs; students who deliberately refuse to repay student loans, etc. etc. Program management protections against such practices should be constantly emphasized and supported as one of the most important roles of the public manager. And it should be made clear that no political interference should ever be allowed to prevent this responsibility.

22. **Government facilities management.** It is almost impossible to comprehend the formidible range and variety of the physical facilities and equipment owned and managed bygovenments. There are thousands of military bases and facilities, police barracks and stations, hospitals, school buildings and government offices. Apparently, nobody really knows how many facilities there are, or how many people are needed to staff and manage them or what all of this costs.

What is certain is that these numbers would be enormous; it is also certain that, whether they are well or poorly managed, they can make a difference of hundreds of billions of dollars in the costs of American governance. And it is also certain that human beings being human, not everything is perfectly managed. To begin with, governments are under constant pressure coming from sources to provide "more". These pressures come from the general public, pushy politicians and crafty special interest organizations. This then created the old traditional dilemmas: when does the oblgation of government reach their limit? When is enough enough? There ought to be more real sources of leverage within governments that constantly seek to prevent the existance of unneeded facilities, unwarranted program expanses, fatal obsolesence, or serious mismanagement.

Another puzzling dilemma in the world of facilities management is the fact that, while some facilities are over done, others are curiously underfunded. There are thousands of examples cited across the country of facilities that break down, lack needed repair, and modernizations and upgradings that are technically feasible but never get undertaken. Often, it is shortage of funds that precipitate these mistakes, but it is hard to explain why these vital, cost-effective funds are not provided. All too often, the fault lies in political cowardice: the lack of political courage to increase public taxes to cover these needs. Threatening political demands to keep open unjustifed facilities in Congressional districts are pressed to prevent employment reduction among constituents.

Then, of course, there are the old traditional problems of <u>bad management.</u>

23. **<u>Untaped assets.</u>** Throughout the huge complex of government facilities dealt with above, there are countless ways in which the government can utilize these assets to generate income. The natural resources agencies such as the National Park Service, the Bureau of Land Management and the Department of Agriculture are managers of mammoth tracts of land, and a great deal of it is scenic or useful or both. The particular issue of land management is heavily overlaid with national policies and concerns about protection of the environment. Lands with enormous economic potential such as areas rich in oil or gas or iron ore or uranium are not allowed for development because of concerns about the invironment. Yet in moderate minds, there would be little wrong to lease out public lands for minerals development or animal raising or for crop production or tourism, or other benign purposes, and these uses need not be any real threat to the environment if properly deployed and managed.

In the Department of Defense, and also in many other federal agencies, that are whole facilities that are either redundant or that possess some possibility to be leased out to outside payer sources. If a facility is, let us say, 75% unneeded, there is the high likelihood that the facility could be closed and rest could be transferred to another government facility, thus saving a lot of marginal funding.

In some cases, goods and services that the government provides for itself could be offered for sale to the public. Access to national parks are sold to tourists. Governments public thousands of books, brochures and technical publications, especially through the Government Printing Office. Tons of technical material have been generated for farmers and food processors by the United States Department of Agriculture. In some cases, the government sells some vital service, and if it is a highly provider it will have customers. A good example is the role of the U. S. Coast Guard ice breakers in breaking through lanes for commercial vessels in the Great Lakes.

24. **Legitimate government roles.** Start a new attitude and a new wave: subject each public program or proposed law creating a program against the question "is this really a government responsibility?" This kind of acid test must be applied with respect to any proposed legislation creating or expanding some government program. The special interests will strongly oppose any denial or retrenchment; here is where common sense and courage are very seriously needed.

25. **Vote buying.** Most governments including those of the United States indulge in the practice of paying out huge public subsidies to curry favor with voters and to "buy"votes. But part of the problem is that almost every such payment usually does have some public value. But it should be argued that such value can and should be provided outside of the largesse of the government. This practice must somehow be curtailed.

26. **Public perceptions.** U. S. interests both public and private must develop and vigorously pursue a program to reduce demands on the public budget. Address Each line item in the budget can be addressed and some determination made as to how the program can be pared down to eliminate marginal beneficiaries and concentrate available funds on those with greatest legitimate needs. Also, a strong campaign can be launched to cut back the rewards to special interests in the budget.

27. **Program decay.** Eliminate/reduce programs that are obsolete, unnecessary, ineffective, unnecessary, too costly, of low value or duplicative. Eliminate small "drop in the bucket" grants, especially those that are merely political payoffs.

28. **More penetrating analysis.** Subject every program to alternatives analysis, cost-benefit analysis, and cost-effectiveness analysis, and force political leadership to justify keeping programs that fail these tests. Require that the results of such evaluations be made public (and incorporated into legislative records). Require that every new proposed law have both an alternatives analysis and a cost-benefit analysis prepared in advance of approval. Develop and insist on the use of uniform accounting standards and practices for all government activities.

29. **Program eligibility.** Increase the statutory age, or other eligibility factor which triggers eligibility for a government program. The world is constantly evolving and the government should take advantage of positive tides to reap whatever benefits accrue from then changes.

30. **Spending freeze.** In order to reduce an excessive budget, the government could exercise one or two governement-wide systemic options: it could force across-the-board cuts for every agency; or it could solicit voluntary budget cutting proposals from each agency. Subsequent failure to meet voluntary target cuts could then precipitate mandatory forced cuts. In any event, no agency budget should go unchallenged. There must be an independent budget review organization to scrutinize both budget formulation and budget execution.

Right now, at the federal level and at many state levels, this function is provided by an Office of Management and Budget (OMB) and it is imperative that such agencies have real and substantial powers to challenge budget content. It is very disturbing to realize that the federal OMB is seen as increasingly simply a loyal element of the President's troops, and less of an honest assessor of budget validity.

31. Make greater use of **user fees**. That is, the ability of governments to charge users for the use of public programs and facilities. One typical example is to charge visitors to public parks a small

fee. Another more expensive example is charging for the use of communications channels mandated and managed by the government.

32. **Cheaper funding options.** Design programs to use loan guarantees which may not lead to costs and are thus preferable than grants, which in turn are cheaper by far than "forever" direct budget expenditures. Similarly, **fixed price contracting** is better than cost plus contracting. In some cases, incentive contracts can be designed to produce even more superior results.

33. **Grants** are gifts of money, but many grants can be designed to give the government some of the same controls as contracts. In addition, many intergovernmental programs involve sharing of costs between levels of government. Some federal grants for example are "80/20" sharing of costs with state governments. In addition, it may be very important for the federal government to require what is known as "maintenance of effort", which means that local governments may not be allowed to substitute federal money for local money, thus not increasing the total amount of funding available.

34. Reduce the number and range of **government insurance programs**, especially in the face of a lot of problems where those insured plan to stick it to the government.

35. **Privatize** government run programs that can be done better or cheaper by the private sector. This requires a formal and very sophisticated type of cost analysis; and of course, it coult be argued in the other direction – to substitute civil service performance for contractor performance.

36. **Reduce free loading in health care**. There are far too many people who are skilled at cheating some part of the enormous and ill guarded health care system.

37. All programs should be pursued at the **optimum pace;** allowing them to be strung out just adds to ultimate cost. DOD weapons systems projects have a bad reputation for stringing out the completion of projects, and to stay on the public contract roles as long as possible.

38. **Reduce rent seeking** opportunities in government budgets, and all forms of improper favoritism, preferment and fake subsidy payments.

39. The **civil service personnel system** is a valuable and relatively effective system at all levels of government to manage millions of public employee posessing a remarkable range of skills. But there are always employees who are ineffective or troublesome, and under present rules, they are very hard to remove, especially if they are union members. Governments should be given special new authority to terminate the employment of employees that perform poorly. But at the same time, there should be a confidential system whereby civil servants can propose reforms in programs and budgets. Now, few career employees feel it is safe to propose improvements for fear of political risks. And the careerists in government should vigorously defend their own worth, even if that means distancing themselves from political domination and coercion.

40. **Human resources management.** In addition to reforms of the personnel system, more attention needs to be paid to the workers themselves. There has been too much neglect of the development of employee skills, frequently excused by allegations of lack of funds, but in fact a dilemma caused by poor management. Automation has reduced the staffing needs of offices just as it has on factory production lines, and often, the government has been slow to get rid of obsolete paper-related jobs and shift to computer based operations. Some agencies still operate like a world of clerks, and need to move up to the reality of offices of skilled and sophisticated people who create and produce.

41. **Structural reform.** Every government agency should be required to eliminate programs of organizational overlap, duplication, redundancy, obsolesence and those that are simply "high cost-low value" programs. It is recognized that it will often be necessary to seek political acceptance of such retrenchments. Politicians must have a workable way to break old commitments, and free themselves to consider change. Lobbying groups must be educated to consider the general public interest and not just their own prejudiced self interest. Members of special interest groups who think they are representing "the public interest" must realize that the stout defense of their own interests may not really benefit the general American public.

42. **Freezes.** Governments may employ temporary freezes of government program deployments, government employee raises, or letting of government contracts. But such freezes must not be forever.

In short, it seems highly likely that governments that become more entrepreneurial and innovative in marketing their capabilities could be more productive and more interesting generators of revenue. As the potentials listed above invite is more moderation, common sense and courage.

VI. THE POWER TO REGULATE

═══════════★═★═★═══════════

T HE U. S. CODE of Federal Regulation has 50 huge chapters, and
now contains an overwhelming 178,000 pages. The official power
to regulate is almost boundless; the potential for abuse is great. There
is almost nothing in American society or the national economy that is
beyond the range of government regulation. At their best, regulations are
valuable protections. At their worst, they are threats to freedom, highly
costly, and sources for public corruption and oppression.

The power to regulate must therefore be broadly and continuously
monitored against serious stardards of morality, common sense and
moderation. Somehow, that which needs regulation will be dealt with,
but not beyond the limits of need, along the following lines:

1. It is unsettling to recognize that there is almost **no practical or
   intellectual definition of the legitimate power of government**.
   Thus, there is an urgent need to define the parameters of acceptable
   regulation in general and on hundreds of case-by-case examples.

2. There is such a thing as "**the regulatory mind**". That is, those
   who have the power to create and enforce regulations believe
   it is their obligation to see to it that a basic regulation must be
   broadened and deepened and made more forceful. The regulators
   must somehow develop a more realistic sense of when to stop.

3. Part of this syndrome is the distinct possibility that such
   extrapolations carry to nature of a regulation **beyond its legal
   intent**, in fact, creating new law by administrative interpretation.

4. It is unfortunately true that regulations are one of the most powerful tools for **government oppression**. This oppression may be merely the tyranny of petty power, but in governments around the world, regulatory power has been used as deliberate forces for far more serious tyranny. The best form of prevention is against the creation of such power, and it must be applied by the whole population from the bottom up.

5. **Irrational regulatory overburden.** In his book "The Rule of Nobody", Philip K. Howard cites a disturbing report by Common Good about all of the laws and regulations effecting a school in the school system of New York city. "Literally thousands of rules, emanating from every level of government, dictate actions by people who are supposedly spending their time educating America's youth. Disciplining a student potentially requires sixty-six separate steps, including several layers of potential appeals. Organizing an athletic evernt could require almost a hundred steps. Bureaucratic forms and requirements are everywhere. Firing a teacher who is inept, or mean-spirited, or burned out, is basically impossble. All these legal requirements, weighing heavily upon principals and teachers, could fill a law library: due process, special education, zero tolerance, No Child Left Behind, tenure, work rules, student rights, privacy rules – to name just a few."

6. Another form of rational protection is to press much more vigorously against the **open ended nature** of regulatory power. There must be better answers to the basic question of when enough is enough.

7. In the United States, there has been a long tradition of **private companies regulating themselves**. Companies have auditing companies auditing their books and records. There are corporate policies designed to protect the interests of the company's customers. There are policies defining and protecting the quality, safety and reliability of company goods and services. This kind of institutional protection is a perfectly sound alternative to the

concept that only the government can and should protect the public.

8. Again, the dilemma of special interest politics raises its ugly head. If some organization can work the political or bureaucratic system for benefits and **special preferment**, it can work the system to aviod government regulation. Thus, regulatory enforcement is part of the broader and far more vexing problem of the avoidance of perverse special interest politics.

9. Again, Philip K. Howard anguishes over another example of bad public politics. "Public unions made it to the headlines in 2010 when sweet-heart pensions negotiated over the years effectively bankrupted a number of states and municipalities. **Political deals with public unions** resulted in laws that allowed public safety workers to retire in their forties, with pensions "spiked" by overtime payments in their final year, so that workers could retire with nearly full pay. In some cases, public workers were rehired by governments the next day, so they were paid double. There is no rime or reason to all of the laws and contracts for public employment. These benefits and requirements just piled up over the years, as successive union leaders used their political clout to "do something" for union members."

10. When one tries to delve into the utterly horrible mass of our **178,000 pages of federal regulations,** it is obvious that there are hundreds of examples of serious wastage caused by the overlap, duplication and even conflict between regulations from different sources. Several agencies may issue regulations dealing with health care, or environmental protection. Hundreds of regulations are duplicated by numbers of agencies at the federal level matched by hundreds of regulations at the state level, or the county level, or the city level. This bureaucratic mess is not only highly expensive, it is highly dysfunctional. There needs to be a new introduction to the strange concept of "simplification".

11. But still – there is the necessity to **keep up.** A recent GAO report pointed out the needs to inspect more foreign drug manufacturing facilities, require better reporting of drug companies on the sale and use of antibiotivd, and develop a strategy to address the use of opiods.

12. One of the adverse features of most regulations is the fact that, once enacted, each tends to be "**forever**", since it seems almost impossible politically to terminate a regulation even if it is admitted to be useless, or obsolete, or dysfunctional. So a powerful idea is that of seeking to enact regulations with fixed lifespans such as five or ten years. The impact of the regulation can be evaluated; the successful ones can be renewed; the failures can be allowed to lapse.

13. As an element of this evaluation, the results can and should be **disclosed to the public,** so that there is at least the possibility that public opposition would embolden timid or cowardly politicians to do the right thing.

14. There is the eternal problem of "**selective" regulatory enforcement**. That is, within a broad and ill defined regulatory arena, it is possible for government officials to fail to enforce provisions that might harm their friends and to push power hard against the unfavored. Regulations usually cost money to comply, so noncompliance can be profitable, and profits can be split with government regulators. Once again, governments need to do far more to evaluate the impact and consequences of their regulations, and to make the results of such evaluations more publicly visible.

15. **The tyranny of compliance costs.** If you are a small business owner, or the manager of some business enterprise, you are certain to view the thousands of pages of federal regulations with fear an loathing. And many individual citizens in some element of their lives also are overwhelmed by the bureaucratic oppression demanded by their governments. This is an argument beyond the question

of whether regulations are needed and proper. It is the question over the costs imposed by the demands for compliance. Large businesses can afford (reluctantly) to hire additional accountants, office staff and expensive lawyers to cope with such demands, but small businesses and individuals cannot. It is perfectly possible for most government agencies to so structure their regulatory demands so that they place only reasonable demands on their "customers". Why are their thousands of stories out there about outrageous demands for compliances, patterns of wretched excess, attitudes of bureaucratic oppression and attack? Any program aimed at regulatory reform should address these issues as one of the mandatory, desirable and constructive objectives of reform.

VII. THE WAR AGAINST CORRUPTION

★ ═ ★ ═ ★

ORRUPTION IS SO UNIVERSAL and so rewarding that if it is serious policy to stamp it out, or at least to reduce it, a whole equally universal and powerful war must be fought against it, including the following types of battles:

1. Horribly, the nature of "corruption" has changed for the worse, going beyond hustling for money to the far more dangerous **movement for terrorism**. Terrorism may be driven by religious passion or cultural zealousness, or political populism, or simple urge for power and the will to oppress. It may now be the most serious role of many governments around the world to deal with these terrorist threats. These threats may be political, economic, territorial, cultural or religious, and many of the threats are transnational in nature. In any event, every government, including the American government must now learn how to protect themselves, the institutions of governance, and the safety and well being of its citizens against this monsterous threat.

2. Much more **stringent controls** are needed over the accounting of government funds and the activities upon which they are spent. The government should always demand a full accounting of all government sources of income, and should require all expenditures to be authorized by law and adequately documented and reported. The number of officials who can approve expenditures should be carefully limited, and their should be a second review and approval process for the actual disbursement of funds. Agency

heads and line supervisors must be held accountable for the actions of their subordinates (gee, I never knew!), and for the actions of government contractors. The fact that a contractor is fully in charge of the performance under the contract does not permit the supervising government official to say "not my fault".

3. Every effort should be made to make it possible for **individual citizens to criticize elements of government** activity which they see as improper or incompetent; and they deserve a system where somebody actually listens to them and does something about their concerns. It is well known that some of the most valuable ideas for the improvement of government performance have come from such citizen assessments. This is already happening; the overpowering range of social media systems has given citizens a powerful new means to express their concerns — if anybody is really listening.

4. Politicians must have a workable way to **break old commitments**, and free themselves to consider change. Many groups which purport to represent the public interest are really only self-serving. Lobbying groups must be educated to consider the general public interest and not just their own prejudiced self interest. Members of all special interest groups must receive this same kind of education. Sometimes, this point seems hopeless. The whole political world is driven by these special interests. Some of them are corrupt, but even if they are properly pursued, they distort the value of taxpayer payments to "their" government.

5. As an adjunct to this argument is the old argument that politicians in both the legislative and executive branchs of governments at all levels should be required to **make public the extent that they are catering to some special interest,** sponsoring bills at the request of special interest organizations, or proposing budget items, taxes, regulations or other measures intended to serve some special interest. Lots of luck!

6. The **careerists in government should defend their own worth**, even if that means separating themselves from political domination and coercion. But it is also incumbent on them to perform at the highest and most effective level as their obligation to the American public. Too many offices in governments and merely bureaucratic treadmills. But this sense of professional responsibility should extend to sturdy resistance to nepotism in hiring, and the employment of relatives and others who are not qualified, or do little real work.

7. Provide a confidential system whereby **civil servants can propose reforms** in budget items. Now, few career employees feel willing to propose improvements for fear of political risks.

8. Regulation tends to be forever, and too many regulations seriously inhibit people's initiative and freedom of action. Any draft law conveying new or expanded regulatory power must be **challenged as to necessity**, relevance, plus/minus impact assessments and cost-benefit value. Nobody seems to really understand the direct and indirect costs of enforcing any regulation, in part because, politically, it is unpopular to ask.

9. **Internal auditors** and investigators must be given strong, unbridled authority within agencies to demand an/all information and data. There should be no element of any government organization that is not subject to audit and investigation. This authority should extend to political appointees in terms of their actions and their own personal finances. One of the most serious problems in the present system is that internal auditing and some investigation is very much "after the fact" – audits are conducted months after actual performance, and the money and the malefactors are usually long gone.

10. **Incentives.** It might be very effective if governments could devise and utilize more various and effective forms of incentives to get people to report corrupt violations.

11. In order to **reduce an excessive budget**, the government could exercise one or two government-side systemic options: it could – force across-the-board cuts for every agency; or it could solicit voluntary budget cutting proposals for each agency. Subsequent failure to meet voluntary cut targets could then precipitate mandatory forced cuts. In any event, no agency budget should go unchallenged. There must be an independent budget review organization to scrutinze both budget formulation and budget execution.

12. **Control regulatory capture**. What this means is that many organizations that are subject to government regulation and partial control will fight back by developing their own set of political connections and allies, and sometimes, their political strength can exceed that of their regulators. Thus, the regulated can "capture" the nature and enforcement of the regulations that are supposed to control them, and reduce or eliminate their impact.

13. **Abolish agency slush funds,** contingency funds, discretionary funds, and secret funds. The real point here is that there is an unsavory record of "raids" on such funds where, because of lack of responsible control, money gets arrogantly misappropriated, or is simply made to disappear.

14. Reduce the federal government involvement in activities that should be the responsibility of state/local government. **Eliminate federal funding for funds that should be supplied by local governments**. All of these ideas for budget cutting apply equally to state or municipal governments.

15. Require all agencies of government to engage in some form of **long range strategic planning** and program implementation planning, which can be used to identify future problems and opportunities and direct resources to them in an optimum manner.

16. It cannot be overemphasized: The most vulnerable element of government is its thousands of contracts. There must be mandatory

insistance on competition as the vehicle for contractor selection, excusedonly when it can be shown that there is only one viable contractor available. Very close control should be exercised over **government contracts** to prevent improper charges, "ghost" staffing, excessive costs, timely performance, and full compliance with government requirements and specifications. Any multi-year contractor should be required to have performance strategies and plans. The concern extends to situations where the government is leasing or selling land or granting some public authority.

17. Penalize those who **ignore public regulations**, deliberately or inadvertently.

18. Develop and insist on the use of **uniform accounting standards** and practices for all government activities.

19. The nature of many laws is that they are vague, loose, ill defined and often toothless. **The laws themselves must be made more effective and compelling.**

Tighter restrictions must be applied in cases of conflict of interest, nepotism and egregious examples of unwarranted preferment. Ant-kickback laws must be made more defining and more seriously enforced. Punishments must be so substantial that they really do deter.

20. Part of this renewed examination of the validity of the legal base is the concern that any law, once passed, is so difficult to repeal or even revise, and thus it becomes "eternal". It may be necessary to devise a form of legal approach where **laws are enacted deliberately for a limited period of time,** such as five years. This would force the law's reenactment, and it provides an opportunity to amend it or eliminate it if reality warrants it.

21. There are some **criminal activities** such as narcotics addiction or smuggling or arms trafficking or illegal alien entry that are local in impact but so widespread and overwhelming that they demand

national solutions and thus serious national government measures to prevent these forms of corruption

22. **<u>Get the top people.</u>** Finally, recognize the ancient reality: If the top people steal big, the lower level people feel entitled to steal small. If the top leadership is corrupt, it emboldens and seems to justify corruption at lower levels in the organization, and leads to secret, careful corrupt alliances and self protections from top to bottom.

VIII. REFORMS IN INTERNATIONAL
PROGRAMS

THERE ARE MAJOR POTENTIALS for cutting costs and improving payoff along the following lines:

1. Support for international organizations have often proved to be money well spent. But too much of that money has been wasted by being **invested in failures,** or "disappeared" by official crooks. Efforts must be made to guard funds more carefully.

2. Nations linked in these international organizations must not shirk their financial obligations, or simply let the **U. S. carry too much of the burden**. The U. S. government can legitimately insist on some fair sharing of all costs – and on insistence that other obligated nations actually come up with the money.

3. A careful and realistic limit must be defined for American responsibilities for all of the problems of the world. The U. S. cannot be expected to be **"the policeman of the world".** We cannot allow our country to be branded as uncaring or inhumane because we are not solving all of the world's political problems.

4. Similarly, a realistic limit must be defined for American responsiblities for social services shortcomings around the world. We cannot be expected to be **"the social services agent" for the world**, nor can we allow ourselves to be branded as cruel

and uncaring because we have not solved all of the world's social problems.

5. There is a quiet concern that too many of these **international organizations have become excessively overblown and bureaucratic** and thus financially wasteful, and some serious effort seems warranted to streamline and upgrade organizational productivity and efficiency.

6. National compliance with most directives coming out of these international organizations is usually voluntary on the part of each member country, and even the worst governments in the world enthusiastically endorse agreements and understandings with which they have absolutely no intention of implementing. Accordingly, many government pledge to provide funding, but the money never arrives. It is very difficult to envision how greater compliance can be achieved, but it is clear that more powerful leverage is needed to **make governments stand and deliver.**

7. Getting into conflict situations is easy. **Getting out is hard**. The U. S. and the U. N. still find themselves embedded in other countries for decades at a time. The UN has been embedded in major rescue programs in Afghanistan, Burundi, the Central African Republic, Cote D'Ivoire, the Democratic Republic of Congo, Kenya, Liberia, Mali, S. Sudan, Sudan. If it is clear that any such intervention is not accomplishing its purposes, then a means should be devised to permit withdrawal. The next big problem of this kind already exists in Afghanistan.

8. The same line of reasoning applies to any number of **internationally provided or financed social services.** The U. N. for example has been operating housing centers in the Gaza Strip for more than 60 years. Again, it is not clear how many of these commitments could be withdrawn because of the almost inevitable humanist damage, but certainly rationalization will not happen if there is no courage to try.

9. There is now a growing need to understand the sources of the formation and **support of terrorist organizations**, and to determine better means for international organizations to combat them. Part of the sensitivity stems from the fact that many terroristss and terror organizations are advocated and supported by Muslim religious leaders and religious schools. Yet, many Muslim governments have stepped up to this dilemma and are now acting to restrict such activities where they are demonstrably illegal and immoral. Thus, it might most logicallly be Muslim governments that will lead the efforts of international organizations to deal with these threats.

10. Unfortunately, a significant number of **aid programs prove to be unsuccessful**, ineffective, of low impact or seriously mismanaged. Aid organizations hesitate to close down these failures because of the desire to avoid accusations of abandonment, or embarassment over their own failures. It should be possible with better leadership to continue to deliver the good programs, but to have the courage to cut out the losers and reinvest the money more productively.

11. It would be wise and productive for the U. S. government and the many international organizations to draw back from the unfortunate tendency to be locked into political populism, and to start practicing the sciences of outcome evaluation, priority setting, productivity enhancement, and other forms of that strange majic called "management".

12. Similarly, there is a disturbing realization that because there are so many bad governments in the world, a lot of money has been given that has been provided for some worthy purpose has ultimately had the effect of **buttressing tyrants** and crooks. Thus, the needy get little and centrist elites get rich. One course of action might simply to be to stop the money flow, and this has increasingly been done, but a second and more rewarding option has become available. Instead of giving funds to suspect government agencies, the funds are being invested in the work of a new wave of

non-government organizations – NGOs – which have a far more acceptable record of responsible service. The World Association of Non Government Organizations (WANGO) lists an astounding number of active NGOs now functioning in 120 countries around the world including the following:

Aging
Agriculture and food choices
Animal health and rights
Business/economic development
Children and youth
Communications and media services
Conflict resolution
Education – primary and university
Environmentalism
Health and nutrition
Human relations
International organizations
Internet services
Laws and legal affairs
Peace and security
Population and human settlement
Refugees and immigration
Relief services
Religion and ethics
Science and technology
Sports and recreation
Trade
Transport
Women's status and issues.

It should be noted that, while most of these NGOs are foreign to the countries in which they operate, a growing number are emerging as native enterprises. There is an innocent assumption that all NGOs will act nobly. But many represent special interests, "causes" for which they are implacable advocates;

13. **Credibility and burden sharing**. The U. S.benefits in many arenas by helping to forge alliances to take on some of the most demanding international burdens. The Korean War, the Vietnam War, the protection of Europe during the Cold War, the war in Iraq, the war in Syria, and many other crises are genuinely multi-national in their dimensions and consequences. In the Muslim world particularly, there are very intensive attacks against the United States as "the great Satan", and the creator of all problems. While this is more propaganda than fact, it is widely believed. It is therefore to the U. S. advantage to be seen as acting as part of a broader alliance. And indeed, such alliances can produce some real burden sharing and the reduction of American costs and stresses. This has never been more obvious that in the growing world of terrorism.

14. A classic example of the kind of dilemmas the nations of the world are facing is the growing concern about hunger and malnutrition. "Hunger" in its broadest sense ranges from conditions of inadquate nutrition to absolute starvation on a cataclysmic scale. Of the 105 nations categorized earlier as in deep trouble, almost all are also nations experiencing **serious food shortages**. The causes are many: often it is war or insurrection or terrorist conflict that destroys much of the country's food production and distribution system. There are an estimates (somewhat overy pessimestic) that those around the world that are categorized as "hungary" have risento 815 million (UN report), or 11% of the global population. More than half of those affected live in countries suffering from various forms of violent conflict. Absolute famine conditions have existed in South Sudan, Nigeria, Yemen, Syria, Burundi, Cambodia, Chad, China, Democratic Republic of Congo, E. Timor, N. Korea, Myanmar, Nigeria, Niger, Sri Lanka, Sudan, Ukraine, Yemen, and most recently, Venezuela. Some of the food shortages have been of such long duration that whole generations of children are too small, too short, too light and suffering from illness and weakness. By UN estimates, the numbers of those in hunger have increased last year at the fastest pace since the beginning of this century. But

reality has not prevented the UN from issuing as part of its "2030 Agenda for Sustainable Development" the assertion that hunger and malnutrition will be "eradicated" by 2030. How? By whom? Well, by each country, including the 105 in deep trouble, and by the same noble leaders who have caused the problems in the first place. And still – the nations of the world must continue to address these problems. The object is not solution; it is mitigation, and perhaps a clear conscience.

15. And now, the world of international organizations have launched themselves heavily into the growing concerns about global warming, and what are seen as the existential threats of the deteriorating environment. The U. S. attitude is fairly typical: how real is the threat; what should be done about it; what is really possible; what is feasible, including the enormous costs being estimated?

16. A recent study conducted for the Congress by the Atlantic Council points out an opportunity closer to home. It assesses the muddle that exists around the provision of aid to foreign countries in the U. S. government establishment, and it proposes that the State Department confine itself the the policy and diplomatic elements of American diplomacy, and the the Agency for International Development (AID) be made the full provider of assistance operations, and the coordinater of the Defense Department and the 24 other federal agencies now engaged in some form of foreign assistance.

17. Further, the Atlantic Council report details the concern that the State Department itself is no vastly overblown, muddled and confusing, and excessively costly, and it proposes the need for a full blown reorganization and simplification of the whole department.

IX. NATIONAL SECURITY

═══════════════★═★═★═══════════════

Accoding to Robert Gates, former Secretary of Defense, about European military activities in troubled Libya "The mightest military alliance in history is only 11 weeks into an operation against a poorly armed regime in a sparsely populated country. Yet many allies are already beginning to run short of munitions, requiring the U. S. once again to make up the difference." Secretary Gates issued a scathing assessment of American defense priorities, and his recommendations bear repeating in detail He stated:

1. The U. S. should stop thinking – and spending –on **general deterrance** and concentrate on real priority missions and specific tasks, and to shift from old conventional thinking in favor of more modern and realistic patterns of special operations against localized targets by combined and integrated forces.

2. It is increasingly apparent that the nature of military engagement has been changing away from major "world" war to smaller localized "neighborhood" conflict. As a consequence, DOD needs to **change its thinking** toward more small level integrated operations in which military personnel function more like police than heavy duty crushers.

3. The DOD must stop **loving every weapons system** and excessive and redundant capability. Gates cites many examples: the Marine Expeditionary Fighting Vehicle designed for amphibious landings – none of which have been conducted for the last 70 years; more

F-35 fighters (at a cost of over $600 billion) when we already have more than we can use; a next generation attack submarine, when current U. S. subs are beyond attack already; the Medium Air Defense System, which is redundant with the current Patriot systems. After spending $ 130 billion on a ballistic missile defense system, an additional $ 30 billion is simply not needed or justified.

4. Specifically, DOD should drastically cut back the purchase of the **F- 35 Lightning II aircraft.** Current F-15s, 16s and 18s are already the best in the world. "The Chinese M-20 is about at their level, but it is only "modestly" stealthy, especially from behind." The F-35 is justifed because it will be used by all Services, and some will be bought by other countries. But 180 have already been delivered, and each Service has insisted on specially designed versions for its own purposes. It is hard to pin down what the ultimate numbers are expected to be built; numbers as high as + 2400 have been reported. But it is almost certain that the ultimate cost will exceed $ 600 billion. The most recent purchase, for 90 aircraft, is scheduled to cost $8.2 billion.

5. Also, DOD should eliminate the **V-22 Osprey tilt rotor aircraft** program as prohibitively expensive, and the fact that its performance in Iraq and Afghanistn was "not impressive". DOD should also eliminatge the preposterous blimp carried cruise missile surviellance system.

6. Similarly, the military already has a very large inventory of the **Abrams tank** – perhaps the best in the world, but often not fully usable in modern "neighborhood" warfare. Future purchases of these tanks seems questionable.

7. Eleven huge **aircraft carriers**? Three more planned?

8. **Research but not production.** It would be perfectly feasible for the DOD to pursue a revised policy where it continues to undertake weapons systems research and development, so that it continues to have the best weapons systems in the world, but to

avoid taking these weapons into the next step of production unless there is a clear and present need to make them operational. R & D is relatively cheap; production is very expensive.

9. **Inventory control.** Gates bemoans the fact that "current inventories of hundreds of thousands of items are already way beyond forseeable need". Add the fact that other studies have reported that too many military warehouses are duplicating items in the four Services, and these warehouses mainain at great expense weapons no longer used, uniforms no longer issued, boots that nobody now wears, and much else that is useless and obsolete and redundant.

10. This logic extends beyond inventory to **the military bases themselves.** There are hundeds of them. Many of them are flatly unnecessary, and they could be closed and their activities performed elsewhere. Others are obsolete, inefficient, and overly expensive for the results they deliver. Others could be combined and consolidated. Again, where is the zeal and the courage to address these concerns?

11. **Human resources costs.** According to Gates: "human resources costs such as pay, benefits, health care and retirement funding have grown so much that 'they are eating the Defense Department alive'" The level of many benefits are seen as unrealistic. DOD, as much as any element of government, it still mired in a world of bureaucratic paperwork, an enormous and utterly debilitating structure of organizational units of vague and often obsolete activities, endlessly running around in tight little circles. Simplify, thin down, automate.

12. **Enormous bureaucracy.** Unfortuately, DOD is heavily over-organized, starting with the questionable continued need for four separate Services, the seeming inability to produce truly integrated operations, the vast oceans of paperwork and paper shuffling, and concerns about overstaffing and the concequent huge costs

of pay, benefits, and ultimately, retirement costs. And the needs for reform must necessarily extend down to the huge numbers of DOD contractors. The need for reform and restructuring cannot and should not be taken as any repudiation of the crucial role of the U. S. military in the world. Better can also mean more. The need? SMALLER-SIMPLER-CHEAPER.

13. In the past, the American government has, through DOD programs, ended up **funding tyrants, dictators, and official thieves**. Many of these problems were defined and justified by the need to "oppose Communism". That rationalization has now gone away, and it is time for the DOD and the government as a whole to more carefully determine the nature of our "friends".

CONCLUDING THOUGHTS

===★===★===★===

ACCORDING TO THE UNITED Nations, there are196 countries in the world and more than seven billion human beings who are both people and "citizens". Providing effective governance for these countries is probably the most complex and difficult thing that citizens are required to do.

Of these 196 governments, probably half of them are weak and incompetent. A few are vicious and destructive, and almost all of them allow or even encourage corruption. In fact, "corruption" is too weak a concept, and the term "pathological" has been employed to describe those policies or actions of governments that are wrong, destructive, abusive and disastrous to their own people, even though they may be perfectly legal.

We can't create a perfect world. It is false and a delusion to expect governments to produce such perfection — as in the "cradle to grave" delusion of state socialism. Human beings and their affairs are unblievably complicated, incomprehensible in their relationships, inherently in conflict, and impossible to fully manage or control. There will always be people or needs that can't be satisfied. This is not necessarily a pattern of failure — it is just the reflection of reality. Increasingly, diversity has moved from being defined as a "problem" to being one of our national priorities. As one observer put it "Black is a Country."

Our governmental world is endlessly and enormously complex. It is difficult even to try to describe the extraordinary complexity and sophisitication of the American governmental system and its ovewhelming power and impact. It is "wall-to-wall" in the sense that it deals in some manner with every facet of American life. It is multi layered in the sense that there are full systems of government at the national, state, county, city and agency level, highly interrelated and duplicative and often in serious conflict. Almost every element of governance reaches down into every sector of American society and culture, which in turn produces a remarkable array of individual responses and the creation of hundreds of thousands of "bottom up" citizen organizations to deal with the impact of governments for good or ill. Special interest political action by these thousands of organizations is so powerful that it seems to dominate the political system itself. It is always to the advantage of these special interests to lock in their wants into national laws and regulations, rather than fight them out in fifty state governments, or hundreds of cities. And yet, the future of the country is largely centered in these cities, and they should be free and in fact encouraged to function in their own best interersts, and not in partisan politics defined in Washington.

It is a delusion to believe that this incredible mass can ever be "managed" in the sense that it is deliberately planned, directed, controlled and modulated. Nobody – nobody – can even count the hundreds of thousands of laws, regulations, and ministerial processes, nor can anybody comprehend the influence of literally millions of pages of laws, regulations, legal opinons and bureaucratic interpretations and processes, all of which demand to be adminstered and enforced.

Such a system is highly vulnerable to manipulation. Hundreds of interests are burrowing away in the hidden reaches of these laws and regulations to advance their own interests, and some are crooks and cheaters.

Thus, it is a world in which it is always vital to keep seeking new and better means to bring the government more under control, clean it up, deny its excesses, and prevent its mistakes. These means will be most effective if they are "from the bottom up."

Presidents, judges, members of parliaments, lawyers, scholars, political scientists, all tell us that, if governments will only obey "the Rule of Law", then all will be well. Unfortunately, it isn't true. The rule of law is vital, but it is not enough. Everything people hate and fear about governments can be made perfectly legal by the creation of perverse laws, and the mechanisms of governments must then be employed for the enforcement of these bad laws.

It is also true that there is a new and pressing need to restructure major elements of the government structure. For example, within the legitimate range of U. S. security needs, the Department of Defense (DOD) is facing the need to rethink its strategies for the future. Gone of course is the day of the battleship, and perhaps the day of the aircraft carrier, increasingly vulnerable to long range guided nuclear missiles, and probably the days of the 70 ton tanks that can't cross most bridges or maneuver in narrow urban streets; or perhaps the day of the high capability fighter-bombers with few targets they can attack. The threat around the world in about 50 countries is now that strike forces of terrorist groups are concealing themselves among innocent civilians. The modern U. S. infantry soldiers must now act more like the police in order to ferret them out. Nuclear weapons are now irrelevant since no sane leader can order them to be used to obliterate cities and slaughter milllions of innocent civilians.

Further, these international organizations have also gotten heavily involved in many efforts to prevent destructive conflict within and between countries. UN and NATO forces have spent years and lives and funds in intervening in crises in many countries. The United States has, from the beginning, been fully engaged in all of these efforts, and usually, the American government, and U. S. private interests have been the largest and most effective contributors. But this then has encouraged an ominous view of this commitment. Whenever a new crisis breaks out, many voices around the world cry out one of two things: "This is the fault of the Americans!" ; or "What is America going to do about this?" The fear then is that the Americans are being demanded to be "the policeman of the world", and that somehow, dozens of horrible conflicts around the world are our responsibilities.

Far too many governments have fallen into the hands of tyrants and self serving elites for whom power is an end in itself, or who violate their public trust to loot the country for personal advantage. The key to the exercise of such power is the ability to misdirect the laws for pathological purposes. But even short of totalitarianism, the nature of politics is often very corrosive. Politics may be more about power than it is about leadership. The political system, whatever its nature, does not necessarily decide what is necessary or right but only what is easily negotiated. But political negotiation – even when many voices are heard – may produce stalemate rather than resolution. There is a legitimate concern that the UN, NATO, and other international organizations are turgid, ineffectual, and intensely bureaucratic, and that the time has come for some genuine rethinking of its real value. In the words of a well-known Texan saying, is the UN "all hat and no cattle?" The United States has several vital relationships which it aabsolutely must face up to, including China, N. Korea, India, Russia and Vietnam. It is not clear that there is anything that can be "solved". These relationships must be dealt with with courage and moderation, and in concert with a set of allies including a more assertive United Nations.

Another arena of extraordinary change has been occurring in the Muslim world. The tides of independence after WWII and the break-up of the Soviet Union have enabled the emergence of Muslims and Muslim governments around the world. What Muslims really want is peace, security, a solid degree of prosperity, and the ability to lead a good and devout life. What they have all too often gotten is a choice between an oppressive or bumbling government and the prospect of control by some horrible terrorist organization. The solution of these dilemmas lies almost entirely within the Muslim community itself; it cannot be imposed or defined by foreign interests, even at the international level.

The lessons to be learned from these experiences is that,even if American governance avoids dictatorship and authoritarian pathology it may still only rise to the level of weakness or cravenness or incompetent muddle. It is extraordinary how fragile public programs are, and how easily they fall into disrepair. And it is disturbing to see how easily government elements lurch into corruption and pathology and how weak are the supposed defenses against them. Pathologies have stolen or squandered scarce funds, misdirected public programs, bred generations of corrupt officials and ultimately severely damaged government's capacity to function. Nobody knows how to solve these dilemmas. Nobody.

Further, the overwhelming influence of special interests in the political system is something that can be dealt with. The American people do not seem sufficiently aware of the degree to which bottom up representative democracy has been displaced by the domination achieved by the practitioners of special interest politics in our political system. The legitimate interests of people and organizations can be retained, while the whole range of political decision making is brought back into its fundamental role of serving the general population of the country. One of the increasing problems in the American system is the fear that political leadership is locked into Democrat/Republican partisan stalemate, which drives out rational evaluation of our problems. The ruling method for evaluating the performance of their roles is not intelligence, or knowledge, or wisdom, but blind adherence to the Party line.

But in the last analysis, despite its occasional lurches and staggers and its occasional serious mistakes, the performance of govenance in the United States remains among the best in the world. It is one of the most heartwarming aspects of life in the U. S. that the great preponderance of human attitude is goodness and humaneness. Part of this excellence is in our systems of government, but the most crucial influence stems from our exceptional American culture. In so many other countries people live in great fear and under great oppression, and have their homes and businesses destroyed, often by their own governments; and get their money stolen by the government – and get killed by the police and the military.

Americans are blessed by a decent, stable, prosperous country created and maintained by their own common sense and courage It has been the object of this book essentially to say "yes, but even we could be better." Given the tragic record of governments from the top down, it is therefore vital to strengthen the "bottom up" elements of national activity, and at the same time people must maintain strong elements toward resistance to threatening top down authority. The new and growing hope is that decent people and organizations all over the world will increasingly rise up in their own defense and bring a new level of moderation and spirit of aid and service **FROM THE BOTTOM UP** to these failing states which are their homes. Our goals must be a sense of moderation, and the political and cultural ability to set real priorities and limits and to have the courage to live with them.

SOURCES

Country Reports on Terrorism, U. S. Department of State November 2009.

Corruption Perceptions Index 2012, Transparency International

Most Dangerously Polluted Cities, All Countries.org. 2011.

Inequality-adjusted Human Development Index, Human Development Report, 2010.

"A Haven for Malcontents", Economist, July 13, 2013, p. 42

"Africans Let Down by Governments", BBC News, 2004

"The World's Ten Most Authoritarian Leaders", World Policy Journal, Fall, 2012.

'Human Development Report: Five Arab Countries Among Top Leaders in Long Term Development Gains", United Nations Development Programme, November, 2010.

"Miserable and Weak Again", Economist, Nov. 16, 2013.

United States Department of State: National Consortium for the Study of Terrorism and Responses to Terrorism: Annex of Statistical Information, Country Reports on Terrorism, 2012.

"Nasty Neighbourhood", Economist, Aug. 2, 2014, p. 41.

World Development Indicators, "Poverty", 2004.

Chandler, Michael, and Gunaratria, Rohan, "Countering Terrorism: Reaktion Books, 2007.

Lankford, James, Senator. "Federal Fumbles", U. S. Government, U.S. Senate publications, Volumes One and Two.

Diner, Dan, "Lost in the Sacred", Princeton U. Press, 2009.

Boston, Andrew G., Ed., "The Legacy of Jihad", New York, Prometheus Books, 2005.

Ayittey, George B. N., "Africa Unchained: The Blueprint for Africa's Future", Palgrave Macmillan, 2005.

Ayittey, George B. N., "Africa in Chaos", St. Martins Press, 1998.

Ayittey, George B. N., "Africa Betrayed". St. Martins Press, 1992.

Zogby, James J., "What Arabs Think", Zogby International/The Arab Thought Foundation, 2002.

Rotberg, Robert, Ed., "When States Fail: Causes and Consequences", Princeton U. Press, 2004.

Villalon, Leonardo A., and VanDoepp, Peter, Eds., "The Fate of Africa's Democratic Experiments", Indiana U. Press, 2005.

Kuran, Timur, "The Long Divergence", Princeton U. Press, 2011.

Bueno De Mesquita, Bruce, and Smith, Alistair, "The Dictator's Handbook", Public Affairs, 2011.

Bhagwati, Jagdish, "Free Trade Today", Princeton U. Press, 2002.

Hayek, F. A. "The Fatal Conceit: The Errors of Socialism", U. of Chicago Press, 1988.

The Quran: The Dilemma, Volume I, The Quran.com, 2011.

Yergin, Daniel, and Stanislaw, Joseph, "The Commanding Heights", Simon and Schuster, 1998.

Bingman, Charles F., "Governance from the Bottom Up", iUniverse Publishers, 2016.

Bingman, Charles F., "Governments From Hell", iUniverse Publishers, 2015.

Bingman, Charles F., "Governments in the Muslim World", iUniverse Publishers, 2013.

Bingman, Charles F., "Changing Governments in India and China", IUniverse Publishers, 2016, (Reissue by new printer).

Bingman, Charles F., "Reforming China's Government", Xlibris Press, 2010.

Bingman, Charles, F. "Why Governments Go Wrong", iUniverse Publishers, 2006.

Freedom House: "Freedom Country Rankings 2011 – Country Rankings

The World Fact Book: "The World's Most Populous Cities, Metropolitan Areas and Urban Agglomerations, 2008.

List of United Nations Peacekeeping Missions, 2015.

Numbeo: "Quality of Life Index for 2012.

UNHCR: "Facts and Figures on Refugees", 2015.

Washington Post, July 26, 2015, "Troubles at electric utility signal depth of Puerto Rico's crisis".

UNDP 2005: "Close to 43 million people worldwide are displaced because of conflict and persecution."

AllCountries.org: "Most Dangerously Polluted Cities", 2004.

Yang, Dali L., "Remaking the Chinese Leviathan", Stanford U. Press, 2004. See also "Governance in China" by the OECD; and "Reforming China's Public Finances" from the International Monetary Fund.

Rotberg, Robert I., "Failed States in a World of Terror", Foreign Affairs Journal, July/August 2002.

Bhagwati, Jagdish, "Free Trade Today", Princeton U. Press, 2002.

Andrusz Gregory, Harloe, Michael, "Cities After Socialism", Oxford, Blackwell Publishers, 1996.

Bingman, Charles F. "China Struggles to Reform", Washington Institute of China Studies, Spring, 2006.

Hayek, F. A., "The Fatal Conceit: The Errors of Socialism", U. of Chicago Press, 1988.

Isbister, John, "Promises Not Kept", Hartford, Conn., Kumarian Press, 1993.

"Making Sense of Subsidiarity", The Center for Economic Policy Research, London, 1993.

O'Donnell, Guillermo, and Shmitter, Phillipe, "Transitions from Authoritarian Rule", the Johns Hopkins U. Press, 1986.

Shleifer, Andrei, Vishny, Robert W., "The Grabbing Hand: Government Pathologies and Their Cures", Harvard U. Press, 1998.

Waterbury, John, "Exposed to Innumerable Delusions", London, Cambridge U. Press, 1993.

Kohli, Atul, "State-Directed Development", Cambridge U. Press, 2004.

Villalon, Leonardo A., and VonDoepp, Peter, Eds. Indiana U. Press, 2005.

Waterbury, John, and Richards, Alan, "A Political Economy of the Middle East", Westview Press, 1990.

Michalski, Mark M., "Trade and Procurement Reform in Poland and China: Responding to the Next Globalization Wave of Interdependent Economies", Journal of the Washington Institute of China Studies, Fall, 2010.

The United Nations Convention Against Corruption, Dec.2003. The UN Declaration Against Corruption and Bribery, 1996.

The Globalist: "A (Very) Brief History of Corruption", Jul. 1, 2012.

Economist: "Bribery: Graft Work", Dec. 6, 2014.

Transparency International: Corruptions Perceptions Index, 2015.

Transparency International: Bribepayers Index, 2011.

Economist: "Corruption and Natural Resources: A Fight for Light", Oct. 24, 2015.

World Health Organization (WHO), "Health Performance Rank by Country", 2011.

The Guardian: "World Educational Rankings: Which Country Does Best at Reading, Maths, Science? Datablog, 2015.

Most Dangerously Polluted Cities, AllCountries.org, 2011.

Detter, Dag, and Folster, Stefan, "The Public Wealth of Nations: How Management of Public Assets Can Boost or Bust Economic Growth", New York, Palgrave McMillan, 2015.

Lomborg, Bjorn, "The Skeptical Environmentalist" Cambridge U. Press, 2001.

Pearce, Fred, "When the Rivers Run Dry", Boston, Beacon Press, 2006.

Economist: "Water Consumption: A Canal Too Far", Sep. 17, 2014.

World Development Indicators: "Assessing Vulnerability", 2004.

World Development Indicators: "Enhancing Security", 2004.

Carter, Ashton B., Perry, William J., "Preventative Defense: A New Security Strategy for America", Washington, D. C. Brookings Institution, 1999.

Cooper, Philip J., "Government by Contract: Washington, D. C., CQ Press, 2003.

Diamond, Jared, "Collapse: How Societies Choose to Fail or Succeed", New York, Penguin Press, 2005.

Drucker, Peter F. "Managing in the Next Society", New York, St. Martins Press, 2002.

Esterbrook, Gregg, "The Progress Paradox", New York, Random House Press, 2003.

Lankford, James, U. S. Senate, "Federal Fumbles: 100 Ways the Government Dropped the Ball:, Volume 1, U. S. Senate.

Lankford, James, U. S. Senate, "Federal Fumbles: 100 Ways the Government Dropped the Ball, Volume 2, U. S. Senate.

Economist Magazine – all issues for 20 years.

International Labor Office, "The Future of Urban Employment", Geneva, 1998.

Ginsberg, Benjamin, Crenson, Matthew A., "Downsizing Democracy", Baltimore, Johns Hopkins U. Press, 2002.

Klitzaard, Robert, Maclean-Aberoa, Ronald, Parris, H. Lindsay, "Corrupt Cities", Washington, D. C., World Bank Institute, 2000.

Marquette, Heather, "Corruption, Politics and Development: The Role of the World Bank", New York, Palgrave, 2003.

Moran, Theodore H., "Foreign Direct Investment and Development", Washington, D. C., The Institute for International Economics, 1999.

OECD, "Regulatory Reform in the Global Economy", Washington, D. C., 1998.

World Bank: "Extending Women's Participation in Economic Development", Washington, D. C., 2003.

SOURCES

=★=★=★=

www.ingramcontent.com/pod-product-compliance
Lightning Source LLC
Chambersburg PA
CBHW030420290526
45786CB00001B/58